Constance Backhouse and **Leah Cohen** are journalists. Constance Backhouse is also a lawyer, and Leah Cohen has worked in various managerial and advisory capacities after obtaining a master's degree in political science.

Sexual Harassment On the Job

HOW TO AVOID THE WORKING WOMAN'S NIGHTMARE

Constance Backhouse
Leah Cohen

A SPECTRUM BOOK

PRENTICE-HALL, INC., *Englewood Cliffs, N.J. 07632*

Library of Congress Cataloging in Publication Data

Backhouse, Constance, Date–
  Sexual harassment on the job.

  (A Spectrum Book)
  Edition published in 1978 under title: The
secret oppression.
  Includes bibliographical references and index.
  1. Sexual harassment of women—United States.
2. Sexual harassment of women—United States—
Case studies. 3. Sex in business. 4. Women—
Employment—United States. I. Cohen, Leah,
Date–joint author. II. Title.
HQ1206.B16 1981   305.4'2   80–22236
ISBN 0–13–807545–X
ISBN 0–13–807537–9 (pbk.)

Production supervision by *Heath Lynn Silberfeld*
Manufacturing buyer: *Cathie Lenard*
Cover design by *Ira Shapiro*
Cover illustration by *John Rowe*

A SPECTRUM BOOK

10 9 8 7 6 5 4 3 2 1

Printed in the United States of America

PRENTICE-HALL INTERNATIONAL, INC., *London*
PRENTICE-HALL OF AUSTRALIA PTY. LIMITED, *Sydney*
PRENTICE-HALL OF CANADA, LTD., *Toronto*
PRENTICE-HALL OF INDIA PRIVATE LIMITED, *New Delhi*
PRENTICE-HALL OF JAPAN, INC., *Tokyo*
PRENTICE-HALL OF SOUTHEAST ASIA PTE. LTD., *Singapore*
WHITEHALL BOOKS LIMITED, *Wellington, New Zealand*

We would like to dedicate this book to our mothers,
Ethel Cohen and Olga Backhouse,
who have always provided us with love and encouragement.

Contents

We would like to thank the following people who have offered encouragement and useful insights during the course of our research and writing: Patricia Dales, Barbara Earle, Anne Hill, Christopher Lindsay, Diana Majury, Mary Jane Mossman, Lionel Orlikow, Dean Paquette, and Beth Symes. We would also like to thank all those people who consented to lengthy interviews. They provided the foundation for our analysis and recommendations for change.

1

Case studies

INTRODUCTION

For a number of years, we have been writing free-lance articles on issues of concern to working women. Regardless of the subject we tackled, the issue of sexual harassment became an underlying theme that so many of the women we interviewed wished to discuss. And so we decided to devote one article specifically to the subject of sexual harassment.

As we began our research, it very quickly became apparent to us that sexual harassment was a rampant feature of all working environments. We were inundated with stories of every description, ranging from subtle psychological coercion to gross physical abuse. It was at this point that we realized no single article could possibly do proper justice to this subject. Although we had both been pursuing independent careers in law and political science, we decided to take some time out to do a rigorous analysis of sexual harassment. What evolved was this book.

There Are a Million Stories

All of the case studies that follow are true stories. But because the subject is so explosive and could cause such devastating reprisals, we have changed the names and certain details in each case to protect the women who came forward.

There are literally thousands of stories. We chose our cases carefully in order to demonstrate that sexual harassment affects all working women, regardless of their age, physical appearance, social status, or job category. We made extensive efforts to interview male harassers. Not surprisingly we were unable to find a single man who would admit to being a harasser, even men who had been publicly exposed. It is our contention that all men erect a self-defense mechanism around this issue, refusing to admit that this behavior is deeply offensive to women.

With one exception all of the women in our case studies recognized that they were being sexually harassed. As the case of the graduate student points out, however, there are a number of women who do not understand, at least in the first instance, that their experience falls within the parameters of sexual harassment. We suspect that this failure to comprehend the dynamics of sexual harassment leaves countless stories untold and undetected.

CASE 1: THE OFFICE WORKER

I think the hardest part was having to tell my thirteen-year-old son. I had to tell him why I'd been laid off. I couldn't lie to my family. When my son and my husband heard the details of how my boss treated me, they both became very angry. My son wanted to go with his father to "punch out" this guy.

This is the case of Ms. Carol Lindsay, a thirty-five-year-old woman who formerly worked as a clerical worker at a small advertising agency. Ms. Lindsay has two children, a thirteen-year-old son and a nine-year-old daughter. She is happily married to a man who was her childhood sweetheart, whom she has known most of her life. As she says, "Ken is not only my husband but my very best friend."

Before she held this job, Ms. Lindsay had been out of the work force for nine years raising her two children. Her work experience before she was married involved clerical and supervisory work in an all-female office. "I never had a problem dealing with men," she said, "before I began to work with the advertising agency."

When she decided to return to the work force, it took her five months of an intensive search to secure a position. Four months after being hired she was fired for failing to comply with her boss's sexual demands.

MS. LINDSAY: I was so excited the first day of my new job. Although I was nervous about being back at work after so long at home, I liked the place and the people, and I planned to work hard and make a success out of the job.

It all began two weeks after I started. My boss, who was the vice-president of the company and the son-in-law of the owner, was a man in his late forties. He was married, with five children. Frank Lodge was a short man, barely over five feet tall. He considered himself a swinger, coming to the office dressed in gaucho style, with jeans, his shirt open to his navel, gold medallions around his neck, and frizzed hair.

He was not particularly well liked, because he was very authoritarian and humiliated his employees publicly, although I must admit he was very intelligent and really ran the company. I would have to say I respected him for that.

My job involved working directly with him, meeting with him five to six times a day in his office. From the very first day I found Mr.

Lodge intimidating. He was always yelling, trying to wear down people's nerves. I was very unsure of myself as a new person, so I kept quiet and would just sit there waiting for his instructions. I was trying hard to concentrate and learn the ropes, so I tried to ignore his remarks.

INTERVIEWER: Could you describe what happened next?

MS. LINDSAY: Mr. Lodge had this really beautiful office. It was expensively decorated, very classy and elegant. In one corner there was a plush purple velvet loveseat. When I was called into his office to confer with him, he would be sitting on the loveseat and he would say, tapping the loveseat, "Come over and sit beside me." I thought this was odd, but decided it was okay because we both had to go over the same set of figures. He talked very softly, so that I had to sit close to hear what he was saying. I became very embarrassed and found myself scrunching over on my side of the seat.

The next time he called me in, I wanted to avoid the loveseat, so I immediately sat down in the chair opposite his desk. His reaction was to close his door and pull his chair from behind the desk around close to mine and to touch my knees. I was very surprised but decided I was overreacting. I felt that the best way to stop it was to ignore it.

But the situation became worse. The office had a conference room in it with a bar, which was often used to entertain customers. Mr. Lodge had a habit of calling me into the conference room and closing the door. On many occasions he would ask me to make him a drink and often asked me if I wanted one myself. I quite firmly said no. His response was to ask if I was afraid I wouldn't be able to control myself. I was somewhat shocked, blushed, but let it go. At that point I didn't discuss it with anyone and felt I owed it to myself to handle it on my own.

The situation deteriorated to the point where he began to suggest that we find a quiet hotel room. Over the weekend I psyched myself up to fight back, because I realized the situation was getting out of hand.

INTERVIEWER: What did you do?

MS. LINDSAY: The next time he shut the door and asked me if I was in the mood, I replied, looking him straight in the eye: "I've got the best at home. I don't need to settle for second best." He ignored my comment completely and came up and whispered in my ear, "Next time you come in my office, I won't let you out." Frightened, I fled from his office.

INTERVIEWER: How did he treat you after that?

MS. LINDSAY: I guess he realized he wasn't going to get anywhere with me. He became very cold and refused to speak to me except to yell about my work. He started to criticize everything I did, making my life unbearable. I realized I was in trouble, so I thought if I worked harder and showed him what a good employee I was, it might help. I began to take work home at night and stayed up late memorizing office procedures.

INTERVIEWER: Did it affect your family life?

MS. LINDSAY: I found myself highly irritable with my children and my husband. I started to withdraw into myself. I lost weight. My husband became concerned, because I was obviously troubled, but he thought it was just part of getting used to a new job. At first I felt I couldn't tell him for fear he would be angry or treat it as a joke. Besides, my pride was at stake. It was my first chance to contribute financially to the family in years. However, it became so obvious that something was seriously wrong that I finally broke down and told my husband.

INTERVIEWER: How did he respond?

MS. LINDSAY: My husband was horrified and outraged. His immediate response was that I should fight back and not take this kind of treatment from anyone. He was very supportive, and I was relieved that I had told him.

INTERVIEWER: How did you come to be fired?

MS. LINDSAY: I still hoped that the whole thing would blow over, and I was working doubly hard. However, for several weeks I noticed that the office manager, a woman in her fifties who was a grandmotherly type, seemed uneasy. Finally, she called me into her office and told me she would have to let me go. My boss had complained that I wasn't working fast enough. He told her I was doing a lousy job. The office manager was sympathetic. She said it was unfortunate, but that when Mr. Lodge took a dislike to someone, it didn't matter how hard they worked. She confided that many other women had been fired for the same reason.

INTERVIEWER: Did you tell the office manager about your sexual harassment?

MS. LINDSAY: Yes, I did. She was astounded. I really believe she had had no idea what was going on. She stood there open-mouthed and then said, "You know, little bits and pieces are now beginning to fall into place. The woman who had your job before you, Shirley Green, must have been fired for the same reason. I didn't realize I was hiring women to. . . . What I mean is it's like prostitution, but without the woman's consent or the payoff."

INTERVIEWER: What happened next?

MS. LINDSAY: Although the office manager could not get me my job back, she promised to give me a good job recommendation on the sly, saying that I was laid off due to cutbacks in staff. But I wasn't prepared to leave it at that. I was too angry. I was still smarting because I hadn't fought back immediately. I shouldn't have put up with it, but I thought it would pass. Who knows how many women Mr. Lodge had harassed? I wanted to stop it.

INTERVIEWER: How did you proceed from there?

MS. LINDSAY: My last few days at work I spoke to every woman in the office. Each and every one of them had had a lewd sexual pass made at them by Mr. Lodge. They said I was lucky. The woman before me, Shirley Green, had been publicly humiliated in front of the whole office. But these women, who did not work directly for Mr. Lodge, felt they had to go along with him. Most of them were single or divorced and desperately needed their jobs. They made it clear to me that they could not afford to support any action I took. The men in the office all knew what was going on. Their response was to smile and chuckle and to speculate whether or not Frank had "scored" this time around.

I managed to track down Shirley Green, who had been able to find another job. She told me Mr. Lodge had also sexually harassed her, to such an extent that she had totally lost her self-confidence. She had wanted to speak up at the time she was fired but was afraid it would jeopardize her next job. But she informed me that she would support any action I took and that she would testify for me if necessary.

INTERVIEWER: Who did you go to for help?

MS. LINDSAY: I immediately contacted the human rights commission and laid a complaint of sex discrimination. It was just awful. They handled the whole thing in a terribly slipshod way. After six months of bickering back and forth they came up with what they thought was a satisfactory solution. They presented me with a check from the company for four hundred dollars in severance pay and a letter from the company president saying that although this was in no way an admission of guilt, they would be prepared to promise that the company would not violate the human rights legislation in the future. I should add that the investigating officer and her supervisor informed me that the commission had gone as far as it was prepared to go. They asked why I didn't just accept the money and let the whole thing go.

I was incensed. I wanted a letter of apology stating that steps would be taken within the company to make sure that Mr. Lodge never harassed another woman. I didn't care about the money. If it had come out of Lodge's paycheck, I might have been interested. But since it came from the company coffers, who cared? What infuriated me was the attitude of the commission. They told me it was expensive to the taxpayer to take it further. They were nasty enough to say that if I had wanted Frank Lodge groveling at my feet, I should have said so when I first laid the complaint. "In this business," they said, "you have to be prepared to give a little." As far as they were concerned, the case was closed.

The trauma of Ms. Lindsay's sexual harassment experience was deep and damaging to her own self-confidence. Although Ms. Lindsay believes that had she been more direct in dealing with Mr. Lodge's abusive behavior, she might have been able to retain her job, our research indicates she would have been fired anyway. Psychologically she might have felt better, since her pride and dignity would not have suffered such a blow.

Her experience with the human rights commission is very unsettling. One would expect that a public agency dedicated to wiping out sex discrimination and protecting human rights would have gone to greater lengths to ensure that Mr. Lodge could never sexually harass another woman. Their conciliatory approach is unlikely to deter Mr. Lodge in the future. What is $400 to a thriving company? Ms. Lindsay was right in demanding a letter of apology and an assurance that Mr. Lodge would be scrutinized henceforth. However, she was wrong in suggesting that money was of no consequence. Large awards do, in fact, put pressure on organizations to stop sexual harassment within their ranks.

Ms. Lindsay is currently looking for a new job. The employment agency she registered with has told her not to mention anything to prospective employers about her experience and her action with the human rights commission. They warned her that to do so would jeopardize her chances of getting another job. Nevertheless, Ms. Lindsay has not been deterred. She has retained a lawyer to put pressure on the human rights commission to take more decisive action. If this fails, she plans to take her case to the civil courts.

CASE 2: THE WAITRESS

It's a very sexual job, and that's how you make most of your tips. That means you have to smile through abusive remarks made by the customer. You have to take a lot of hassles, everything from comments to being propositioned outright.

Waitresses are a particularly vulnerable occupational group. Whether they work in high-priced elegant restaurants or the greasy spoon around the corner, whether they are portly grandmothers or young slender, attractive women, they are all subject to sexual harassment. Not only must they hustle for tips from customers, but they must also put up with sexual abuse from co-workers and bosses.

As the case of Ms. Rosalie Adams demonstrates, this sexual abuse can often border on rape and leave its victim devoid of dignity and stripped of her self-confidence. Rosalie Adams is a twenty-three-year-old single woman who at the time of writing was out of work. As she says, "I've had one waitressing job after another, and it always turns out the same. I either come across or my life is made miserable. It really does something to your head putting up with this everyday. You start to feel like a piece of meat, not a real human being."

INTERVIEWER: How did you become a waitress?

MS. ADAMS: I grew up in a welfare family, one of eight kids. I dropped out of high school at fifteen and took the first job I could get. I had to get away. My father was an alcoholic, and my mother totally unable to cope. She tried her best to keep the family together cleaning other people's homes, but there was never enough money. My first job was in a neighborhood diner; you know the type of place. My customers were local factory workers and truck drivers. I was pretty naïve at the time and put up with a lot of crap.

I still remember how terrified I was of my boss. He used to come in every morning and yell in front of everyone, "Hey, Rosalie, are you getting any action?" I could have died. He would come up and slap my bum and try to grab and kiss me on the neck. The other women were a lot older and more experienced. They had to put up with his crude comments all day too. They told me I'd get used to it. I never did.

INTERVIEWER: Did you work there long?

MS. ADAMS: No. I held a series of jobs over the next eight years. With each new job I tried to improve my situation. I thought if I worked in a classier place, I would be dealing with a better class of people. I really thought the abuse would end. I wanted to be good at my job. Over the years I became very efficient, spent a lot of money on my appearance, and even took a self-improvement course so that I could learn how to walk, talk, and dress.

You know, it was terribly surprising. The sexual abuse became more subtle. It wasn't up front like in the diner, where the customers leered, grabbed, pinched, and made crude remarks. These so-called gentlemen, with their fancy three-piece suits and stylish haircuts, just had a different line. In a way it was worse. They would tell you how attractive you were, never looking at your face, just at your body. Lots of them really thought that any woman who waitressed was open to prostitution, or at the very least an easy lay. I got offered money more times than I can count. It made me realize I just wasn't a person as far as they were concerned.

INTERVIEWER: Why did you put up with it?

MS. ADAMS: When you're a waitress, your basic pay is so low that you can't live on it. Surviving depends on your tips. So what are your options? If you come back with smart comments, even if you've given excellent service, you stand to lose your tips. And if you keep it up, you'll find yourself on the street without a job. You're forced to smile, be pleasant, and grit your teeth when some idiot grabs at you, puts you down, or propositions you. Those are the facts of life.

Most of us can't get other jobs. The waitresses I know have very little education and are often single parents with no support from their ex-husbands. They can't afford to be unemployed. It would be nice if we could take courses and become office workers, but that all takes time and money. None of us have those privileges.

INTERVIEWER: Would you tell us about your most recent experience?

MS. ADAMS: It was the worst situation I've ever been in. On the surface the job looked terrific. I was working in a beautiful old hotel as a waitress in the main dining room. The clientele were rich upper-class types. The tips were really good. I was finally able to save a little.

I was sort of surprised at what they asked me to wear. It was a very tight, full-length, revealing dress. There were slits on the side almost up to my hips, and the neckline was very low-cut. I was required to wear a fresh rose in my cleavage every day. I hated the outfit. It was extremely difficult to walk in it without swaying your hips. I tried practicing to walk so that nothing shook.

INTERVIEWER: How did the customers respond to you?

MS. ADAMS: Our customers were often crowds of male executives on big expense accounts. The usual scene was that they began with suggestive comments, ogling my body and asking to smell the rose in my cleavage. Sometimes when one of them would get really drunk and obnoxious, he would grab me and pull me down so that he could smell the rose.

A couple of times a week I'd be propositioned outright with offers of anywhere from $50 to $200. They just assumed that I was a prostitute. I became really upset and tense around these men. I had never experienced such a constant attack on my body and on my dignity.

There was one man in particular who got on my nerves. He was a regular customer, a real smoothie, about thirty-five, dressed like a swinger, coming on to anything in skirts. He kept telling me that my perfume drove him wild. I finally told him I never wore perfume and to lay off. The next time I passed his table, he said in a very loud voice so that everyone around could hear, "I'm sure I can smell your perfume. Maybe it's your FDS." I was so embarrassed that I wanted to drop through the floor. If I hadn't needed the job so badly I would have slugged him.

But the customers weren't the half of it. I was also hassled by the bartender and the male kitchen staff. When you're a waitress, you have to keep in the good books of the guys backing you up. If the bartender takes a dislike to you, he can slow down on your orders to the point where you get no tips at all. The kitchen staff can sabotage you in other ways. The food can be cold, it can arrive late, and orders can be all mixed up. So you see how crucial it is to have a good working relationship. I really tried hard to get along with these men, but they were impossible.

INTERVIEWER: What did the bartender do?

MS. ADAMS: The bartender told me outright that I'd have to come across sexually. I was just sick. No one had ever been that explicit. I felt backed against the wall and tried to put him off. At the same time I was trying to cope with the characters in the kitchen. The head chef thought it was very funny to hoot at me as I came into the kitchen to pick up my orders. He went so far as to carve a penis out of a large carrot and hold it at his crotch level, pointing it at me as I walked through. He did this for days. The rest of the men who worked in the kitchen would laugh hysterically. The other women tried to ignore the whole thing. I could tell they felt badly, but what could they do? Most of them could barely speak English and were really afraid of losing their jobs. Although several did come up to me and try to tell me they sympathized.

I might have been able to hack all that, but it didn't end there. The final straw was when my boss tried to set me up with some of his best friends. As he put it, "It would be just a cozy little dinner with about eight men." I was to serve the meal and "be especially nice," as he termed it. He said there was a lot of money in it for me.

That was it. I started to yell at him, "I'm here to work as a waitress, to do my job the best I can. I do not provide sex on the side. Where do you get off acting as my pimp?" He became very angry and told me that all his girls knew the score. Who did I think I was? The Virgin Mary? That was life in the big city. He said I was lucky to be working there period. He could get anyone he wanted. Didn't I know jobs were tough to come by? If I didn't want to end up on the street, I'd better change my attitude fast.

I just saw red. I told him I was prepared to continue working, but just as a waitress, and that no one was going to treat me that way. I had my rights, and I was sick of putting up with these oversexed pigs. At that point he told me I could pick up my pay and leave.

INTERVIEWER: What happened next?

MS. ADAMS: I had no choice. What could I do? Waitresses don't have unions. We are marginal workers. Who cares about us? I knew if I complained anywhere, no one would believe me, and even if they did, they wouldn't be able to do anything. So I hit the streets, looking for another job. I didn't want to go near a fancy place. I convinced myself that a café would be easier to handle.

After a week or so of looking, I landed another job. It was a really nice, quiet restaurant, near the university. My boss was quite a young guy, and when I applied for the job, he seemed very pleasant. My very first day he asked me to work late, to help close up. When I was changing out of my uniform, he walked into the back room, smiled, and said, "We should really get together. You know you're a very pretty girl, and I could make this job really nice for you."

I was just stunned. Here we go again, I thought. I looked him straight in the eye and said, "Mister, get your grubby paws off me and get out of here before I scream." He laughed and tried to pull me closer. I picked up my purse and swung at him as hard as I could. He staggered back and yelled hysterically, "You're fired, you bitch. Who do you think you are? Unless you get out of my restaurant immediately, I'll call the police and charge you with assault."

I yelled back, "Like hell you will. I'll charge you with attempted rape." But I knew no one would ever believe me. And then I fled. I was crying so hard I could barely breathe. That happened about two months ago. I've been so upset that I can't bring myself to look for another job.

I don't know what to do anymore. The thought of having another sleazy character try to feel me up makes me physically ill. I shake every time I think about it. It's enough to make you hate all men. I can imagine how rape victims feel. It just never lets up.

The older women tell me it only gets worse. The men assume you're desperate and are happy for any attention. I guess we all put up with it because men hold all the cards. They have the money and the power. I think the only hope is for women to organize and fight back. I would be prepared to take a stand if I could find several other women who would fight with me.

Ms. Adams's case is particularly striking in any analysis of sexual harassment. She was the victim of both physical and psychological coercion on the job. You cannot dismiss her situation as exceptional, since the majority of women do, in fact, work at marginal, low-paying jobs like waitressing. Women in these jobs do not make a sufficient minimum wage to survive without tips. They are forced to come across as sex objects. This leaves them open to relentless harassment, not only from their bosses and co-workers but also from their customers.

Ms. Adams, like other waitresses we have spoken to, appreciates that as an individual there is little she can do. One woman trying to fight against sexual harassment is either fired or forced to quit. Greater potential for success lies in collective action. As Ms. Adams said, she would be prepared to take a stand if only she could find several other women who would support her.

CASE 3: THE CONSTRUCTION WORKER

I like my work, but it's lonely without other women. The men have finally accepted me, after a long struggle, but there are still some problems. I would never go back to low-paying women's jobs. I can finally earn a decent living for myself and my two kids.

This is the case of Sandy Mitchell, a thirty-eight-year-old divorcee who has two teen-age children. When her husband left her ten years ago, she enrolled in an apprenticeship training program and subsequently became a construction-site electrician. Before her marriage she had worked at marginal jobs as a waitress and file clerk.

MS. MITCHELL: When my husband left me, I was very depressed and worried sick about paying the bills. I had no idea where he was, and there was little hope of him sending money. I knew that if I worked as a waitress or an office worker, we wouldn't be able to survive and we'd probably end up on welfare. I was also angry. I had been married for ten years and had finally acquired a house, a car, and decent furniture, and I wasn't about to give them up.

All my life I had liked mechanical things. I was much better than my husband at doing repairs around the house. Everybody had always kidded me, saying I was a real character and reminded them of "Josephine the Plumber," like on TV. I knew very few women, if any, who did men's work such as plumbing, cabinetmaking, welding, and so on. But I decided to ask around and see if I could get into some sort of course.

After looking into a number of areas I decided I would like to be an electrician, so I approached the electricians' union and asked to be admitted to the apprenticeship program. The man who interviewed me tried his best to discourage me. He told me it was dirty work, that the men talked rough, that there wouldn't be any special ladies' facilities, and that women really didn't belong in a man's field. But I argued with him and told him my situation, saying that all I wanted was a chance.

INTERVIEWER: What was the initial reaction when you first began to work?

MS. MITCHELL: It was incredible. The men were shocked when they saw me march onto the construction site wearing workmen's clothing and special safety boots. I was twenty-eight at the time and I guess I was a reasonably attractive woman. Their first ploy was to hoot, holler, whistle, and stamp their feet every time I walked by. That didn't bother me, I was expecting it. And I was prepared to put up with it.

INTERVIEWER: Did things improve?

MS. MITCHELL: No, they got worse, much worse. It became pretty obvious that I was darn good. I was efficient and a quick learner. You only have to tell me something once, and I never forget it. I guess they hoped I would quit after a couple of weeks. When they realized I was serious, good at what I did, and determined to stick it out to the end, they became openly hostile.

INTERVIEWER: What sort of things did they do?

MS. MITCHELL: They started to get physical with me. Every chance they got, they would grab at my body. I can't count the number of times I was pinched. But they were fooling around with the wrong lady. I'm a good athlete and had been taking self-defense lessons for years. I punched a couple of people really hard in the solar plexis, you know, the stomach. I don't think they'd ever encountered a woman who fought back. I also informed everybody within earshot that I had my brown belt in karate. The physical abuse stopped abruptly.

But they adopted other tactics. They tried to break me down psychologically. One of them even put a dildo in my lunch bucket. I started to receive obscene phone calls at home. I was also sent threatening letters. It was just awful, and it really did get to me. I started to feel very alienated and lonely. Here I was spending eight hours a day with these guys, and not one of them could accept me as an equal co-worker.

INTERVIEWER: Did you complain to anyone?

MS. MITCHELL: At first I thought I could handle it myself. My friends and family kept telling me to quit, that a construction site was no place for a woman to be. My two sons were the only ones who were supportive. They kept saying, "Mom, you can't let those guys push you around."

I finally got so upset and angry that I complained to the union. My union rep just laughed. He said, "What did you expect? Roses? If you're not tough enough to take it, you should get out. The guys all tease each other, why can't you take it?" He was just hopeless.

Just as I was about to quit, the foreman on the site approached me and told me he'd been watching me. He said I was "some lady" and "the best apprentice" he'd seen in years. I told him I was really discouraged and fed up with all the hassles and sexual come-ons. He told me that if I stuck it out, the men would eventually give up. They would get used to me and probably decide I was some kind of "freaky" woman.

INTERVIEWER: So you decided to stay?

MS. MITCHELL: Yes, I did. And I did a number of things. I started to carry a wrench in my back pocket as a warning to the more obnoxious grabbers and pinchers. I posted a bulletin informing the men that if the letters and calls persisted, I would take legal action. I wasn't kidding. I actually consulted a lawyer to see if I could really do anything, but he didn't hold out much hope. But of course the guys didn't know that. Anything to do with the law scares the hell out of them. And I stopped being silent when someone yelled crude remarks at me. I yelled right back. This really upset the men. Women aren't supposed to swear. It took the wind right out of their sails. It took months, but eventually they started to treat me like one of the guys.

INTERVIEWER: Do you advise women to move into nontraditional areas?

MS. MITCHELL: Yes. Most definitely. There's good money in it, a union to back you up, and it's very satisfying work. You actually help build something. You're part of a team. Of course, not all women are interested. They think it's unfeminine and not ladylike. But if you're realistic and you want to earn a decent living and you're not a professional, I would advise women to seriously consider the trades.

INTERVIEWER: Do you think women in nontraditional areas get more sexual harassment than other women?

MS. MITCHELL: Yes, I really do. The men see you as a real threat. You're moving into their territory, an all-male club. You have to remember, these are pretty macho types. They have the "little wife" at home cooking, cleaning, taking care of the family, afraid to speak up or complain. And here I come along, a divorced, independent woman who thinks she has a right to work alongside them. I earn the same salary and expect the same benefits. They want to push you back where they think women belong.

Sexual harassment is a good way to get back at you. It's their way of saying you're a nonperson, only a sexual object. They're right, it's completely humiliating, one of the toughest things to fight. It dehumanizes you when people are grabbing at you and yelling obscenities. It makes you feel very vulnerable and afraid. I was just fortunate that I was tough enough to be able to wait it out.

INTERVIEWER: Do you have any ideas how to stop sexual harassment on nontraditional worksites?

MS. MITCHELL: I have a few ideas. It would have helped me if there had been other women working with me. You need the companionship and the support. It would be terrific if we could come onto sites in groups. It would be a lot less frightening.

I also think women are pretty naive. I certainly was. I expected the yelling and the hooting, but I wasn't prepared for physical come-ons, the phone calls, and the letters. Not to mention the dildo in my lunch bucket. There should be some way to train women in handling sexual harassment. Maybe we could work in groups to come up with strategies to stop this sort of behavior.

I've thought a lot about it. There should be courses for women moving into the trades, teaching them basic self-defense, what to expect from the men, and how best to cope with it. The union guy could sure use a course. He was an insensitive clod. He had a responsibility to help me in some way or at least listen to me. I have to give it more thought, but I'm sure if we had the money and the time, we could stamp out sexual harassment. It's tough enough trying to do unusual work without having to put up with sexual harassment.

Obviously, women entering careers that have been largely male domains until recently face more blatant and flagrant forms of sexual harassment. Ms. Mitchell is an exceptional person in that she withstood the sustained attack of her co-workers for a long period of time. Sexual harassment is a very frightening weapon that men in groups, such as on construction sites, use against what they perceive to be a woman intruder. There was nothing subtle about their behavior. It was carefully designed to push Ms. Mitchell to the point where she would quit.

For many women with limited options to earn a decent income, nontraditional work is tremendously appealing. It is their right to pursue any career they wish. If women are to be successful in entering nontraditional areas in significant numbers, Ms. Mitchell is right. They must prepare themselves carefully. The biggest obstacle they will encounter is sexual harassment.

CASE 4: THE GRADUATE STUDENT

Seven years ago, when my professor came on to me, I didn't realize that what I was experiencing was sexual harassment. It was such an unpleasant incident that I put it completely out of my mind. It wasn't until I came across a definition of sexual harassment in the newspaper that I began to understand more fully what had happened.

This is the case of Penny Simon, who is now a thirty-two-year-old college teacher. Seven years ago she was studying for a graduate degree in psychology at a very prestigious university.

Her case provides a good illustration of how many victims of sexual harassment do not comprehend how they are being exploited. Some of this can be attributed to the socialization process under which the majority of women grow up. Women are taught to avoid confrontation and unpleasant, threatening situations, even when they are being sexually coerced. They hope that through avoidance the situation will either resolve itself or disappear.

INTERVIEWER: What led to your being harassed when you were a graduate student?

MS. SIMON: Professor Carter was my thesis advisor. I was required to attend one of his seminars and as a result saw him on a regular basis. I should say that I was a particularly naïve twenty-five-year-old. Although I maintained a tough, independent exterior, I was really very inexperienced and relatively untouched by life. I had held summer jobs, but I had never actually worked full-time. I considered myself an academic and had ambitions to teach, myself, one day.

At the time, I had been with Professor Carter for about a year. I was quite thrilled when he offered me the opportunity to work as his research assistant during the summer break. He offered me about $125 a week, which was an extraordinarily high amount in those days. I jumped at the chance.

I should mention that Professor Carter was a man in his fifties, married, with two children. There was something about him that worried me. It was as if there was something very unpleasant just below the surface. But I thought I must be imagining things and tried to dispel my uneasiness. My upbringing was such that I had been trained to be nice and polite in all situations, especially to a superior such as a professor.

Shortly after I began to work for Professor Carter, he took me aside and explained that he hoped we could be very intimate. He said that he had been watching me for months and had noticed that I often came late to class. He accused me of doing this deliberately to attract his attention. It was his interpretation that I had been looking at him suggestively throughout the year.

I had no idea what he was talking about. I came late to his classes because I found them boring. I looked at him only when he was lecturing. I'm sure I didn't stare at him any more than any of the other students. It's just natural to look at someone who's lecturing to you.

Instead of speaking up, I just smiled and didn't say much. I probably should have quit the job, but that didn't enter my head. I didn't want to lose the opportunity. I thought I could handle the situation, and I remained quite friendly. It's hard for me to believe I could have been so stupid.

INTERVIEWER: Did this behavior continue?

MS. SIMON: Yes, it did. I remember doing research in his office and coming across bits of paper with poems about me that he had written on them. I found this very disturbing but chose to put it out of my mind. He also had a habit of popping over to my apartment uninvited. I lived a few blocks from the university, and he would come on the pretext that he was delivering a book or some notes to me.

I was very uncomfortable, but I had no idea how to handle it. So I remained very nice. He knew I had a boyfriend about whom I spoke often, but that seemed to have no effect. It was very embarrassing that everyone in the psychology department just assumed that I was having an affair with Professor Carter.

On several occasions he actually kissed me in his office. I drew back, mortified, confused, and feeling utterly helpless. It left me with an incredibly dirty feeling. But again I was too nice to speak up. I was starting to feel very cheap about the whole experience. Luckily the summer was coming to an end, and I was planning to go home for several weeks before the fall semester began. I hoped that would be the end of it.

INTERVIEWER: Was it?

MS. SIMON: No. When I arrived home, my mother informed me that a professor had called several times, always leaving messages that I should return his call and referring to himself by his first name. My mother was very upset and couldn't understand why he was being so familiar.

I just shrugged it off, because I felt it would have been impossible for me to explain my circumstances to my mother. I told her all of the graduate students called the professors by their first names, although this wasn't true. I'm not sure she believed me, but I wasn't prepared to pursue it. I knew she would disapprove of my behavior.

A few weeks later I received a parcel in the mail from Professor Carter. It contained half a dozen books, each with a special inscription, not exactly suggestive but slightly condescending. It made me sick. My stomach actually turned at the sight of the books. I had a feeling that beneath his veneer of niceness was something very ugly. But I dimissed the whole thing as a freak experience. To make sure there could be no further incidents, I switched thesis advisors at the first opportunity when the fall semester began.

INTERVIEWER: Were there any reprisals?

MS. SIMON: I must have been extremely lucky. He was annoyed and behaved quite coolly toward me but, as far as I know, did not act in a vindictive way. Years later I learned that I had been just one of many female graduate students who had had the same experience.

INTERVIEWER: Did it have any effect on your self-confidence?

MS. SIMON: Yes, I think it really did. Even though I knew I was a victim and that he was taking advantage of me, I berated myself for handling this so poorly. It really stays with you. I guess I never did forget. I've always felt that it represents something dirty in my past, like a blot or a black mark. I remember the time as a long, grotty summer. It took away any feeling that I could have had about doing good work. The whole period represents something negative. There was no development or growth.

INTERVIEWER: Have you had any further experiences of sexual harassment in your working life?

MS. SIMON: There are shades of it at work. I'm still too nice. I still feel very uncomfortable when men come on to me sexually. I don't think that's sexual harassment, but it's unpleasant anyway. It's that same old thing. Men know who to come on to. I'm sure I'm seen as vulnerable because I'm always so nice. It's all so insidious. And I suspect it has a lot to do with the fact that I'm not always "up front."

INTERVIEWER: Do you think all women are open to sexual harassment?

MS. SIMON: I would say that half the women I know are like me, ideal victims for sexual harrassment. It has a lot to do with our upbringing and our attitudes toward men. We just go along with things even though we find them unpleasant and frightening. We've been told all our lives that male attention is flattering. Nobody ever talked about how humiliating and coercive it can be at times.

I realize there are circumstances where men use their power to demand sexual favors. However, I know a number of very strong women who would never let themselves be victimized. It's unthinkable for them. They would just stand up to their harassers and wouldn't take any nonsense. They're sure of themselves and very confident. Sexual harassment doesn't happen to these women.

We chose a graduate student as a case study because we wanted to demonstrate that the future of a graduate student can be contingent on the goodwill of her supervising professor. This situation is much like that of all working women. Students are as vulnerable to sexual harassment as women in the workforce are. Reprisals and repercussions can be just as devastating. A professor can effectively ruin a student's future career with a bad reference and by contributing little to her academic growth.

Ms. Simon's case illustrates how so many women internalize their feelings of repulsion. Instead of focusing her anger on her professor, Ms. Simon was left with a feeling of self-loathing, referring to her experience as a blot and black mark on her past.

She still hasn't come to grips with the fact that sexual harassment isn't a selective phenomenon. All women can be victims, whether they are assertive or extremely passive. What Ms. Simon fails to appreciate is that a self-confident woman can be just as humiliated and manipulated when faced with a sexual harasser who has power and influence over her career.

CASE 5: THE PROFESSIONAL

I consider myself a feminist, and I've always thought of myself as an assertive person. That is why it was so devastating to discover that I was totally incapable of standing up to the man who was harassing me.

Katherine Foster is a twenty-nine-year-old lawyer who worked for a large establishment law firm. Ms. Foster is a very self-assured, confident professional woman who has been active for some years in the women's movement. A year after she joined the law firm, she was forced to resign from her position because of what she describes as a "long and insidious battle with sexual harassment."

MS. FOSTER: When I began working for the law firm, most of my work involved acting as a junior lawyer, assisting one of the senior partners in the firm. Mr. Scott was a highly respected corporation lawyer who was politically well-connected and a shrewd and successful attorney. He was a man in his late forties who was married to a lovely woman and had three children. I was quite excited to be working with him. He did his job marvelously and seemed very much prepared to share the wealth of his experience with me. I realized this would give me a great advantage in future years, and hoped to learn everything he could teach me.

The job required a very close relationship, since we worked together a large part of every day and often well into the evening. Things were going very well, I felt I was growing and learning, and Mr. Scott saw that I was given more responsibility all the time. My self-confidence was at an all-time high. I was convinced that I was well launched into what would prove to be a very successful and fulfilling career.

INTERVIEWER: What happened to change all that?

MS. FOSTER: Six months after I began there, the relationship started to alter, although I didn't notice it at the time. Mr. Scott started asking me to accompany him to two-hour "working" lunches just about every day. I thought nothing of it and in fact was pleased that I was being given more opportunity to participate in the decision-making process. I though that my work was so good that he was actually seeking out my advice. Soon after this, Mr. Scott started suggesting that we work later and later in the evening. It became customary for us to work until quite late and then have a late dinner together before going home.

Although we mostly discussed work at these lunches and dinners, the conversation began to take a new turn. We told each other stories from our personal backgrounds and discussed our personal lives. In fact, I didn't see this as an intrusion. I just assumed that we were becoming close friends. We worked well together, why shouldn't we be friends? The men in the office had similar relationships with each other.

One evening after a lengthy and relaxing dinner, during which Mr. Scott had questioned me intently about my previous romantic liaisons, he suddenly confessed in an extremely roundabout way that he wanted to have an affair with me. He said he wanted to make a clean breast of it, that he had felt guilty for making me work late so often when part of his motivation had been personal interest.

INTERVIEWER: What was your reaction?

MS. FOSTER: Although I must admit I was somewhat flattered that such a powerful man found me personally stimulating, I also recognized I was in a compromising and extremely dangerous position. I definitely didn't want to have an affair with Mr. Scott. I was at the time involved with a man whom I had known for many years, and was completely happy with our relationship. However, Mr. Scott's ego was on the line. Terribly frightened of offending him and possibly ruining my chances for success in the firm, I knew I was treading on thin ice. In an attempt to salvage the situation I told Mr. Scott that I was so surprised I couldn't comment.

I knew I was going to have to give him an answer, and I spent the weekend figuring out how I could tell him no politely, without jeopardizing my job. Mr. Scott had a reputation for extreme ruthlessness when crossed. I came back to the office on Monday and delicately informed him that I admired and respected him very much, but that I was completely happy with the man I was seeing and that I was not interested in him in that way.

INTERVIEWER: How did he respond?

MS. FOSTER: He made it obvious that he wasn't prepared to take no for an answer. The next few months, my life was miserable. He took every opportunity to bring up the subject of our impending affair—at lunches, at dinners, even in the office. I kept saying no firmly but politely.

Personally, I was devastated. I began to wonder why I had got the job in the first place. Here I thought I was hired for my ability, and now it turned out that my major attraction may have been my body. I was too embarrassed to tell anyone about it, even the man I was involved with. My health began to suffer. The tension involved in trying continually to fend him off without risking his ire was almost too much for me.

I began to experience painful constrictions in my chest—I was convinced I was heading for a heart attack. I was alarmed enough one weekend, when the pain became very severe, to rush down to the emergency ward of the nearest hospital. The intern who examined me told me I was physically fine and questioned me about tension and anxiety. The whole thing was so distressing that I broke into tears and began to sob. The intern, visibly distressed, asked me if I felt suicidal. When I told him no, he gave me a prescription for Valium.

I was mortified by the whole situation. I was appalled that my stress was manifesting itself physically, since I had always considered myself a strong, capable person. But I was also angry and annoyed at the intern who prescribed Valium for me. He must have thought I was a total neurotic. I knew that many members of the medical profession tended to prescribe tranquilizers unnecessarily for women, and I was deeply insulted that I found myself a recipient of such a diagnosis. The intern just assumed I was neurotic without knowing any of the facts of my situation. I had gone to the hospital fearing I might be having heart problems. Once I learned I was not, that was all I wanted to know. I threw away the Valium in disgust.

INTERVIEWER: What brought you to the point where you resigned?

MS. FOSTER: Mr. Scott's persistent advances went on for months. At one point he threatened that he would have to move me because my very presence was so disturbing to him. As he put it, "Unless you have an affair with me, I can't continue to work with you." I still thought I could handle it and should contain it between Mr. Scott and myself. I tried to stall him and avoid a real confrontation.

The final straw occurred about a month later. One of the other partner's secretaries came to Mr. Scott to complain that she was being sexually harassed by her boss. I knew from the office rumor mill that she intended to complain to Mr. Scott, and I was waiting to observe his behavior carefully. He had the classic defensive reaction. He thought she was lying and told her she was "a big girl" and should know how to take care of herself. He definitely had no intention of intervening on her behalf. Within days of the encounter she resigned suffering severe physical and psychological trauma associated with stress.

I was very upset that Mr. Scott had handled the situation so poorly, but I really got furious when he called me into his office and told me his version of her story. He expected me to support his treatment of her! I told him flatly that I believed her account and walked out.

Several days later I told him that I would be resigning. Fearing for my future career and recognizing that he could destroy my chances of securing another position, I was too frightened to tell him why I was resigning. I lied and told him that I wanted to travel for a while.

INTERVIEWER: Did it ever occur to you to complain to an agency outside the law firm?

MS. FOSTER: I didn't think I'd have much of a case, because his behavior had been too subtle. In fact, I learned later that the whole office had assumed that we'd been having an affair. There were no witnesses; there was nothing I could document. It was simply my word against his. I realize now that I should have built a case and trapped him through the use, perhaps, of a hidden tape recorder. But even with good evidence I stood to lose as much as he did. I was not prepared to become a sacrificial lamb, even though I feel very strongly about women's issues. The press would have had a field day, but I would have been blackballed in the legal profession.

INTERVIEWER: Do you think, as a professional woman, that you are as vulnerable as a marginal worker?

MS. FOSTER: A lot of people think professional women should be able to handle sexual harassment. It's not true. We are just as vulnerable, maybe even more so. We move in very small circles, and one bad reference could effectively ruin your career. Very few of us are independently wealthy and well connected enough to withstand a character assassination. I know a lot of my peers who have never been sexually harassed just scoff at the notion that professional women can be as humiliated as can other working women. But if the rumors are any indication, I suspect that many professional women have had similar experiences to mine and are just too embarrassed to talk about it and to admit that they were unable to handle it. We just quietly leave, hoping to minimize the damage.

INTERVIEWER: Do you think there are any solutions?

MS. FOSTER: As a lawyer and feminist I have a strong belief in collective action. There are legal remedies to fight this behavior, but the price is too high for any one individual woman to pay. Unless several harassed women band together, the legal forum is unlikely to provide much of an answer.

I think sexual harassment is a reflection of a basic inequality in the workplace between men and women. Until that changes, men will continue to treat women as sex objects, not as professional colleagues.

Professional women, like all working women, suffer from sexual harassment. It manifests itself, generally, with more subtlety. There are rarely the grabbing, leering, pinching, and crude remarks that one associates with more marginal workers. But the effect is the same. Ms. Foster felt humiliated and intimidated, as did many of the other women interviewed. She felt powerless to confront her harasser directly and bluntly.

Her major concern centered on salvaging her future propects. In her opinion a direct confrontation or a legal battle would have jeopardized her professional life. In some respects she appears more vulnerable than the other women, since she would have greater difficulty job hopping than more anonymous workers do. The good reference is critical to her career. Secretaries and waitresses are not as dependent on their previous employer's assessment of their work. Professionals move in a very small, tight circle, with its attendant privileges but with its obvious pitfalls—as exemplified by Ms. Foster's experience with sexual harassment.

CASE 6: THE STRIPPER

People think stripping is the bottom of the barrel. It's viewed as taking no talent. The women are seen as nobodies. Odd as it may seem, we have a sense of pride in our dancing. Music is important to most of us, and there are some nights when it satisfies a strong creative desire.

Sugar La Rue, a twenty-eight-year-old exotic dancer and stripper, performs regularly in nightclubs and at stag parties in many large North American cities. Ms. La Rue is a tall, striking brunette with deep hollows under her hazel eyes. Her life, she admits, is very exhausting. "It's not only the hours you keep, but to dance creatively night after night demands a tremendous amount of energy. It's totally draining."

Ms. La Rue openly professes to be a sensual person, who considers dancing an important art form. "I am proud of my body and I enjoy displaying it. But that doesn't mean that I am immune to sexual abuse. People assume that strippers will put out for anyone who asks."

INTERVIEWER: Can you tell us about some of your experiences?
MS. LA RUE: Let me make it clear that my bosses no longer try to force me
to sleep with them. Once you have any experience as a stripper, you

quickly become hardened. You're suspicious, you're guarded, you're always on the lookout. You've clearly come to grips with the fact that you earn your living with your body, and you don't give anything away for nothing.

But it wasn't always that way. I'll never forget when I first moved into the big city looking for work. I was sixteen years old and came from a backward, straitlaced rural town. I wanted to escape from the lives I saw my mother and sisters leading. There was no fun or excitement in their lives. Just hard, hard work with nothing to show for it.

I've always loved dancing, since I was a little kid. I wanted to become a professional dancer. However, I quickly realized that you had to have money and connections to break into professional dancing. So I decided to look for a job as a go-go dancer. I had heard that the money was good and that the club owners were always looking for fresh talent. I walked into a downtown nightclub and asked to see the owner. I was completely taken aback at his appearance.

I had expected an underworld type. Instead out came an elderly man, dressed in a white satin shirt and black velvet pants, with four or five flashy, expensive-looking jeweled rings on his fingers. He told me his name was Mickey Stone. I told him I wanted a job as a go-go dancer. He laughed and said, "Nobody hires go-go dancers anymore. If you want a job, you will have to work as a stripper." I was shocked but took him at his word. I had left home with very little money, and I was determined never to go back. If I had to strip to break my way into the world of dancing, a stripper I would become.

He asked me to come into his back office. He said that was where he interviewed all prospective strippers. I was nervous but I decided to follow him. Once we were in his office, he locked the door and offered me a drink.

INTERVIEWER: What happened next?

MS. LA RUE: He told me that before he hired anyone, they had to show him their act first. That sounded reasonable to me. So I agreed. He turned on the stereo and told me to go to it. I had no idea what I was doing. I had never seen anyone strip before. But I was a good dancer and was able to move well to the music. When I took my clothes off, I made sure that my back was facing him. I must have spent at least five minutes dancing, facing the rear wall, too embarrassed to face him. I was frightened that if I turned around, he would laugh at me, that my body was not voluptuous enough, not good enough. Near the end of the record I did finally turn around and danced numbly on until the music stopped.

Mickey looked bored and definitely unimpressed. "Not bad," he said, "but you have a lot of teasing to learn. I'll have some of my girls teach you a few tricks and you should turn out okay! I'll pay you twenty-five dollars a night, and you can start tomorrow."

I smiled dumbly, relieved, and started to put on my clothes. "Not so quickly," he said. "Come over here and sit down on the couch. I like to get to know the girls that work for me." I knew I was in for trouble. I mumbled something incoherently and continued dressing. My only thought was to get out of there as soon as possible. "Look," he said, "all I want to do is take a few pictures of you. All the girls have to have their pictures taken for a promotional portfolio. It's part of the job." It seemed pretty fishy to me. I just didn't trust him. When he saw my hesitation, he told me if I wanted the job, I better let him take the pictures. I tried to stall, saying, "Maybe tomorrow. I have to leave now."

It was at this point that he lunged at me. He was surprisingly strong and had me pinned to the floor in no time. He put his hand over my mouth and with his other hand undid his fly. I tried to bite his hand and struggled with all my might, but I couldn't stop him. It was over very quickly. He got up, did up his fly, and said, "Check in at seven tomorrow." That was it. He walked out of the room smiling. I lay there in a heap, utterly humiliated and in a state of shock. It was hard to believe what had happened.

I knew there was nothing I could do about it. I couldn't turn to my family or friends because I didn't want to let them know that I had auditioned as a stripper. I realized the situation was compromising, and everybody would think I had asked for it.

INTERVIEWER: But you continued stripping as a career?

MS. LA RUE: When I got dressed and was about to leave, an older woman came up to me and asked me if I were a new girl. She couldn't have helped noticing how distressed and disheveled I was. I started to cry, and she took me by the arm and walked with me over to a nearby restaurant, where she bought me a cup of tea.

I blurted out the whole story, sobbing the whole time. She was very kind and sympathetic. I guess she would have been about my age now. She offered to let me stay at her place and help me get started. She told me that stripping was a good way to earn your living and that I should feel proud of my body and my ability to dance so well. "Mickey is a pig," she said. He tries to take advantage of all the young and inexperienced girls. The older girls try to keep their eyes out for any newcomers and warn them in advance. She was very sorry that they hadn't warned me in time. "We protect our own," she said.

She made me feel a lot better about what had happened, and I decided to give stripping a chance. I didn't really have a choice anyway. I was down to my last dime. When I next auditioned, I made sure it was on the stage of the nightclub and not in the owner's office. I was much tougher, and no owner has been able to take advantage since.

INTERVIEWER: Do you have trouble with the customers?

MS. LA RUE: We all do. It's an occupational hazard. Customers are always crude. But sometimes when they get drunk, it goes further. I have had grown men drunkenly sprawl on the stage, trying to look up my legs, pulling at my costume. Sometimes it gets so bad that I have to leave the stage. It can be pretty rough at the end of the evening, when I am trying to leave the club and go home. Some of the more obnoxious customers often linger after closing and try to accost me on the street. If I could afford it, I would take a cab home every night.

INTERVIEWER: What do you think the effect of all this has been on you?

MS. LA RUE: You learn to tune men out. You concentrate on your dancing and the music. Before long, the audience becomes one faceless blur. Most of us have contempt for men who frequent strip joints. Unfortunately, they don't come for the dancing; they come for a cheap thrill.

It does get to you after a while, though. When I get home, I have to climb right into a hot shower to purge myself. Sometimes I get really depressed. But the real problem is the way that society views stripping. They see strippers as hunks of meat, the dregs of humanity, without feelings or dignity. The general view is that we are nymphomaniacs, ready to go to bed with anyone. It's simply not true. I, like other women, have every right to decide whom I will sleep with.

INTERVIEWER: Do you know what happened to the stripper who first befriended you?

MS. LA RUE: I've lost touch with her. She stopped stripping several years ago. I guess she became too old. In this business they are always looking for younger bodies. It's a short-lived career. I understand that she has become a seamstress. I certainly hope that she is making out all right. I owe her a great deal, and I will never forget how she helped me.

I also try, as do other older strippers, to look out for the new girls. I know it's a competitive business, that we are always fighting with each other for the best jobs, but we still support each other on the issue of harassment. It's a common problem for all of us. And if we don't help each other, who will?

Both men and women commonly feel that "workers of the flesh" deserve what they get when it comes to sexual harassment. Few people sympathize with their considerable problems, even in extreme cases such as Ms. La Rue, who was raped on her first job interview. But this attitude is both callous and unjust. Strippers, like all female workers, have a job to do and feel that they have a right to work in an environment free from sexual harassment.

As long as one woman is being sexually harassed, regardless of her line of work, all working women are in jeopardy. Our research indicated that different people hold different perceptions about what is provocative behavior. Most people think strippers are provocative. Many people feel that waitresses don't deserve much sympathy. Some people think an attractive receptionist who dresses stylishly wants sexual attention from men. It's all a question of degree. No woman is asking to be sexually harassed. To attribute blame to strippers validates the argument that all women ask for what they get.

As Ms. La Rue said, "I realize that most women who are sympathetic to strippers see us as the most exploited group of working women. But as far as I'm concerned, all women are exploited. Prostitution and stripping aren't the causes of sexism. They are the result."

CASE 7: THE GOVERNMENT EMPLOYEE

I was horrified because I thought a human rights commission was an agency in power to protect women from this kind of sexual abuse. I was shocked and dismayed to discover that this kind of corruption went on there too.

Paula Singer is a forty-three-year-old married woman with three children. Several years ago she worked as an investigation officer for a human rights commission. Because she was sexually harassed by the director of the commission, she gave up what could have been a very promising career. Her story also involves a number of other cases of sexual harassment within the same office, which came to her attention after she left the job. Her involvement with these cases occurred because her next job was as a personnel officer within the same government.

MS. SINGER: At the time I began with the commission, I was divorced and on my own with my three children. A year after this I developed a steady relationship with a man I later married. Simultaneously I noticed a subtle change in the director's attitudes toward me. This was particularly evident at our annual staff Christmas party. He kept pressuring me to stay later and told numerous jokes about being a "freethinker" sexually and speculated about who would be sleeping with whom at the end of the evening. I felt very uncomfortable and left, making excuses that I had to meet my boyfriend.

From that time on, until I resigned, the director made continuous derogatory comments about the man I was seeing. He kept saying that marriage was "an old-fashioned institution" and that he couldn't understand why I was even considering it. This seemed rather contradictory in light of the fact that he had been married for twenty years and had four children. As far as I knew, he wasn't remotely contemplating a divorce.

At this time the agency was undergoing a reorganization. New opportunitites for advancement were opening up. The director informed me that my work was excellent and that I definitely had a future there.

A few weeks later I attended our annual staff conference, which was held at a small remote town several hundred miles north of the city. The director made a point of sitting next to me on the bus that had been chartered. For the entire trip he talked on about my future career and stated repeatedly that we had to spend more time together talking about it.

That evening there was a reception prior to the dinner. The director consumed a fair amount of alcohol. He began coming on in a very heavy-handed way. He kept insisting that he wanted to dance with me and how we really must get together to talk further about my future. We then proceeded to dinner, where he cornered me and told me that we should "have some fun" together that evening. I was very nervous and made my excuses. I told him I wanted to go back for a sauna at the hotel with the other women.

He kept insisting that we get together and that I dispense with this other man. He told me that discussions that were to be held later in the evening would be very important to my future. But I went back to the hotel with a number of other women and proceeded directly to my room. The minute I entered, the phone began to ring. I was positive it was him, and I refused to pick it up. I knew his ego was on the line and I was looking for a way to turn him off without annoying him. The phone must have rung for two hours into the night. The next morning he was very abrupt with me and asked me what time I got back to my room. Understanding full well the precarious position I was in, I was careful to tell him that I arrived back fifteen minutes after the last time that I knew he had called. He was extremely cool to me for the remainder of the time.

Right away I started looking for a new job. His insistence that I get rid of my relationship was very unsettling to me. By this time I had already married my boyfriend. We'd actually only been married for two weeks. The director remained very cool toward me and kept telling me how unfortunate it was that I had missed out on those discussions.

Within weeks I did in fact find another job. The director was furious when he found out I was leaving. He burdened me with extra work in order to delay me, but eventually he had no choice and had to let me go. Just before I left, he arranged for a farewell party, where he expressed his anger about my rejection of my future with the commission. It is my conviction that I only escaped just in time to avoid a bad reference and a totally impossible situation.

INTERVIEWER: Was that the end of it?

MS. SINGER: For me personally, yes. But in the next while, due to my position as a personnel officer, I became aware of other women at the same agency who were being similarly harassed. This time the harasser was not the director, but his second-in-command, John Sackville.

The first incident I heard of concerned a woman who had applied for a job as an investigation officer. She had spoken to Mr. Sackville about the possibility of securing a position. He told her that he was prepared to use his influence on her behalf if she would agree to go to bed with him. She couldn't believe it. She thought that a government office set up to protect human rights would stop that very kind of coercive behavior. But she told me she would not make a formal complaint because she was convinced that no one would believe her and that furthermore she would be treated like a "crazy" and end up as a victim.

INTERVIEWER: Were there any other incidents?

MS. SINGER: Yes, there was one that really sticks in my mind. Mr. Sackville was having a long-standing affair with one of the female officers from a regional district. Although it was a voluntary relationship, he held out the promise of a promotion to head office if she would leave her husband. Everyone in the office knew about this, and the women especially found it demoralizing. They were shocked that Mr. Sackville would use his position in this manner, and they also resented this woman exploiting her sexuality for an unfair advantage.

The female officer in question agreed to leave her husband and come to head office if Mr. Sackville would also leave his wife. He assured her that he was prepared to do so, so she moved. Shortly after she arrived at head office he made it clear to her that he had no intention of ever leaving his wife. Not long after this the relationship cooled considerably. Mr. Sackville then tried to divest her of her promotion by implying that her work was unsatisfactory, since she was obviously "promiscuous" and would embarrass the agency by sleeping with her clients.

INTERVIEWER: How was this resolved?

MS. SINGER: As far as I know the antagonism continues. Mr. Sackville was not successful in having her removed. But there is one other very important case. Just at the time that Mr. Sackville's relationship cooled with this woman, he began to pursue another female officer who had been happily married for many years. Jane Collins had been with the commission for six years and was considered to be a superb officer. Her future seemed promising. Despite Ms. Collins's best efforts to discourage Mr. Sackville, he persisted.

INTERVIEWER: What were his tactics?

MS. SINGER: Ms. Collins worked in a regional office and required consultation with Mr. Sackville on a regular basis. Mr. Sackville refused to come to her office and would only agree to discuss business over dinner. On one occasion there was an out-of-town conference which they both had to attend. In the evening, after the day's sessions, Ms. Collins's husband visited her briefly in her hotel room. Mr. Sackville was furious and publicly introduced a proposal at the next morning's session, attempting to set a precedent that no relatives could attend any portion of the conferences in future.

A month later Ms. Collins was informed that she would have to come to head office and stay in a hotel for about six weeks to catch up on a backlog of cases. Her husband, who occasionally had business in the city, often took the opportunity to spend the night with her when he could. Even though Mr. Sackville knew this, he kept up a barrage of calls, making sexual overtures even while her husband was in the room. Ms. Collins's husband was very upset and wanted to have a confrontation, but she insisted she could deal with it herself. She felt that the best way to proceed was to be polite and civilized. But the pressure started to take its toll. Ms. Collins's self-confidence was visibly shaken.

Ironically and perhaps disastrously, while all this was going on Ms. Collins was given a case to investigate involving sexual harassment. She needed Mr. Sackville's cooperation in order to pursue the case effectively. He made his support contingent upon her cooperation with his advances. At her wits' ends, she went to the director of the agency, my former harasser. He denied ever having had any other complaints of this nature before about Mr. Sackville. In fact he accused her of being hysterical and wondered why she couldn't cope with this problem herself. He told her she should be "more straightforward." She was so insistent that he promised to look into the matter and get back to her.

INTERVIEWER: Did he do anything about the complaint?

MS. SINGER: Although Ms. Collins contacted the director on several subsequent occasions, he was very evasive. Finally, she documented what had happened and personally hand-delivered it, so that he couldn't deny knowledge of the problem.

The result was that Mr. Sackville was moved to a very prestigious position, which gave him enhanced visibility and greater career opportunity. Ms. Collins was so upset that she finally came to me and told me the whole story. I took the matter up with the director of personnel. He told me I should warn Ms. Collins that unless she kept quiet she could only lose and would end up as a sacrificial lamb. I personally was told to leave well enough alone. As the personnel director said, "That's the way of the world. Mr. Sackville is a very capable person and is one of our star people." I was so angry and frustrated that I went over the personnel director's head and marched in to see the senior official in the department.

INTERVIEWER: Did he respond any better?

MS. SINGER: Not at all. Mr. MacLean expressed extreme annoyance that I had taken it upon myself to come to him. He asked me how I expected him to be a neutral adjudicator to both parties when I was doing my best to bias him. He went on to say that now that he had full knowledge of the case, he was forced to take some action. In future he didn't want to hear any more about sexual harassment. As far as he was concerned, it should be resolved at a lower level, preferably in personnel, and he should be left unbiased in case of a future hearing.

His parting shot was that he found Ms. Collins to be rather attractive himself and that she had probably played a part in the entire unfortunate affair. The personnel director was furious that I had gone over his head. He again reiterated that Ms. Collins should "just drop it" and that in any event the promotion of Mr. Sackville would resolve the problem. His exact words were, "Sometimes you have to sleep with people to get ahead. Women who don't understand this fail to understand part of the basis of sponsorship."

INTERVIEWER: What are your feelings about the commission now?

MS. SINGER: I think it's insidious that an agency that is set up to defend human rights is riddled with sexual harassment. They can't seem to recognize the distinction between their role as defender and the fact that they are perpetrators. Here we have all these female officers, trained to negotiate fair settlements in equal rights disputes, rendered powerless by injustice within their own agency.

What I find pathetic is the willingness of all women, even those who are trained to fight for human rights, to passively accept their situation. They try to make the best of the circumstances. They believe you should be civil and at all costs polite. They keep hoping that if they avoid the situation, it will go away. What's so sad is that none of us bring it on ourselves. We are victims, just like someone who is robbed or assaulted. It says a lot about society's attitudes toward working women.

This case is particularly indicative of how deeply rooted coercive sexuality is. Here we have a human rights agency, which for some women is the agency of last resort, internally infested with sexual harassers. This may provide a partial explanation of why human rights commissions generally handle the issue of sexual harassment with such indifference. Obviously, if a director and his second-in-command at a human rights agency sexually harass women with such ease and frequency, they must be totally insensitive to the ramifications of this behavior.

As all these cases point out, women suffer tremendously from sexual harassment, which is a very poignant form of sex discrimination. The men who work for human rights are especially chosen for their expanded social consciousness and their understanding of how detrimental discrimination in any form can be. Yet they fail to recognize that they are abusing their power by using it to coerce vulnerable women into unsolicited sexual relations.

2

An expression of power

DEFINITIONS OF SEXUAL HARASSMENT

"Any sexually oriented practice that endangers a woman's job—that undermines her job performance and threatens her economic livelihood" is defined as sexual harassment by the Alliance Against Sexual Coercion (AASC). AASC is a collective that has been formed with the ultimate goal of ending sexual coercion in the workplace.

Working Women United Institute (WWUI), a nonprofit organization, also established to fight sexual harassment, defines it as "any repeated and unwanted sexual comments, looks, suggestions, or physical contact that you find objectionable or offensive and causes you discomfort on the job."

Karen DeCrow, a former president of the National Organization of Women (NOW), claims that sexual harassment "is one of the few sexist issues that has been totally in the closet. It is an issue that has been shrouded in silence because its occurrence is seen as both humiliating and trivial." Gloria Steinem, of *Ms.* Magazine has referred to sexual harassment as "the taming-of-the-shrew syndrome. It's a reminder of powerlessness—a status reminder."

THE RANGE OF BEHAVIOR

Sexual harassment can manifest itself both physically and psychologically. In its milder forms it can involve verbal innuendo and inappropriate affectionate gestures. It can, however, escalate to extreme behavior amounting to attempted rape and rape. Physically, the recipient may be the victim of pinching, grabbing, hugging, patting, leering, brushing against, and touching. Psychological harassment can involve a relentless proposal of physical intimacy, beginning with subtle hints that may lead to overt requests for dates and sexual favors.

All women are targets for this type of male behavior in normal social settings and to some extent on the streets. When this kind of activity is transferred to the work setting, women's vulnerability increases dramatically. It can poison a woman's work environment to the extent that her livelihood is in danger. There is the implicit message from the harasser that noncompliance will lead to reprisals. These reprisals can include threatened demotions, transfers, poor work assignments, unsatisfactory job evaluations, sabotaging of the woman's work, sarcasm, denial of raises, benefits, and promotions, and in the final analysis, dismissal and a poor job reference. In no uncertain terms, it is made clear to the woman that she must give in to the harasser's sexual demands or suffer the employment-related consequences.

Women working at the bottom of the economic scale are subject to the grosser expressions of sexual harassment. They often encounter crude suggestive comments and crass physical assaults. Professional and managerial women are not immune to sexual harassment. Their treatment is more subtle, and instead of the outright physical abuse they are subject to psychological intimidation. They receive offers for after-work drinks, expensive lunches and dinners, and business trips, with the implicit message that sexual favors are expected. What this implies is that men up the ante for professional women. They are seen to have more economic independence, so men assume it must take more to impress them. It is part of the theory that every woman has her price.

In defining coercive sexuality, it is not always necessary that there be job-related reprisals attached to the sexual invitation. An unsolicited sexual advance made by a person with the authority to hire and fire is inherently coercive. The mere asking of the question places the woman in jeopardy. The employer-employee relationship embodies clearcut power implications.

At a social gathering, a meeting between a male president of one company and a female file clerk of another company is feasible and open to normal social ramifications—in theory, at least, the woman can accept or reject the invitation with impunity. The same would not be true for these two people in an employer-employee relationship with its inherent power implications. Unfortunately, the work environment lends itself to exploitation, especially when we are not dealing with a meeting of equals.

In a society where a woman is fundamentally defined as a sex object, and men hold most of the positions of power and influence in a hierarchical work structure, it is inevitable that sexual harassment has become a pervasive feature of many working environments.

SURVEYS OF SEXUAL HARASSMENT

In an effort to define statistically the presence, extent, and handling of sexual harassment, a number of surveys were undertaken in the United States between 1975 and 1977.

In May 1975, Working Women United Institute conducted a survey in the Ithaca region of upstate New York. Of the 155 women surveyed, 70 percent reported that they had experienced sexual harassment at least once; 92 percent of the respondents considered it a serious problem; and even among those women who had never experienced sexual harassment, 63 percent considered it serious.

In WWUI's survey, of the 70 percent who had been sexually harassed, 75 percent ignored it. The harassment only continued or worsened. Of those who ignored it, 25 percent were penalized by unwarranted reprimands, sabotage of their work, and dismissal. Only 18 percent of those harassed complained through established channels. No action was taken in over half of the reported cases. In one-third of the cases negative repercussions, such as increased workloads, unwarranted reprimands, and poor personnel reports, resulted.

In the same survey the women who did not complain cited the same reasons:

- 52 percent felt that nothing would be done
- 43 percent felt it would be treated lightly, or they would be ridiculed
- 30 percent felt they would be blamed, or there would be some repercussions

In 1976 *Redbook* magazine conducted a survey among its readers to solicit their views on sexual harassment. The editors of the magazine were astonished to discover the overwhelming response: Nine thousand readers took the trouble to reply; 88 percent of the respondents had experienced some form of sexual harassment; 92 percent considered the problem of sexual harassment serious. *Redbook* reported that out of their total respondent pool, only 25 percent thought that a harasser who was reported would be asked to stop "or else."

A naval officer used the *Redbook* questionnaire to poll women on his base in the town of Monterey, California. Of those who were polled, 81 percent replied that they had experienced some form of sexual harassment.

Of the 875 women in professional and clerical positions polled in 1976 by the Ad Hoc Group on the Equal Rights for Women Committee at the United Nations, one-half of the women reported that they had at some time either personally experienced sexual pressure or were aware that such pressure existed within the organization. Slightly less than one-third of the staff members who were harassed complained. The reason frequently given for not having done so was the perceived absence of proper channels through which to lodge a complaint.

In the fall of 1977 Professor Sandra Harley Carey, a sociologist with the University of Texas at San Antonio, surveyed 481 working women, all of whom replied that they had suffered some form of sexual harassment.

Of these women 16 percent said the sexual advances by male co-workers or the boss were so disturbing that they resigned. Sexual advances mentioned by the women included leering or ogling (36 percent), hints and verbal pressures (37 percent), and touching, brushing against, grabbing, or pinching (3 percent). Male supervisors asked 18 percent of the women away for a weekend, and 6 percent said they were promised rewards for their other-than-business activities.

The survey found that few of the women took any action against the men involved. "A woman is socialized to be the victim and not to fight," Professor Carey said. A few of the women reported incidents to supervisors, but such reports "were fruitless."

All of these surveys confirm the pernicious effect sexual harassment has upon its victims. More specifically, 48 percent of *Redbook*'s respondents had themselves quit or been fired from a job due to harassment or knew someone who had; 75 percent reported being "embarrassed, demeaned, or intimidated" by harassment; 81 percent felt angry; 50 percent were upset; 24 percent were frightened; and 21 percent felt guilty. There were also frequent complaints of powerlessness, self-consciousness, feelings of defeat, diminished ambition, decreased job satisfaction, impairment of job performance, and adverse physical symptoms such as headaches, nervousness, insomnia, and anxiety attacks.

These surveys indicate that sexual harassment is a problem of epidemic proportions. The pervasive secrecy surrounding the issue is a function of fear of reprisals. This fear is more than justified, as exemplified by a *Harvard Business Review* poll of 1,500 male managers on management issues relating to women. Most of them said they "did not feel their organizations had any responsibility to alter their employees' attitudes towards women."

WHY WOMEN ARE SILENT

Sexual harassment is a problem that most women have sublimated, although it is endemic to the workplace. Their reluctance to confront the issue bluntly stems from a number of valid fears. Women are either embarrassed or humiliated that they are the targets of sexually coercive behavior. But more than that, they are intimidated as subordinates in the hierarchical structure, fearing that a direct confrontation would result in threats to their livelihood. Finally, women generally do not want their husbands, boyfriends, parents, and children to know of their predicament. They fear that they will be ridiculed or made to feel guilty that they in some way were responsible by encouraging the harasser.

These are not idle fears. Women have had ample opportunity to observe what happens to those women who do publicly complain about this kind of job situation. They have repeatedly seen these women ridiculed, intimidated, and ignored. Most male supervisors treat it as a joke or as an indication that the woman is a "troublemaker," vindictive, unstable, or of questionable morals.

Since most women do not believe that they will be able to stop sexual harassment by speaking up, they will go to great lengths to signal their unavailability. They may dress down or in severely tailored clothes, wear wedding bands, invent boyfriends, or behave in a very cool, reserved manner. But the subterfuge can cause almost as much stress and anxiety as the harassment.

Middle-class and professional women respond to sexual harassment with the same wall of silence as do working-class women. Sexual harassment cuts across class lines, leaving all women feeling that they have lost control and experiencing a sense of doom.

WHY DO MEN SEXUALLY HARASS?

Sexual harassment is not an expression of sexual desire. Men who sexually harass are not behaving as lovers, but as bullies. It is a demonstration of power politics, an assertion of power that happens to be expressed in a physical manner. It is the ultimate reminder to women that their fundamental status in society is that of sex object and that they hold their positions in the workforce only on male sufferance.

The motivation behind sexual harassment becomes clearly apparent when one examines the problems of women who are working in nontraditional jobs. Women who are moving into occupations that have historically been all-male find that they, even more than other women, are targets of extreme and concerted forms of sexual harassment.

As affirmative-action programs begin to show results and more women are able to find jobs in these areas, male supervisors and coworkers have fought back with the last weapon available to them: sexual coercion. The situation has become so serious that the United States Department of Labor was forced to publish proposed regulations in 1977 requiring construction contractors to maintain a working environment free of harassment, intimidation, and coercion. *The New York Times* reported that women around the country "tossed their hard hats in the air" in relief.[1]

A woman's age, appearance, and status do not appear to determine whether or not she will be a victim of sexual harassment. As a woman-object in a subordinate position she is vulnerable. She is not desirable in herself but represents the extension of the husband-wife relationship carried to its extreme. It is the perpetuation of the active-male/passive-female syndrome. The man presumes, as in the dating game, that there is no harm in trying. At the office as in the home, the woman is seen as an economic dependent—dependent on her boss for her living. Sex goes with the territory in the psyche of a sexual harasser.

WHO ARE THE SEXUAL HARASSERS?

Male perpetrators of sexual harassment cannot be defined as psychologically disturbed, perverted, or even immature. They could be any man. As long as it is an accepted notion that women are objects—easily manipulated and a sexual perk—the most ordinary of men are capable of sexual harassment.

Similarly, the most powerful and famous of men are equally capable of this behavior. In *A Sexual Profile of Men in Power,* the authors describe an incident of sexual harassment perpetrated by President Lyndon Johnson:

The assumption which [President Johnson] shared with so many politicians was that women were merely one of the many perquisites of high office, objects to be used at his convenience. The most telling illustration of Johnson's imperious way with women was the story of a girl on his staff who was awakened in her bedroom on the Texas ranch in the middle of the night by a searching flashlight. Before she could scream, she heard a familiar voice: "Move over, this is *yore* President."[2]

Bosses, supervisors, co-workers, clients, and customers can all be perpetrators of sexual harassment. Bosses and supervisors obviously have a great deal of power over a woman's job and can threaten her with serious employment consequences for failure to comply with sexual demands. Co-workers in most cases have little direct power over fellow employees, but have a unique opportunity to poison the working atmosphere and can make working life intolerable. Clients and customers can threaten to take their business elsewhere and cancel contracts with the woman's firm.

In some cases even employees supervised by a woman can cause her difficulty with their sexual advances. Two instances of this latter phenomenon came to our attention during the course of our research. In one case a college professor was forced to fend off male graduate students who saw sexual advances as a way to curry favor. In the other a woman who owned a real estate agency lost her best salesman: He quit, telling her he couldn't work for her unless sex came along with the job. In determining who can be a sexual harasser the relevant point is whether the man in question can create job-related reprisals for a female worker who refuses his sexual advances.

TWO CATEGORIES OF HARASSERS

At the outset of our research we hypothesized that sexual harassers appeared to fall into two categories: the one-time offender and the relentless repeater. The former, we discovered, was often a man in crisis. A death in the family, the approach of middle age, or a divorce had precipitated aberrant behavior. The latter, it seemed, had assessed that sex went with the territory. It was akin to double cream in one's coffee, a carpet in one's office, or more precisely, the exercise of one's prerogative over women subordinates. Relentless repeaters, in many of the cases we uncovered, harassed scores of working women throughout their careers.

As the research progressed, we were surprised to discover that the relentless repeaters were in the majority. A man who might at first look like a one-time offender, upon subsequent examination, often turned out to be another relentless repeater. In many cases men sexually harass women after they experience some blow to their manhood from work. Our society encourages and tolerates men who take their frustrations out on women. Different men have different tolerance levels. Thus some men sexually harass more frequently. And there is always a first time. But once a sexual harasser sees that this behavior makes him feel more powerful, that he won't get into trouble, and in fact may get applause from other men for his actions, he is likely to sexually harass again.

In our society, male sexuality is equated with power, virility, strength, and domination. In fact, men rarely suffer censure from aggressive sexual behavior. Their peers offer encouragement, admiration, and accolades for sexual conquest.

Precisely because male sexual advances are so inextricably intertwined with the image of the "male conqueror," a rejection is tantamount to a failure of manhood. The wounded male ego reacts by escalating the attack to the stage of sexual coercion.

There are some men who never indulge in sexual harassment. Their religious proclivities, their ethical standards, and their personal code of morality preclude extramarital sex or aggressive, unsolicited sexuality. For many of these men, sex is not an expression of power but rather a part of interpersonal relationships. Unfortunately their numbers are small, but their response when they learn of the phenomenon of sexual harassment is unbridled.

THE VICTIM'S REACTION: SEXUAL HARASSMENT SYNDROME

A small percentage of sexually harassed women report that they felt flattered in the initial stages of the sexual advance. This is not surprising.

Our entire society emphasizes that women should measure their status by their success in attracting men. The pervasive belief is that women are flattered by sexual come-ons.

The majority of sexually harassed women, however, do not feel flattered. They recognize only too clearly how precarious their position becomes when sexual initiatives can be combined with job-related reprisals. Even the small numbers of women who are flattered at the outset find to their dismay that when the harassment continues after they reject the advances, flattery quickly turns to fear and anxiety.

Many victims suffer from "sexual harassment syndrome." Fending off unsolicited and offensive sexual advances every working day causes tension, anxiety, frustration, and anger. Most women find their job performance suffers as they are forced to take time and energy away from work to deal with sexual harassers. The anger they feel at this unjust treatment is often internalized as a deep sense of guilt. Society wrongly views sexual harassment as sexually motivated. Women are socialized to think that it is their responsibility to control sexual matters. When they are unable to do so—and in an employment situation, there are very few women who can deal with sexual harassment from supervisors and other men with authority over them—they believe it is due to some shortcoming on their part.

The tension, fear, and anger build up inside sexual harassment victims who have nowhere to turn for relief. Most victims experience psychological depression and despair. Many suffer physical ailments such as stomachaches, headaches, nausea, involuntary muscular spasms, insomnia, hypertension, and other medical illnesses caused by continual, unrelenting anxiety and frustration. A surprising number are reduced to the point of psychological and physical breakdown, to such an extent that they require hospitalization.

THE MALE RESPONSE

A court battle charging that Yale University faculty members had sexually harassed their students is currently pending. Although five women students and a male assistant professor filed a class action suit, contending that male faculty members had engaged in sexually offensive conversations and behavior resulting in a multitude of harms, the university responded in a defensive, cavalier manner. As one Yale spokesman said, "It's not a new thing, but it is also not a major problem." Another university official who claimed to be in touch with large numbers of faculty members and administrators added, "There is a strong argument that if women students aren't smart enough to outwit some obnoxious professor, they shouldn't be here in the first place. Like every institution, Yale has its share of twisted souls."[3]

Yale is an Ivy League university whose reputation is based on scholarship and the pursuit of high ideals. Yet when faced with evidence of moral corruption within its own ranks, its response is a strident, arrogant denial. There is no suggestion that the most fundamental precepts of fair play demand, at the very least, an internal investigation. The onus is placed on the female victims, suggesting that if they were competent, mature women, they could have handled it.

The example of Yale University is indicative of the general male response. Sexual harassment strikes a central nerve in the psyche of all men. Those men who are somewhat sympathetic to the effects of overt acts of violence on women, such as rape and battering, cannot accept the notion of sexual harassment as a widespread problem. At best they attribute it to the isolated acts of a few perverted, immature, or disturbed men.

The hostile, defensive, ridiculing response that the subject of sexual harassment elicits is indicative of the fact that most men can imagine themselves as perpetrators. The milder forms of sexual harassment are viewed as part of the general sexual byplay that is endemic to all working environments. To admit that sexual harassment is deeply offensive and humiliating to women is an unpleasant expression of the coercive power that men exercise over women, even when they are in the position of paid workers.

Most people appear to believe that office flirtation in itself is not a bad thing—that it is a normal interaction between sexually healthy men and women. It adds an element of intrigue, romance, and even mystery to everyday working life. However, in a society that designates the male as the conquering sexual hero and the female as the docile, submissive puppet, sexual byplay has a great potential for damage. The actors in this work-world drama are not equal, so that flirtation can quickly become coercion.

To bring sexual harassment into the open will force the vast majority of men to rethink what they have traditionally construed as "harmless fun." Women, they will discover, are not discussing an obscure, relatively minor problem, but one of the basic symptoms of sexism in our society.

UNFOUNDED MYTHS

Throughout the history of women at work, sexual harassment has been grossly misunderstood. A number of the more predominant myths about sex on the job still find widespread acceptance despite the fact that they bear no relation to reality.

1. Women Who Object Have No Sense of Humor

The reaction of many people to women who are beginning to speak out against sexual harassment is that they lack a sense of humor and are overreacting to what is essentially harmless behavior. This is absurd. Sexual harassment, with the prospect of imminent reprisals affecting working conditions and future career plans, is neither humorous nor harmless. It is degrading and humiliating. It threatens women's economic livelihood and in many cases causes physical and psychological reactions that are severe enough to lead to hospitalization.

2. A Firm No Is Enough to Discourage Any Man

An astonishing number of people dismiss any discussion of sexual harassment with the peremptory answer that all any woman has to do is to refuse her harasser's advances firmly. They completely ignore another societal myth that when a woman says no, she really means yes. They also ignore the fact that the situation is not between equals. By its very definition sexual harassment involves sexual advances from men who have power to bring employment-related reprisals down on women who refuse them. A man who has greater economic, physical, and social power can override a woman's protests regardless of how firm and unequivocal they may be.

3. Middle- and Upper-Class Working Women Do Not Suffer from Sexual Harassment

Many of those who will admit that sexual harassment exists refuse to recognize that it is a problem for women of all classes and is as serious a job impediment for managerial and professional women as it is for lower-echelon employees. Professional and managerial women cannot handle sexual harassment any better than working-class women can.

Although middle- and upper-class women may hold positions of some status in their organizations, their harassers hold power and authority over them. Job-related reprisals can be used as effectively against these women as against lower-level employees. In fact, professional and managerial women move in smaller circles and therefore in some cases stand to lose even more from a sexual harassment incident than do other women. In professional circles or specialized fields, word quickly leaks out. These women are less able to bury evidence of their past work experience. All their harasser has to do is to mention casually that the woman was fired or quit because she was emotionally unstable or could not get along with co-workers and supervisors and she may be black-balled for good.

Underlying the myth that higher-status working women are not sexually harassed is what we shall call the Archie Bunker theory. To make the argument that lower-class women receive more sexual harassment is to insinuate that the lower-echelon men who supervise these women harass more than their upper-class counterparts. Since the beginning of industrialization this argument has been presented. It is a discriminatory, class-based theory, and according to all the evidence it is manifestly inaccurate.

4. Women Often Make False Accusations of Sexual Harassment

As with all sexual crimes, society seems to fear that many women will accuse men of sexual harassment without justification. Victims of other crimes and antisocial behavior never seem to face the credibility barriers placed before women. Such attitudes are the result of hostile, misogynist views about women and are patently unfair.

A woman who is courageous enough to bring forward a complaint of sexual harassment will face disbelief, ridicule, and accusations of enticement. Often she will lose her job because she complained openly. If her complaint becomes public knowledge, other employers will be reluctant to hire her in the future. Women who make charges of sexual harassment have little to gain and a great deal to lose. Recognizing these repercussions, women would be foolhardy to bring false complaints.

THE LINK TO VIOLENCE AND RAPE

Violence against women in society refers to both specific and general abuse. It includes battering, rape, and other forms of physical domination. It also encompasses the attitudes that imply that women are "fair game." Sexual access to women and physical domination of women are considered to be male prerogatives according to the prevailing attitudes in our society.

Attacks against women—including rape, battering, molesting, assault, and sexual harassment—have been tolerated or even encouraged in many ways. In the movies and on TV, the super macho male is presented as the ideal masculine type. Comedians make jokes about beating their wives. In the legal system, rape victims are often humiliated by lawyers who try to insinuate that they "asked for it." And assault by a husband against a wife is rarely even treated as a crime.[4]

It is not surprising, therefore, that sexual harassment, one of the more subtle forms of violence against women, is a "secret oppression." When women are treated with such derision when they attempt to defend themselves against extreme forms of violence such as rape and battering, they can hardly be expected to be assertive and open about sexual harassment.

As in all forms of violence against women, by speaking up women run the risk of being classified as enticers. One would expect that other women would be supportive and sympathetic. This, unfortunately, is not the pattern, as exemplified by the attitudes of women jurors at rape trials. These women generally perceive raped women as less than innocent. That is understandable, since identifying with the victimization of raped women makes all women feel extremely vulnerable. It is easier to assume that rape does not happen to moral, upstanding women and that rape victims are inherently lacking in moral fiber and somehow deserving of their fate.

The problem is compounded for victims of sexual harassment. Their ordeal is not as graphic as in rape and battering. Sexual harassment takes its toll in a long-drawn-out battle of nerves, where the woman is generally the loser. She may lose not only her job but her self-confidence and self-esteem. She is left with the ugly feeling that there is something fundamentally wrong with her. Even though rape is still treated with abnormal disdain and indifference, the public consciousness has been somewhat heightened in the last five years, specifically by women's individual and collective efforts to demonstrate that rape is a vile, reprehensible crime. As yet, sexual harassment is hardly acknowledged as a condition of working women's lives, let alone as a crime.

POTENTIAL TO BIND WOMEN

Sexual harassment is one of the most compelling problems confronting women in society. It stands at the crossroads, encompassing both economic coercion and an aspect of violence against women. Since it affects all working women, it has tremendous potential to bind women together. For all women who have ever personally suffered from sexual harassment, there is a tremendous sense of relief in learning that their sexual harassment is not a personal problem but rather part of a societal issue. Women who have been indifferent, neutral, defensive, or even hostile to the women's movement may alter their thinking when confronted with a phenomenon that does not differentiate between women in terms of class, race, or economic and social status.

SOCIETAL PATTERNS PLAY A SIGNIFICANT ROLE

Societal patterns of sexual behavior lay the foundations that permit sexual harassment to become a normal part of the working environment. From the earliest point of teen-age dating, men are expected to take the role of the sexual aggressor. Women are not seen as free to initiate sexual activity on their own.

Although notions of the "sexually permissive" society are beginning to alter traditional double standards, it is still true that "nice" women are not free to dispose of their own sexuality according to their personal desires. From birth women are taught to preserve their virginity for their future husbands. Women are taught to evaluate their worth in terms of their sexual and reproductive capacities. They are expected to make the best bargain possible on the marriage market, exchanging these assets for future financial and emotional security.

Once they have made such a bargain, society enforces it. Women are expected to consent to sexual relations with their economic provider regardless of their personal wishes. The law explicitly provides that a woman cannot be raped by her husband. The provision of sexual services is part of the marriage contract, upon which a woman cannot renege. Similarly an employer takes on the role of economic provider for female employees. Unfortunately sexual favors often become part of the bargain.

Since women are put in the position of bartering with their sexuality, it is not surprising that men attempt to persuade and coerce women into granting them sexual favors, trying to get the best deal they can. Their actions range from mild persuasion to physical assault. The tactics to some extent depend on the man's personal assets. If he is rich, powerful, and attractive, his "charm" may be all he needs. If this is not enough, he may be able to use economic coercion, which is often readily available in the employment setting. Men who lack all of these assets rely, in some cases, on physical force.

When coercive sexuality manifests itself through physical force, as in rape, the criminal system and society take action to punish the offender. Lesser forms of coercive sexuality—of which sexual harassment is a prime example—are ignored. As a result society turns a blind eye to most sexual coercion. The most unsettling aspect of our findings was that the majority of people with whom we discussed sexual harassment were unable to distinguish between coercive and consensual relationships.

Whenever we would begin to discuss instances of sexual harassment, people would bring up examples of office romances, ignoring the fact that such relationships were mutual.

There is a world of difference between a man and a woman who express mutual attraction and proceed to engage in a relationship freely and without any element of pressure, and the situation where a boss independently insists on an affair with his subordinate, who stands to lose her job if she refuses. The inability of most people to distinguish between the office romance and sexual harassment is a frightening indication of how often sexual harassment must go on. The coercive element in such relationships is so completely invisible that people are unable to distinguish between consensual affairs and blatant abuse of authority for sexual purposes.

That is why sexual harassment is an issue that must be dealt with at all costs. To force society to recognize that sexual harassment is a crime against women is to force it to take issue with the coercive sexuality inherent in all of its fundamental attitudes and practices.

3

The history of sexual harassment

SEX AND VIOLENCE IN TORONTO, 1915

On the evening of February 8, 1915, Charles Albert Massey, a prominent member of one of Toronto's wealthiest and most powerful families, walked up to the door of his Walmer Road home after work. Suddenly a shot rang through the air, and the bullet pierced Massey's left breast. A newsboy up the street witnessed him stagger out of the doorway when a second shot felled him to the sidewalk. He died almost instantly.

The police arrived and were searching through Massey's house when they heard noises from the attic. One policeman called out, "Come on down, you had better surrender!" A voice called back, "Come on up!" When the police climbed the stairs to the attic, the sight that met their eyes was a pale and trembling housemaid with a revolver still clutched in her hands.

The police told the woman she was under arrest for murder, whereupon she sobbed bitterly, saying: "Yes, I shot him. He ruined my character. Take me away from here; he has ruined my life." She was promptly arrested and taken to jail to stand trial for her employer's murder.

Carrie Davies, the accused housemaid, was a short, fair-haired girl of eighteen. Her life until this moment had been much like that of any other eighteen-year-old girl in the same station of life. Two years earlier she had immigrated to Canada from her home in England. Her older sister had traveled to Canada several years before, had found work, and had married and settled in Toronto. Carrie's widowed mother, who was going blind, found it increasingly impossible to support her large number of children in England, and Carrie felt it necessary to move to Canada to look for work so that she could send money home to help support her family. Her sister had loaned Carrie the money to pay her passage, and when she arrived in Canada, she had immediately gone to live at the

46

Massey home as a domestic servant. All of the money she received as wages she used to repay her sister for the loan and to send back to England, along with weekly letters to her mother and brothers and sisters.

Why had Carrie shot her employer that fateful day? The family of the dead man told reporters she was under a spell and mentally deranged. They suggested she be put away without prosecution or court proceedings. Massey's sister-in-law told a Toronto newspaperman that although she knew that it had been hinted that Massey might have been indiscreet and acted improperly toward the girl, that whole story was ridiculous. "No person who knew my brother-in-law will believe that for a minute," she said. "If Mr. Massey had acted improperly toward her, why did she remain in the house? Why didn't she say something to one of us?"

Carrie's trial began in Women's Court in Toronto City Hall on the morning of February 25, 1915. It drew a crowd—chiefly composed of women—that almost stormed the City Hall corridors. Three policemen were needed to keep back the overswell.

The trial generated considerable sympathy for Carrie among Toronto citizens, and numerous letters to the editor were written to the newspapers in support of her acquittal. To pay the costs of her legal defense, a defense fund was set up, which collected more than $700 from over one thousand contributors.

Carrie took the stand to give her evidence. She told the court that several days before the murder, Massey's wife had gone off to Connecticut to visit relatives, leaving Massey, Carrie, and Massey's young son alone in the house. Two nights before the murder Massey had held a dinner party, with lots of guests and lots of liquor. After the guests had left, he asked Carrie if she had seen him "run his hand up and down a certain lady's stocking." Carrie testified:

I didn't answer him, but just looked hard at him. He also said he had a lady friend of his own. He caught me by both hands around the waist and said he liked little girls. Then he kissed me and I struggled but he kissed me again. He was trembling and very much excited.

Carrie managed to break away, but shortly after this Massey called her up to his bedroom to make his bed. Carrie told the court what occurred when she tried to obey his instructions:

As soon as I went in, he began looking through Mrs. Massey's bureau drawers and brought out her underwear. He wanted me to try them on for him, and then he came towards me and tried to throw me on the bed. I struggled, pushed him to one side, and ran out of the room, upstairs, to my quarters. I locked my door while I dressed, and then left the house and ran to my sister's.

When she reached her sister and brother-in-law's home, Carrie told them her story. While they were alarmed, they told her she would have to return to the Massey home or she would lose her job. Torn between duty and fear, Carrie gave in to her sense of duty and, warned by her sister to be careful, she returned home that night. She avoided Massey by hiding in the cellar until he left for work in the morning. Under cross-examination, Carrie stated during the trial:

I was unable to work all day. I kept thinking of what had happened. He was my master and he kissed me and that worried me. When I saw him returning home that evening, I lost control. All I could think of was what he was going to do to me. He took advantage of me yesterday, and I thought he would do the same today. I shot him in self-defense.

The defense lawyer had several doctors conduct a physical examination of Carrie to ascertain whether she was still a virgin. During the trial the doctors took the stand and assured the court that their examination indicated Carrie was a virgin and had remained "a pure girl." In his summation to the jury, the defense counsel exhorted them to acquit this poor girl, whose actions had merely been conducted in self-defense, "to preserve her priceless and crowning jewel of womanhood."

After a half-hour deliberation the members of the jury returned to the packed courtroom, visibly affected, to announce their verdict: not guilty. The newspapers reported the pandemonium in the courtroom upon this announcement:

An instant after the foreman of the jury delivered the verdict, three hundred throats shouted in one tremendous cheer, such as never rang through a Canadian courtroom before. Meanwhile, the pale-faced girl, with the ostrich trimming of her hat trembling over her pale face, stood in the dock supported by two women. She leaned forward and clutched at the rail. The two women led her over towards her sister and Carrie fell into her arms. Tears welled up in the judge's eyes. In fact, there were few dry eyes in the courtroom.[1]

The dramatic acquittal of Carrie Davies demonstrated a phenomenon that has existed throughout the history of sexual harassment of working women. The court and the public recognized that the sexual abuse Carrie had suffered warranted her resort to self-defense, but there was no discussion about the morality of her employer's actions. Instead the trial focused upon Carrie's morality. That the defense lawyer felt compelled to introduce medical evidence of Carrie's virginity is both sad and shocking. There seemed to be a pervasive feeling that Carrie's valiant efforts to preserve her "jewel of womanhood" were to be admired as the actions of a pure woman. But what should a woman's virginity have to do with this? If Carrie had not been a virgin, would she have been convicted?

Surely the point was that Massey's unsolicited sexual advances constituted a crime against his housemaid, regardless of whether she was a virgin or a promiscuous woman. His conduct was the issue, not her reputation. What occurred during this trial was that in the age-old tradition the crime of men was neatly turned into a matter of the "character" of women. The parallel to modern-day attitudes is clear. In considering the topic of sexual harassment in the 1970s, the focus shifts away from male action to questions about whether women invite sexual harassment, whether women exploit their sexuality in the workplace, and whether women sexually harass men.

THE FOCUS ON WOMEN'S MORALITY

Modern-day attitudes indeed find their roots in history. During the Industrial Revolution the appalling working conditions nurtured a very ripe environment for sexual harassment. A number of royal commissions were set up to investigate the plight of the working class. None of these investigations examined the prevalence of sexual abuse. Instead they inquired into the question of immorality on the part of working women.

In Britain the reports of the Factory Commission in 1883 and the Children's Employment Commission in 1843 explored in some depth the low state of morals *among the workers* in all industries. No distinction was made between voluntary relationships and sexual advances from superiors, with coercion threatened as a penalty for noncompliance. The commissioners found that immorality among dressmakers and domestic servants was proverbial. Among the strawplaiters chastity was said to be "at a sad discount," while prostitution "was at a high premium." The moral condition of lacemakers was said to be "nearly as low as the plaiters." Prostitution was "rife among them from the same causes—scanty earnings, love of finery, and the almost total absence of early moral culture." Low standards in all industries were determined to be due not so much to congregating of men and women together in the workplace, as to the lack of education, the want of decency in their homes, and bad conditions all around.[2] Moral degradation was found to be due less to a debasement caused by the system than to the standards believed to be prevailing among the working classes generally.

Wanda Neff, in *Victorian Working Women*, states:

The coarse surroundings of a young girl in the factory, the prevalence of indecent language, the absence of dressing rooms, the necessity of working in scanty clothing on account of the heat, the precocious sexual development which was believed to result from the heat and confinement, the long hours, and the night work which made it necessary for her to be out late on the streets alone, the exhaustion which led to thirst, and the monotonous labour which brought a craving for excitement, were all studied carefully in relation to their effect upon morals.[3]

By turning around the question of responsibility for sexual licentiousness to an attack on women's morality, the social commentators of the time did women a grave injustice.

The situation in North America was similar to that in England. A Canadian royal commission was set up in 1886 to inquire into and report upon the relations of labor and capital in Canada. It provided a good example of this deflection of attention from sexual harassment to women's "immorality." The commissioners interviewed over 1,800 witnesses in Ontario, Quebec, New Brunswick, and Nova Scotia, including 102 women whose work ranged from textile work in cotton mills, woolen, and knitting factories, through manufacturing work in shoe factories, match factories, and tobacco industries, to millinery and dressmaking.

The commissioners searched diligently for immorality, assuming it to be a necessary consequence of the mingling of the sexes in the factories. However, even in their investigations of "immorality," the commissioners were a little off base. Their questions indicated an overwhelming concern about whether overhearing "immoral" language in the factories by factory girls would cause them to become immoral. They expressed a view that women and men should enter and leave the factory at different times so that the women would not hear the "bad words" uttered by the men.

The state of factory toilets amounted to a virtual obsession with the commissioners. Witnesses were asked whether separate "conveniences" were kept for men and women, how high the water closets were which separated the men from the women, and whether men were ever seen trying to get into the women's conveniences when the women were in there. Persistent inquiries were made about the presence in factories of women in "interesting conditions," that is, pregnant women— particularly unmarried ones. An unmarried pregnant woman was referred to as "the guilty party," and it was felt that no pregnant women should be mixing with young children at work.[4]

Ultimately, the commission did bring itself to ask several witnesses whether the behavior of foremen and factory owners toward women workers was "gentlemanly." Most of the women witnesses failed to provide any direct evidence on this, largely out of fear of reprisal. (The majority of women who testified even refused to permit the publication of their names, fearing dismissal or maltreatment on the part of their employers.)

Some of the women, interestingly, argued with the commissioners that the morality of factory women was unbesmirched and that the commission and press reporting of its hearings were exaggerating the "goings-on" in the mills. In a roundabout way these women recognized the injustice being done to them by the focusing of the commission on the question of morality of women rather than on injustices in the workplace.

There were, however, some oblique references to sexual harassment of factory women contained in the testimony of certain witnesses. The Archbishop of Quebec, E. A. Cardinal Taschereau, wrote to the commission stating:

It is necessary to provide means for the protection of morals in the factories and outside of them, before entering and after going out. It also happens sometimes that employers make an abuse of their authority, and the law ought to be severe. [5]

The following exchange took place between the commissioners and Pierre Pleau, a machinist from Montreal:

Q: What was, in your opinion, as the father of a family, the moral condition of the Ste. Anne factory during the time that you worked there? Did you see any reprehensible acts committed in the factory?
A: I saw things pretty "tough" as we say.
Q: Did they occur often?
A: Yes, several times, but as they were people above me, I had nothing to say.
Q: Do you mean to say that the manager and the superintendent of the factory did not maintain order in the establishment?
A: No, in this particular, they were a little too free with certain women. [6]

Another interesting discussion was held with Z. Lapierre, a boot and shoe manufacturer in Montreal:

Q: Is the girls' room separate from the men's room?
A: No.
Q: Have you any dressing room provided for the women?
A: No.
Q: They have to dress in the same room as the men work in?
A: There are only five girls working in the whole factory, and they can easily dress themselves without being seen by the men if they choose. [7]

One wonders at the truth of this last offhand comment. The lack of privacy these five women endured probably gave rise to serious sexual harassment and a great deal of suffering.

HISTORICAL MISINTERPRETATION

Despite the so-called findings of these commissions, no accurate data about the morals of working women during the Industrial Revolution are available. Friederich Engels, however, did speculate at the time that roughly three-quarters of the factory hands between the ages of four and twenty in England were unchaste[8]—something impossible to prove.

Modern historians have made the case that industrialization caused an increase in the rate of illegitimate pregnancies. One well-known historian, Edward Shorter, attributed this increased illegitimacy to the sexual emancipation of women working outside the home. Work led to sexual liberation, according to Shorter, causing women to become self-seeking, to rebel against traditional constraints, and to seek pleasure and fulfillment in uninhibited sexual activity.[9]

Other historians have disagreed with Shorter, arguing that women's work outside the home did not provide an experience of emancipation (due to poor pay and hard work), and that increased illegitimacy rates were due to an absence of traditional constraints such as family, local community, and churches. The absence of these constraints, along with increased mobility, kept men from fulfilling their promises to marry women with whom they had had sexual relations.[10]

Surprisingly, even modern historians have not considered whether sexual harassment of women by their supervisors or factory managers played a part in the rising illegitimacy rates. No longer protected by a family-unit, domestic type of industry conducted at home, and facing extremely severe living and working conditions, these women may have been compelled to comply with the sexual demands of their superiors in the workplace. This situation, combined with widespread ignorance about birth control, may in fact have played a significant role in the rising illegitimacy rates of the time.

Historical omission and misinterpretation have marked all facets of history where women are concerned. Until very recently history has largely been the recounting by men of the past experiences and exploits of men. The role played by women through the ages has been virtually ignored. Where it was considered, gross distortions are evident. Thus it is not surprising that details of sexual harassment of working women through history were rarely recorded, and when the matter was considered at all, the question became one of women's morality.

Modern-day women historians, naturally angry with this interpretation, have spent their energies rebutting previous accounts of female immorality. They, too, have failed to examine the issue of sexual harassment and its impact on working women through the ages. A great deal of reconstruction waits to be completed before the true story of the experiences of working women through history can be told. Despite the omissions and misinterpretations of historians, however, some accounts of sexual harassment have been left, and it is to these we will turn now.

FEUDALISM

During the Middle Ages and the feudal era, a custom existed that was referred to as the *droit du seigneur*, the right of the first night. Custom stipulated that all vassals or serfs were required to give their feudal lords the right to take the virginity of their brides. The only way this could be avoided was where the bride or the bridegroom paid a specific amount of produce in redemption dues.

While this may seem different from the normal forms of sexual harassment on the job, in fact, in feudal times the feudal lord was the employer of his vassals and serfs, and their brides became his sexual property. The exploitative practice of *droit du seigneur*—certainly a form of rape—appears to have been enforced regularly in certain parts of Germany, France, Italy, and Poland.

SLAVERY

Slave women, like the brides of feudal vassals and serfs, were seen as sexual property. Women were critical to the institution of slavery throughout the ages. They were forced into dual exploitation: as laborers and as reproducers. Their physical labor and their sexual favors belonged outright to their male masters. Slaves had no legal right to refuse sexual advances from their masters, since legally the concept of raping a slave simply did not exist.

Forced into the roles of field laborer, house servant, and breeder, a female slave was frequently used by her owner for his sexual and recreational pleasure. This sexual privilege was a hierarchical right that spilled over to the slave owner's neighbors, visitors, and younger sons eager for initiation into the mysteries of sex. Lower-class males, acting as overseers in the employ of the slave owner, also exercised their sexual prerogatives with slave women, using the fact of physical bondage and the power of the whip when necessary. Gross manifestations of sexual harassment were obviously a recurrent feature of the slavery system.

COTTAGE INDUSTRY

It is often assumed that the first women workers were produced by the Industrial Revolution. This view is totally unsupported by facts, since for centuries before the Industrial Revolution most women labored in their homes at a wide variety of tasks in rural domestic, cottage, and agricultural industry: brewing, dairywork, the care of poultry and pigs, the production of vegetables and fruit, spinning flax and wool, nursing and doctoring, clothing manufacture, preparation and preservation of food, cleaning, laundering, soapmaking, and candlemaking.

All production was for the family, and all members of the family labored from sunup to sundown. Few women worked outside the home as wage earners, and when they did, the sum would be paid directly to the male head of the family and not to the woman herself. With work so inextricably bound into the family unit, one would expect work-related sexual harassment to be limited.

During the next stage of economic development, at the beginning of industrialization, most women continued to work at home, but instead of producing solely for their family needs, they began to produce goods that were marketed to industrialists. A large group of middlemen grew up who acted as go-betweens to dispense materials and instruction to the women working in their homes and to collect the finished products.

This type of cottage industry was to continue into the twentieth century in certain trades. Wages were paid by the piece and were set so low that few women, despite unremitting toil, could earn a living wage. In addition they were powerless to resist the petty exactions and tyranny imposed by greedy and dishonest middlemen. These women were often charged a commission by the middlemen and were often obliged to take payment in inferior goods sold by the middlemen at inflated prices.

Credit was readily offered by these men, and once in debt the women were powerless to resist whatever deductions and conditions they imposed. Complaints were often voiced by these women about being forced to pay for materials they never received, not receiving payment promptly, and being fined for late or allegedly defective work when in fact the work was returned on time in satisfactory condition. They were often forced to walk long distances to the shop of the middleman only to be kept waiting for long periods of time.

Allegations were made by numerous women that middlemen of bad character used their power to victimize women, and almost invariably they came to prefer work in the factories to subcontracted work in their homes. It is not difficult to speculate on the amount of sexual harassment to which home workers must have been subjected.

THE INDUSTRIAL REVOLUTION

With the Industrial Revolution and the growth of the factory system, women's traditional work was moved from their own homes to the factories. This was a period of rapid urban growth characterized by large-scale migrations of men and women into the towns and cities in order to earn wages to make a living. Specialized production for commercial exchange replaced traditional household manufacture. The economic and social change of the period injected uncertainty, variety, and mobility into women's lives.

Small family-run farms were converted to more industrial large-scale agricultural enterprises. Wage laborers were utilized to farm these larger units under a gang system. Bands of workers of both sexes, working under the direction of an overseer and moving from farm to farm, were common.

A farmer desiring to have a piece of work done applied to a gangmaster, who contracted to complete the work for a specific sum. He then selected from the people in his employ as many men, women, and children as he thought necessary for the task and sent them to the farm under an overseer, whose business it was to accompany them on their journey and supervise their work.

The Government Inquiry in England into the Employment of Women and Children in Agriculture in 1834 universally condemned the gang system. By threats and physical blows women and children (whom the gangmasters found more easily driven and managed than male laborers) were urged beyond their strength. The accounts of some gangmasters were shocking in their descriptions of brutality and sexual license. The inquiry reported that the overcrowding and employment of both men and women from all districts led to "immorality" in most cases.[11]

Women who worked in the mines in the nineteenth century were also a source of grave concern to English society. A royal commission appointed in 1840 to investigate working conditions of women and children in the mines reported that they were engaged in tasks of appalling drudgery under almost indescribable conditions. In a great number of the coal mines the men worked in "a state of perfect nakedness" and were assisted in this state by females of all ages, "these females being themselves quite naked down to the waist."[12] As "hurriers," women loaded small wagons with coal. Young girls "hurrying" for men, working beside them in scanty garments and, alone with them for hours of the day in isolated parts of the mines, were totally at their mercy.[13] According to the commission, all classes of witnesses testified in the strongest terms as to the immoral effects of these conditions upon the women workers.[14] Again, it is part of the pattern of investigations in this era that immorality was blamed on the women and sexual impropriety was envisioned as a class failing—as occurring between men and women workers of the lower classes, rather than between men from supervisory or managerial ranks and working women in their employ.

THE FACTORIES

Women factory workers in the latter half of the nineteenth century and the early part of the twentieth century worked under nearly intolerable conditions, and they, too, suffered sexual harassment on the job.

The many women who experienced sexual abuse in the factories and shops suffered their humiliation and fear in private. Although sexual exploitation of young girls by men in power was a source of outrage among the female workers, few could afford not to play by the rules. Elizabeth Hasanovitz, a young Russian Jewish immigrant to the United States who became a factory operative and later a union organizer, was one of the few women who fought back and recorded her experiences.

In her autobiography, *One of Them*, Hasanovitz described one incident of personal sexual harassment.[15] She had been unemployed for some time when she had finally managed to find a job. In desperate financial straits she went to her boss to try to collect her wages after working for two and a half days, even though payday was not until later in the week. Her boss attempted to make her grant him sexual favors before giving her her wages. She recounted the incident as follows:

When the bookkeeper had my pay made out, she left. I still waited for the money. The boss sat at his desk writing. I had no courage to disturb him, so I sat and waited. At last he stood up, straightened himself, and smiled at me.

"So you are in hardship—too bad, too bad."

Then he took my pay, looked at it, fixed his eyes on me, and asked: "Is that all you get?"

"No, I get thirteen, but this is only for two days and a half," I said, already regretting to have aroused his pity.

"But my dear girl, that would not be enough for you. Don't you need more than that?" . . . I sat trembling with fear. . . .

"Wait a moment: I will give you some more."

But no more had I time to refuse when he grasped me in his arms. I screamed, and with superhuman strength, threw him from me and ran into the hall. . . . How I hated men, all of them without exception! I stood up before the mirror and studied my face, trying to find out if there was anything in it that awakened men's impudent feelings toward me. . . . If only I could discredit that man so that he would never dare insult a working girl again. If only I could complain of him in court! But I had no witnesses to testify the truth; with my broken English I could give very little explanation. Besides that, if I were working in a shop and were called to court the firm might suspect some evil in me and send me away. So I left him alone and never went to collect my money, although I was in a frightful need.

Individual women trying to fight back against sexual abuse were rarely successful, as this example points out only too clearly. However, once women working in factories and shops were unionized and union grievance committees were set up, charges of sexual abuse became one of the major complaints made by female workers to union officials. While in some cases the union was willing to attempt to resolve such situations, the attitudes of many union organizers were similar to those prevailing in society at large.

The attitude that sexual harassment was a female problem and not a crime against women was clearly expressed in this excerpt from a letter written by one female union organizer to another in 1912:

Insofar as moral conditions are concerned, well, this should not have been made the chief issue in the strike. . . . You know as well as I, that there is not a factory today where the same immoral conditions do not exist. You remember factories where we have worked and . . . both of us know that the cloak factories and all the other shops in the city, in New York and Chicago, every one of the men will take to the girls, take advantage of them if the girl will let them, the foreman and superintendents will flirt with the girls, and this is nothing new to those who know that this exists today everywhere. True that I have 17 affidavits in my possession now, but read them over and you find the same old story, that the foreman asked a girl to come into his office and hold hands, etc., etc. This to my mind can be done away with by educating the girls, instead of attacking the company.[16]

This union organizer was expressing her opinion that sexual harassment could be solved best through the education of the women, a concept that is clearly irresponsible and ineffective. To locate the problem as a matter of women's behavior is absurd. All the education in the world would do little to help a woman in desperate financial straits who was faced with a sexually coercive employer. The working conditions in the factories during the nineteenth and early twentieth centuries were highly exploitative and clearly conducive to gross manifestations of sexual harassment.

In Victorian society it was assumed that women were always to be dependent upon a man. If they were single, they were expected to live with their father or brothers; if they were married, they were to be supported by their husbands. Their wages were set so low that, even by the admissions of contemporary writers, working women could not support themselves, let alone any dependent children. Equal pay was unheard of even where women and men were working side by side at the same work in the same factory. In fact factory owners openly proclaimed that the reason they hired women workers was because they could pay them less.[17] When trade unions began to organize and pressed for higher wages, women were sometimes reluctant to join in. This reaction was natural enough, as employers usually reverted to male employees as soon as union organization boosted the conditions and wages of work.[18]

Much male public opinion failed to distinguish between women workers and prostitutes. Both were in some sense escaping from male authority and control and both were unprotected. This made them an easy prey for male lust. One example of this is the situation of women working in the Lowell Mills in New England. It was assumed that there was a connection between the working woman who sold her labor and the prostitute who sold herself.

Newspapers of the time published stories from local doctors and prominent citizens of the immoral activities of the female employees in the Lowell Mills:

There used to be in Lowell an association of young men called the "Old Line" who had an understanding with a great many of the factory girls and who used to introduce young men of their acquaintance, visitors to the place, to the girls for immoral purposes. Balls were held at various places attended mostly by these young men and girls, with some others who did not know the object of the association, and after the dancing was over the girls were taken to infamous places of resort in Lowell and the vicinity and were not returned to their homes until daylight.[19]

Public discussion of sexual harassment of working women in the factories, what little there was, revealed class antagonism. Whenever it was admitted that working women were suffering from sexual abuse on the job, discussion would focus on the fact that the first generation of industrial chiefs belonged to the uneducated classes—rough, coarse, strangers to etiquette, family traditions, and moral considerations.

While it was felt that charges that these men frequently used women in their mills for their amusement were exaggerated, it was also agreed that these women employees were dependent upon the overlookers, managers, and other men in authority. It was a matter of general acknowledgment that the new industrial chiefs were not the type of men who would be likely to place checks upon the behavior of their male overseers. No one publicly admitted that sexual harassers belonged to all classes.

DOMESTICS

If the picture portrayed by nineteenth-century literature is accurate, female servants, particularly the young, vulnerable maids, were often forced to become the sexual playthings of the members of their employers' families. Working conditions of live-in domestics in the nineteenth and twentieth centuries were arduous and made them extremely vulnerable to reprisals from employers. A factory worker may have had to work twelve hours or more for a subsistence wage, but when she left at the end of the day her personal life was her own. Servants, however, had very little time off (often one afternoon a week and the occasional Sunday). They were tied to their workplace and their employer's supervision twenty-four hours a day.

A domestic servant was afforded little privacy, dignity, or freedom to socialize with others. Forced to live under the same roof as her employer, she was constantly at his disposal. This must have made the situation intolerable where an employer expected sexual favors to go along with the rest of the duties exacted from domestic servants.

Once these illicit liaisons were discovered, the female servant could expect to be fired on the spot without recommendations, to sink to the gutter. The domestic servant who lost her virginity or, even more serious, became pregnant could no longer anticipate marriage. If she bore an illegitimate child, she would be dismissed from her job and shunned by society. It was a firmly held belief in Victorian society that an unmarried woman who had lost her virginity (or in the vernacular of the day, had "fallen") was unredeemable. An unmarried woman who was no longer "virtuous" would find herself ostracized, with little hope of finding a husband or regular employment in the future.

As a last resort, unemployed domestic servants frequently turned to prostitution. Faced with dismissal by their employers, domestic servants suffered greater insecurity than did factory or office workers in similar situations. They lost not only their means of earning a living but also their home. The insecurity, isolation, and loneliness that characterized domestic service made unemployed domestics particularly vulnerable to the recruitment efforts of madams and pimps.[20]

In fact there is evidence that the most common occupation followed by women before they became prostitutes was that of domestic service.[21] Ironically, this knowledge of the pattern-of-employment shift from domestic service to prostitution itself increased the frequency of sexual harassment perpetrated against domestic servants. Domestic servants were particularly subject to sexual harassment because their employers perceived them as already maintaining a lower morality.

One fascinating account of sexual harassment of a domestic servant was written over a century ago by Louisa May Alcott, herself the victim of this abuse. Faced with financial problems, Alcott had accepted employment as a companion to a middle-aged lady. She quickly learned, to her dismay, that she was also accountable to the lady's brother, who thought he had hired the attractive woman for his own pleasure.

When Alcott resisted his attentions, he assigned her dirtier and heavier household work. Despite spirited resistance Louisa May Alcott was unable to convince her employer to stop his amorous advances, and she was eventually forced to leave the job rather than submit.

WAITRESSES

North American waitresses at the turn of the century had similar problems. Two black women talked about their experience in Atlanta in the 1930's:[22]

ISABEL: Some of the girls wanted to work downtown as waitresses, you know, and I asked my daddy if I could—to earn extra money. Daddy said, "You will never work downtown. Not the way white men think about black women."

EVA: Yes, a black woman was fair prey, you know.

ISABEL: You see, a white man that might not dare accost a white girl is safe in his advances on a black girl. Why? Because in court her papa or brothers or any black man—even a black lawyer—wouldn't dare stand up against one white man.

EVA: The answer to all that was to protect us from it ever happening. But the idea was that if you were a black girl outside your area, and a white man decided to insult you . . . nothing could be done.

SALESCLERKS

Sexual harassment of women salesclerks in the nineteenth century seems to have been widespread. Wages were extremely low, and despite long hours, department store regulations concerning dress left salesclerks little money for food. They went hungry much of the time and often left their jobs in desperation to become prostitutes. According to one historian, male supervisors and floorwalkers took advantage of their plight and urged individual women to give them "concessions." A woman who refused found her job in jeopardy.[23]

OFFICE WORKERS

In North America, white-collar office jobs were viewed as highly favored positions. Women who held these jobs were generally native-born, as were their parents. Immigrants and black women rarely managed to obtain such positions. The appeal of office work was that it was cleaner and less strenuous than factory work as well as more socially acceptable. However, the hours of work were long and the salaries low. Sexual harassment was visited upon these working women as well, in the form of advances of men who also worked in the offices and who felt the young women were fair game and would not dare to protest.

LEGISLATION

In April 1890, the Canadian federal government introduced into the House of Commons an amendment to the criminal law to make it a criminal offense for a person who had a female employed in his factory to seduce her or to use the power that his position gave him to destroy her virtue. The legislation, however, required that the woman be of previously chaste character and under the age of twenty-one, and it only applied to women working in factories, mills, and workshops. Upon conviction the employer was liable to two years' imprisonment.

Extensive debate was held in the House of Commons over this legislation, with some members arguing that the age should be extended to thirty years, citing that "very painful cases" had occurred "where the age was over twenty-one, and where the impoverished condition of the unfortunate woman, and her state of subordination, were the causes of the seduction."[24] Some members also argued that the legislation should be extended to cover servant maids and women in offices and in theaters. One member of the House of Commons stated that he knew that young women who were "employed in subordinate parts in theatres were frequently seduced by the managers," and were "constantly liable to be affected by the temptation placed in their way that they would get good parts if they submitted to the advances of the manager."[25]

Other members were not so enamored of the legislation. Several objected to the extension of the age to thirty, arguing that after the age of twenty-one women were very well able to take care of themselves. One member expressed skepticism on the entire issue: "I have never heard of an instance of advantage being taken of a woman who was not pretty willing to accede." He felt that due to the opportunity this legislation would give women to "blackmail" their employers, men in charge of factories would be placed "at the mercy of the female sex." Not only would it open the door to blackmail, but it would put a premium on women falling. He believed that women "might even find it profitable to fall, who would otherwise have kept themselves straight."[26]

Still other men who spoke during the debate were defensive, mentioning how "fascinating" some women were and the need to protect themselves and to see that legislation was not enacted that would be likely to lead young men into trouble. One speaker was downright hostile: "We know very well that many a girl has the reputation of a previously chaste character, and that her chastity is, like the phases of the moon, very changeable."[27]

The ultimate vote in the House was to extend the age to thirty and pass the legislation, restricting its coverage to factories, mills, and workshops. The Senate amended the age to twenty-one, and it was enacted in that form.

The section came up for amendment in 1920, and a number of changes were made. Although the section was extended to apply to women in all forms of employment, the wording of the section was changed from "woman or girl" to read "girl." The intent behind this was to make the section inapplicable to married women, and it was subsequently interpreted as not applying to married women by the courts.[28] (The present wording of the section now refers to "female person" and presumably covers both married and single women.) Finally, in cases under this section the judge was to instruct the jury that they might acquit if they found the accused not "wholly or chiefly to blame."

The attitudes of the time—as reflected in the debates in the Senate—had not changed much since the initial enactment of the legislation. One senator provided the rationale for lifting protection from married women: "After a woman is married and has one or two children, it is absolute nonsense to talk of her requiring legislation of this kind."

Another senator was quite vociferous about the perils of covering domestic servants under this legislation, stating that it would "expose every householder to being blackmailed by a domestic servant." He recalled that the Senate members had found this matter cause for some amusement in the past but stated that domestic servants of the day were not in the position in which they had been forty or fifty years previously.

They are perfectly independent; it is the master or mistress who are now dependent. Every honourable gentleman knows that today the domestic servants as a rule go out in the evenings and remain out until 10 o'clock or later; and they are not always engaged in saying their prayers when they are out. To hold that the master of the house is to be deemed liable for the mistake that a girl of that kind makes is very unreasonable, and as I say, it opens the door very wide to blackmail. I think this is really pernicious legislation.[29]

This type of reasoning underlies much of the historic concern about the issue of legislation to protect women from sexual abuse at the hands of men. The overriding fear of many men appears to have been not the plight of the victimized woman but what might happen to a fine, upstanding fellow if a vengeful female lied and cried that she had been assaulted.

American historians have investigated a series of studies which endeavored to make the connection between low wages and vice, culminating in the "Purity Crusade" of the Progressive era.

The concern for the working girl shown by the middle class reformers who conducted these studies was double-edged; working women often saw it as condescension and resented the implication that they were morally weak.[30]

The legislative response focused on protective legislation. The goal was to enact legislation providing women with shorter working hours than were required of men. There were various waves of agitation for protective legislation in the nineteenth century. By 1908 the principle of legislative limitation of women's hours was upheld by the United States Supreme Court.

Mary Bularzik in her *Radical America* article, "Sexual Harassment at the Workplace: Historical Notes," argues that fear of sexual harassment was one of the main motivating forces pushing for this legislation.

Threats to morals were prominent among these "dangers" of employment to women. The general opinion was that women workers were subject to harassment of superiors, and thus should be prohibited from certain occupations and night work, for their own protection.[31]

THE TWENTIETH CENTURY

Twentieth-century trends in the workforce have witnessed a growing number of female workers employed outside the home. Women from the poorer classes have always worked outside their homes, but growing numbers of middle- and upper-class women, both single and married, have entered the workforce in recent years. While in the 1920s the tendency was for single girls to work until they got married, once married, social pressure required that middle-class women stay at home. As well, many employers, including the federal civil service, adopted rules insisting that women resign upon marriage.

During the world wars,. however, North American women were recruited to fill the jobs left vacant by the soldiers at the front and the new jobs created by the wartime development of industry. Single and married women went out to work, although this was largely seen as a temporary measure, and the concessions of tax relief and day care centers provided to working women were withdrawn at the end of the wars.

After World War II the increase in the female labor force was due mainly to an increase in the proportion of married women aged thirty-five to fifty-four wishing to work. The structural change in the workforce, with a great expansion of white-collar and service industries, provided a large number of new jobs of the sort traditionally thought of as "female," and the growing numbers of working women filled these spots. Rather than being distributed evenly over the occupational structure, women have continued to be slotted into a few jobs and have remained practically absent from most others.

This increase has of itself increased the incidence of sexual harassment on the job. There are simply more working women to be harassed. It is only very recently, however, that the term "sexual harassment on the job" has become a common topic of discussion and women have begun to demand that such abuse cease.

There are many theories why this is such a recent phenomenon. One is that since more women are working, there are more instances of sexual harassment and that this has brought the problem to a head. Another is that middle-class women have begun to recognize they will continue to work outside their homes for the majority of their lives. This, it is argued, causes them to take threats to their working status—such as sexual harassment—more seriously.

Another theory ties the discussion of sexual harassment to that of rape, pointing out that rape, too, was a closet issue about which few people spoke out until recently. Women rape victims feared reprisals and personal attack from a society that viewed rape victims with some suspicion and distaste. In the last few years the women's movement has attempted, with some degree of success, to categorize rape clearly as a crime against women and to turn attention away from other irrelevant issues.

Sexual harassment can be seen as a subissue of rape, and in the more enlightened climate of the present, women are less afraid to challenge sexual harassment in the workplace and to fight against injustice. Finally, as the first brave individuals fight back to stop the perpetrators of sexual harassment, the public attention focused on their cases causes media and public discussion of the realities of sexual abuse and intimidation on the job.

Women are beginning to recognize that they are not alone, but rather are part of a larger phenomenon. With growing awareness of the political ramifications of this issue, women are recognizing that the juxtaposition of societal attitudes that see women as sex objects, with a hierarchical workforce, causes untold havoc in their working lives. Together they are beginning to fight back and search for solutions to this problem, which has beset them throughout the history of work.

4

Personnel, management, and union perceptions

1. WHAT YOU CAN EXPECT
FROM PERSONNEL AND MANAGEMENT

The Worst You Can Expect

One of the most revealing interviews we had involved a vice-president of personnel of a large retail concern. The man in question occupied a rather opulent office, replete with mahogany desk, deep leather chairs, plush blue broadloom, and a crystal chandelier. His office on the thirty-second floor overlooked a magnificent view of the city and the harbor. Mr. Smith, as he shall be referred to, belongs to the most prestigious business organizations, such as the chamber of commerce, is an active member on many community boards, such as the Boy Scouts of America, and considers himself a forward-thinking, enlightened businessman.

We had been trying to arrange for an interview with Mr. Smith for several weeks but had been constantly put off by his claims of urgent business trips and meetings. Mr. Smith had cautioned us on the phone that he was only prepared to allot fifteen minutes to the interview and that he suspected that he would have little or nothing to contribute on the subject of sexual harassment of working women.

Sitting nervously behind his vast mahogany desk, his left leg shaking, Mr. Smith began the interview by informing us that by broaching the subject of sexual harassment we were more intimidating than anyone he had met in a sexual situation. Before we could begin to introduce our questions, Mr. Smith launched into a polemic on the role of women in his organization. He said, "Women in our business do not have the propensity to run the board of directors. They don't have that kind of career goal in our industry."

Fearing that the fifteen minutes would be taken up by a lecture on women's innate limitations in business, we interjected a definition of sexual harassment. Before we could finish, Mr. Smith exclaimed,

Good night! I am not aware of sexual harassment, but I am aware of lots of other relationships in the organization. I've never heard of one example of sexual harassment in the sense of a superior harassing a subordinate. But I have heard of it the other way around. By that I mean a subordinate, such as a secretary, coming on to a boss.

As our discussion continued and we cited specific examples, Mr. Smith somewhat amended his comments. He expressed the notion that at the lower echelons, that is, where working-class, less-educated men predominated, it was conceivable that women were sexually harassed. But he stated emphatically that more sophisticated, educated men do not behave in this manner. As he said, "At the very lowest levels of business there are a lot of Archie Bunkers. They protect the status quo. If any group in business has done more to slow down the possibility of women moving ahead—it's them."

Mr. Smith was determined to pursue the subject of the office romance, which he believed was more pertinent than incidents of sexual harassment, despite the fact that we pointed out that professional and responsible surveys indicate that most women experience some degree of sexual harassment at one point in their working lives. He went on to say,

I have seen friendliness develop between people of the opposite sex where it has been perceived by others in the organization as unfair, since the woman often receives special privileges such as choice work assignments, coveted prime vacation time, and so on. It could backfire. That's the most terrifying thing. When this happens, we move one of the individuals.

When we questioned him as to who would be moved, he conceded that the woman is usually in a subordinate position to the man even if she happens to be a professional or a manager. Ultimately the woman is moved, since she is the most expendable. We said, "This is very interesting, and a real problem in the business environment. But, Mr. Smith, are you saying that there is no sexual coercion of women on the job?"

Mr. Smith became highly agitated and flatly stated, "I don't buy this coercion." "Are we deliberately lying?" we countered. He replied,

I think it's just two writers looking for accidents to happen. Any woman can turn any man off. I think the whole thing is a hoax. I'm very sorry if I'm boring you, but all I'm doing is telling you the nature of reality. Women have all the advantages in our society.

A tiny smile crept over Mr. Smith's face. He paused briefly and continued, "Women can definitely sexually harass men, but I can't fathom men harassing women." He continued sanctimoniously,

Besides, if sexual harassment would manifest itself in our organization, lots of people would notice it before it actually got to the stage where it could be defined as sexual harassment. I suspect that prior to reaching the level of sexual harassment there would be some sort of tendency to flirt or enjoy the other's company.

He concluded the interview with the blanket statement "There is never a case where a man would come on to a woman without some encouragement."

At this point Mr. Smith glanced at his watch, exclaiming that forty-five minutes had gone by. He quickly ushered us out of his office, commenting that it had been a mutual waste of time. "Not at all," we said. "Your comments were truly fascinating." His secretary, who had been hovering at the door through most of the interview, smiled broadly at us as we passed her desk.

If a woman was a victim of sexual harassment in Mr. Smith's organization and complained, she would not receive an unbiased hearing. More precisely, she could not anticipate receiving anything remotely resembling justice. Although Mr. Smith's comments and observations are particularly harsh and an expression of a pervasive negative attitude toward women in the workplace, he does represent business at the top.

He is a powerful individual whose opinions count and whose actions affect the lives of thousands upon thousands of women, either directly or indirectly. Mr. Smith is a business leader and a pacesetter. What he says, what he believes, are a good reflection of what women are up against when attempting to fight sexual harassment within the organizational structure.

Mr. Smith is saying that sexual harassment does not in fact exist; that women, although they are almost uniformly subordinate in relation to men, are the sexual aggressors. And he admits quite candidly that women are expendable and the most likely to be moved when a conflict arises. After all, the organizational investment is generally in men, as they are inherently more valuable to the organization in terms of status and productivity.

Mr. Smith is a vice-president and can afford to be outspoken. He does not see the issue of sexual harassment as worthy of consideration. For that matter, he does not believe that women suffer from discrimination or unequal opportunity. As he said, "Women have all the advantages," although he neglected to point out what specifically these advantages are.

Mr. Smith is only one of many people we interviewed in a personnel or managerial function. Our research involved a wide range of work situations, from small concerns with as little as thirty employees to large institutions employing thousands of individuals. We contacted people in business, government, and academia, ranging from manufacturing, sales, financial institutions, universities, and foundations to public utilities. The status of the interviewee encompassed vice-presidents, personnel directors, and middle- to high-level managers. Depending on the status of the individual, remarks tended to be tempered as we moved down the organizational ladder.

Women directors and managers all acknowledged the concept of sexual harassment. The more closely linked to senior management and policy making, the more open and outraged the women became. The women furthest from the center of power admitted that they could do little to protect the victims of sexual harassment.

First Principles of Good Personnel Policy

Our next discussion was with Mr. Brown, as we shall call him, the personnel director of a large insurance company whose workforce is 60-percent female. Mr. Brown, like Mr. Smith, was highly nervous and intensely uncomfortable. His was the only enclosed office on a floor that housed several hundred, primarily female employees, most of whom were clerks, secretaries, and first-line managers.

Mr. Brown began the interview by commenting, "I may have my head in the sand, but really, girls—is it a big problem? I've received no complaints in fifteen years as a personnel director, nor have I observed any evidence of sexual harassment." Mr. Brown smiled and continued, "although we do have one female manager who surrounds herself with attractive male subordinates."

"Mr. Brown," we asked, "how would you handle a case of sexual harassment should the situation ever arise?" Mr. Brown replied,

Well, I would go back to the first principles of good personnel policy. I would want to get the facts from the complainant and the man being accused. I would try to work it out between the two of them. I wouldn't want to take it to the man's supervisor. If the man admitted he was being *silly*, I would tell him to stop and hope that he would.

"However," he continued, acutely embarrassed, "if he denied harassing the woman, I would have to investigate further."

We asked Mr. Brown what course this investigation would take. He replied, "I would want to look into the previous history and track record of both people. After all, all criminal acts should not be treated in the same way. It depends on the circumstances." At this point, he made the analogy to a theft at a large department store such as Sears Roebuck. He pointed out, "One would want to investigate the mental condition, family history, economic and social circumstances, and so on, of the accused thief." What he failed to recognize or acknowledge in making this analogy is that he would only investigate the accused, not Sears Roebuck, the entity that had been robbed.

In sexual harassment, both parties are on trial. As Mr. Brown laboriously explained,

I would check to see if either the man or the woman had a history of playing around. I would be particularly protective of a mousy girl. But an attractive girl who dresses in an attractive fashion would not make me feel very sympathetic. I would be less hard on a man who came on to an attractive girl. In these situations, there is generally some sort of initial romantic attraction. It's hard for me to imagine that an attractive girl can be taken advantage of—sexually. Mousy girls who never flaunt themselves, who are not provocative—yes, I would be concerned about them and could imagine them being taken advantage of.

He went on to say, ending vaguely, "It would be difficult to prove in any event. After all, how could a company step in and deal with a subordinate, by overruling a manager?"

We then asked Mr. Brown what he thought of the idea of introducing educationals on the subject of sexual harassment. He replied, "Educationals might worsen the problem. Some women might go looking for sexual harassment where it didn't exist. Educationals are dangerous. We would have all these ladies out there crying wolf."

Mr. Brown, like Mr. Smith, wields an enormous amount of power. Neither Mr. Brown nor Mr. Smith really acknowledges the problem of sexual harassment. Mr. Brown makes the initial assumption that both parties are on trial. Quite openly, he admits that companies protect their investment and would be hard put to discipline a superior. The question of dispensing justice is not of primary concern. Far more relevant is the corporate investment in the manager. Of course organizations would prefer that sexual harassment not be a feature of their working environments. However, if sexual harassment is brought to management's attention, its overriding objective is to protect its investment.

Interestingly, Mr. Brown divides women into two categories. There is the attractive, innately provocative woman, for whom he has little sympathy—the implication being that attractive women ask for trouble by virtue of being attractive. Then there is what he terms the "mousy" woman. The "mousy" woman has his sympathy but not his protection or support. No doubt Mr. Brown has some concern about hierarchical injustices, but he is in fact acknowledging that a personnel director's job is ultimately to protect management.

Defensive Management

There is another class of personnel director, represented by a man whom we shall call Mr. White. Mr. White works as the personnel manager for a small manufacturing concern employing several hundred people, with most of the women in support jobs such as clerks, secretaries, factory-line assembly workers, and the odd first-line manager. Mr. White was extremely defensive (as opposed to embarrassed or abrasive). Like Mr. Smith and Mr. Brown, he could not recall one single incident of sexual harassment in his twenty-odd years as a personnel manager.

When we described the range of acts that sexual harassment encompasses, he exclaimed, "I haven't personally noticed pawing. I might myself," he laughed, "be accused of pawing, depending upon how one defines it." He went on to say, "I have, on the other hand, heard of incidents where there is mutuality. What I mean is that two people, a man and a woman, are fooling around. That's life! However," he stated,

I can believe that women harass men, and that women exploit their sexuality. I remember one female assembly worker who had to be asked to get a baggy sweater. Her sexual explicitness wasn't directed at one person, just at males in general.

Although Mr. White denies that sexual harassment exists, his immediate response is that women sexually harass men and exploit their sexuality whether or not they are subordinates, peers, or superiors in the hierarchical structure. Mr. White is an amazing example of the male ego's ability to protect itself. In essence Mr. White tries to dismiss sexual harassment as a joke. He can imagine sexual harassment perpetrated against a woman, as evidenced by his remark that he himself might be accused of pawing women.

This rather mild, good-natured middle-aged male manager cannot accept the notion that sexual harassment is a form of economic rape. If a woman becomes the victim of sexual harassment, noncompliance may threaten her livelihood. Women's general economic condition as marginal, low-level, poorly paid workers, with little or no attachment to real power, places them in double jeopardy.

Sexual Harassment Is Rampant—But What Can I Do?

In the course of our research, we did, in fact, encounter one male manager in government who readily acknowledged that sexual harassment was rampant in the workplace. This man, whom we shall call Mr. Freeman, had given the subject of sexual harassment considerable thought, since he was constantly being confronted with incidents. It was his observation that the more educated a man, the greater degree of frustration he experienced and the more likely he was to act out this frustration in the form of sexual harassment perpetrated against female subordinates. However, he commented that a well-educated man would most likely perpetrate psychological coercion. He would suggest a dinner, a hotel, a weekend affair, with the implicit threat that noncompliance would incur his displeasure and could result in reprisals against the woman in question. Mr. Freeman believed that less-educated men tended to be more physical in their approach—leering, pinching, grabbing, and so forth, and possibly making crude, suggestive comments.

Mr. Freeman recalled a case where the secretary to a senior manager complained of sexual harassment. In his memory, having been privy to numerous incidents over the years, this case was the only one where the manager was actually fired. The woman had endured both physical and psychological abuse over several years, finally becoming physically ill and mentally distressed.

The manager in question would often come up behind her, embrace her, grab at her breasts, pinch her, endlessly tell dirty jokes, and finally ask the woman to dinner and an evening of "sexual favors." Although the woman explained that she was happily married and was in the workplace to work and was not remotely interested, the manager persisted, becoming increasingly abrasive and threatening.

Mr. Freeman admitted that the man was not fired specifically for sexual harassment, but rather for embezzlement—a fact that his secretary had documented and reported to Mr. Freeman. The sexual harassment was an add-on issue and perhaps the final straw.

In all the other cases of sexual harassment that Mr. Freeman had observed, the women generally resigned. One case particularly disturbed him. A male manager in the engineering department had sexually harassed seven separate women, all contract workers. All seven had left prior to the end of their contracts, ranging from six months to two years. Mr. Freeman had been especially careful in his selection of women to work with the offending manager after the first two incidents came to his attention. The following five women had been either older, unattractive, or strident feminists. All to no avail. The manager persisted in pursuing each woman in turn, demanding dates and one-night stands. When each woman in turn refused, he became abrupt, supercritical of her work, and generally overbearing.

Although Mr. Freeman was able to document all seven cases, only two of the women were prepared to complain higher up the hierarchy—that is, to the office of the most senior civil servant. Mr. Freeman wryly concluded that the women received a very unsympathetic audience, since the senior civil servant was busy harassing one of the women on his own staff. In the end, the complainants simply left in disgust. The senior civil servant informed the woman he was harassing that she would have to leave unless she consented to an affair. He claimed that her very presence was too disturbing to him.

Mr. Freeman held out little hope for justice in the organization. He said, "People at the top are so ingrained in their attitudes—namely, that with power comes sexual privilege. All women are fair game to these men." Mr. Freeman went on to say, "It's a no-win situation. Unless you can contain it, you should expect repercussions from the harasser, who is generally the superior."

In Mr. Freeman's opinion, women should avoid taking their cases to a personnel manager or management. As he said,

The personnel director will most likely go to the sexual harasser and have a quiet little chat and a good laugh and express any number of the following statements:

- She brought it on herself.
- She can take care of herself.
- She was obviously willing.
- She is vindictive, as a result of a love affair gone sour.
- In fact, this is one isolated incident, not a serious problem.
- She is a troublemaker.

Mr. Freeman advises women to start looking for another job before the situation becomes critical and unbearable. If the situation reaches the crisis stage, it will be difficult to secure a reference from the harasser. As he says, "A woman is in real jeopardy if she can't get along in government. Who will hire you in private industry, if you are fired by the government?" He goes on to point out,

I appreciate that many women are not in a position to switch jobs at will. I realize they have real financial responsibilities and cannot afford to be unemployed for even a day. For those women, I suggest they hire a tough feminist lawyer who will take the case as a personal challenge. She should act as their advocate, directly confronting the harasser and threatening him with reprisals unless he stops.

"The point is," he states, "you should contain it between the victim and the harasser. The moment it goes further, the woman is sure to lose."

Mr. Freeman was one of those rare individuals who was prepared to speak up about what he perceived to be a grave injustice and a crime against women in the workplace. He freely admitted that the personnel function is a pawn of management, basically ineffectual, and conceivably destructive to the victim. It was his experience that a woman who complained to personnel would eventually be fired on some pretext. Ultimately, he believed that if women could instill a healthy fear of reprisals in male harassers, they could stop the perpetuation of sexual harassment.

Beware the Corporate Hack

One male vice-president in his late thirties attempted to analyze sexual harassment in light of what he termed "the sexual revolution." Mr. Kraft, as we shall call him, is the vice-president of corporate affairs for a large manufacturing company. It is his job to analyze the "real world"— economically, politically, socially, and so on—so that the corporation keeps in touch with current trends.

Large corporations often recognize that they must monitor economic, political, and social phenomena that affect their business objectives. If, for example, one must promote a few women to keep the government from intervening, then the vice-president of corporate affairs is responsible for suggesting a plan of action that will keep the corporation one step ahead of the government. In essence, these men are imagemakers and business trendsetters in the realm that has come to be known as "corporate responsibility."

Mr. Kraft ordered a special lunch for us that was spread out informally on a coffee table and included sandwiches, salads, desserts, coffee and tea, and even liquor if we wanted it. We settled back into a very comfortable sofa while Mr. Kraft took off his jacket, loosened his tie, and lowered himself into a deep velvet chair.

Mr. Kraft, in answer to our question of whether he was aware of sexual harassment within the organization, replied,

I am not denying that it is a serious problem. But in today's world, it's a question of expectation. Men are conditioned to expect that men in power play around. Women, however, are still coping with a double standard that says, "Nice girls don't do that." So we have a situation where men generally wield an enormous amount of power over women and can coerce women into coming across sexually. After all, if men and women aren't equals, what options are open to women? Besides, the work setting provides a good way of sexually harassing women. The organization is actually paying you for the time spent in such endeavors. And you have a good chance of succeeding with a woman who can't demand money, as does a prostitute. Men generally see sexual harassment as part of the work game.

Mr. Kraft pointed out, however, that he could not recall any cases of sexual harassment in his own company. When asked how a woman should handle it, he said,

There are women who can turn you off sexually without turning you off. Sexual harassment is, after all, an ego problem. You must somehow get the message across that you aren't interested but would still like to continue with the job.

He reflected a moment and continued, "A woman could say, 'Look, you are a nice person; this isn't personal; I'm just not interested in a sexual relationship with you.'"

Mr. Kraft, as had others we interviewed, advised women to try to deal with the problem directly—by confronting the harasser. "If it becomes serious," he added, "you should go to the harasser's boss. It's a tough situation. If the harasser is a successful man, he won't be fired. But the company knows that if they can't resolve it internally, the woman might be prompted to seek a legal remedy. Ideally," he said, "repeaters should be isolated or fired. In a larger company, people can more easily be moved. Our company has initiated a special mechanism to deal with personnel problems." "How does this mechanism operate?" we asked. He replied,

We employ a psychologist and a social worker, who counsel employees and also act as ombudsmen when such a conflict occurs. They try to resolve the issue at the lowest level possible. It's an alternative for low-level employees, since, for example, if a woman who is sexually harassed goes to the counselor and it is decided that her complaint is legitimate, she would have the weight of management on her side. If, alternatively, she decides to sue the company, regardless of who is right, management will close ranks and fight her.

After saying all this, Mr. Kraft conceded that it was a no-win situation for the woman, especially if she was a specialist. "Where," he said, "could she be transferred to?" Still, he would advise a woman to save "her big guns for the last"—that is, hiring a lawyer.

On a philosophical note, Mr. Kraft contributed this observation: "As you get more women into senior positions, women collectively will disapprove of sexual harassment, but with some clout. But," he cautioned, "women should be aware that they are judged by what they wear and what they talk about. If they wear suggestive clothing—they are asking for it. Also a sexy woman won't be taken seriously in business." He lamely went on to conclude, "If a man touches a woman or women, one should look at this in the context of his total behavior."

Mr. Kraft is an equivocator in that his remarks were an odd mixture of what he construed to be "with it, now, straight talk" and a basic chauvinism, so ingrained that he isn't remotely aware of how contradictory he is. On the one hand, sexual harassment is a serious problem. On the other hand, he acknowledges that a successful man would not be fired and that a professional woman is hard to transfer. His company's ombudsman policy would be ideal if one could really believe in impartiality in light of his other comments.

Mr. Kraft fails to appreciate that the woman is not on trial, the man is. He is the offender, the perpetrator, and she is the victim. In the end, Mr. Kraft provided a real insight into corporate gamesmanship. Be nice, be modern, watch for those trends, but take care of our investment—the male manager. Do such a good juggling act that nobody can accuse you of being a poor corporate citizen.

The Ineffectual Female Manager

All of the women personnel managers uniformly acknowledged that men sexually harass women in the workplace. Depending on their status and attachment to power within the organization, they differed in their approach in dealing with the problem.

Ms. Cooper, as we shall call her, is the personnel manager of a large insurance company employing thousands of women in support and line positions, with a distinct minority functioning as low-level managers. Ms. Cooper is a woman in her fifties, one of five who has worked her way up into middle management. She is aware that her achievement is unique and tenuous at best. In the course of the interview it became apparent that she felt obliged to defend the role of a personnel manager, claiming that in fact she had some power to redress injustices.

When asked if she had ever received any complaints of sexual harassment, she replied, "I'm surprised, actually, that I can't think of any incidents going on now. I recognize that I have received very few complaints over the years because women are afraid to bring it into the open." Ms. Cooper, although she was defensive of the personnel function, went on to say,

If a woman encounters sexual harassment, I would suggest that she try to deal with the man who is causing the problem. If this fails, then she should go to either personnel or management, depending upon where she thinks she will receive a more sympathetic audience.

She added,

Of course, you need more than sympathy. The woman must also make her selection in terms of who she thinks has the authority to take decisive action. And in the final analysis, if the woman hasn't top management's support, she might as well leave.

We related to Ms. Cooper the negative reception we had received from most of the male managers we had interviewed. "Why," we asked, "are women managers more willing to recognize sexual harassment?" She answered, smiling, "I suspect that most women managers have been victims of sexual harassment themselves and therefore have more direct knowledge and experience."

"Ms. Cooper," we continued, "so many of the men we interviewed were convinced that women exploit their sexuality in the workplace. From your own experience and observation, do you think that this is true?" Ms. Cooper answered emphatically,

I would doubt very much that a woman would get very far relying on her sexuality. An organization by its very nature cannot afford to have incompetent persons in responsible jobs. Besides, male managers attempting to promote a woman whose sexual favors they are enjoying do not operate autonomously. I, personally, cannot recall a single instance where a woman succeeded by exploiting her sexuality.

In conclusion, Ms. Cooper had this to say about any form of sexual activity at the office:

Business and pleasure categorically do not mix. A woman would be smart to avoid even forming close friendships with members of her own sex. You really can't afford to be friendly with one person in particular, since your impartiality in decision making would be challenged and ultimately compromised.

Ms. Cooper obviously has genuine sympathy for victims of sexual harassment but personally can do little to protect the woman. As she said, "If it were possible, I would use peer pressure to stop the harasser, and if that failed, I would enlist the support of senior management. I believe that if all these approaches fail, the man should be fired."

However, she doubted that in a real-life situation the foregoing scenario would take place in her company. At best, she thought that she might be able to secure a lateral transfer for the woman. It would be very difficult if the woman were a professional. Her options, according to Ms. Cooper, are even more limited than a clerk's or a secretary's.

Ms. Cooper is a good example of a woman who has good intentions and a sense of justice but no real power to effect any changes. She's a good company woman with a conscience, but she is aware that if she pushes too hard, her job may be on the line.

The Real Role of Personnel

Ms. Masters, as we shall call her, is a personnel manager at a medium-sized North American university. She is responsible for the personnel function as it relates to the support staff, which is largely female.

Ms. Masters began the discussion by offering a definition of the personnel function. She said,

The personnel function cannot exercise any real power. We operate in an advisory capacity to management. Remember, this is a staff function, not a line function, and as such we do not have the authority to instruct the line people how to behave. Only management is empowered to do that.

We asked Ms. Masters how she would react if she received a complaint of sexual harassment. She said,

I suspect a woman would be very reluctant to come forward, since she would recognize that it is her word against another's. The other, of course, is generally a superior. But if I did receive a complaint, I would treat it as any other employee relations problem. I would listen to the facts and try to determine if anything could be done.

She continued,

Normally I would see the person complained of. I recognize, in the case of sexual harassment, that confronting the male harasser might make the situation worse for the woman. I think there would only be one real option, and that is to help the woman find another position, especially if the situation was intolerable. I admit, it would not really solve the problem. The man would look for yet another woman to harass. What I would attempt to do is to find a woman with a strong personality who could stand up to this man.

Ms. Masters very candidly admitted that she is almost powerless to handle an incident of sexual harassment. She agreed with all the people previously interviewed, namely, that the woman must be moved, not the man. Even though she has a keen appreciation of the nature of the power in the organization and how limited she is in relation to the line function, she believes that a subordinate with a strong personality could stand up to a male harasser in a superior position. It is a strange perception and obviously ludicrous in light of her own analysis of power. Ms. Masters, who is in a superior position to the majority of women harassed, has never considered the possibility of speaking up to the harasser on the subordinate's behalf or at least exercising her advisory function by acquainting senior management with the problems. Ms. Masters is honestly afraid. It is puzzling that she doesn't fully recognize that so are nearly all the victims of sexual harassment. After all, if your livelihood is at stake, it is difficult to be a "strong personality" when you are almost assured of losing your job.

Women Attached to Power

We did encounter one female personnel manager who was aware, sensitive, and refreshingly gutsy in her analysis and approach to sexual harassment. Ms. Lyon, as we shall refer to her, worked for a manufacturing concern that was partially unionized.

When asked if she could document specific incidents of sexual harassment, Ms. Lyon recalled two that had come to her attention in her ten years with the company. She said,

Case number one involved a youngish, first-line supervisor with a small clerical staff. He was experiencing a marital breakdown at the time. He simultaneously harassed three women on his staff, mostly through verbal suggestion. It all came to a head when two of the women reached the limits of their endurance and complained to his immediate supervisor. The man was fired, but not solely for the sexual harassment, although it was the most disturbing element in this case. His poor performance on the job was probably the major reason.

Case number two was more difficult in terms of evidence. A young woman complained of sexual harassment of both a physical and a psychological nature. The harasser was her immediate supervisor. The man in question grabbed, leered, asked for dates, and suggested physical intimacy. Her firm refusal evoked a torrent of verbal abuse and constant put-downs. The woman became emotionally distressed and finally complained to management, claiming that other women had left before her because of this man's behavior. Management stalled. They were reluctant to take action especially without corroboration. Finally the woman quit, her confidence shaken; she was severely emotionally disturbed.

Ms. Lyon was the only personnel manager who either knew of or was prepared to speak about sexual harassment in specific terms. Although other women personnel managers acknowledged it, none could or would relate case histories.

Ms. Lyon had some very definite opinions and observations. In answer to our question about what she personally would advise a woman to do, she replied,

In very practical terms, this company is a union shop, so my first reaction would be to try to instill some confidence in the employee that the union could protect her if necessary and that her job was not at risk. I have observed that most women are terrified about speaking up. I would advise a woman to speak up and tell the man to stop immediately. At times the only recourse is to walk out on verbal abuse.

Ms. Lyon continued,

In a peer situation this may work. I'm not sure it's effective behavior against a superior. If a woman who is being harassed has female co-workers she trusts, she could ask them to support her.

Ms. Lyon, unlike all the other personnel people interviewed, maintained, "The personnel manager should go after the man, not force the woman to move to a new environment. After all, it is the man who has created the situation. The woman is the victim, the one who has been coerced." Ms. Lyon did go on to admit, "I doubt if a man would be fired in many cases. But at least the personnel function should exercise what power it has by warning the harasser and making him aware that he is being watched. If, for example," she said, "the woman decides to transfer and the next woman is harassed as well, the harasser should be told in clear terms that he will be removed from his supervisory function unless he stops."

Reflecting on the situation, Ms. Lyon stated, "If we want to stop sexual harassment of women, we must go back to the cradle. By that I mean we must develop a kind of educational support system so that men and women really believe that they are equals."

"Do you know of any incidents where women exploit their sexuality," we asked? Ms. Lyon replied,

I have never personally witnessed this situation. It is my observation, though, that ambitious, exceptionally attractive women are at a distinct disadvantage. They have to get beyond that and be taken seriously as professional, competent women. Besides, a man would be a fool to promote a woman because he enjoys a sexual relationship with her. If she turns out to be unqualified, the personnel function will have evidence of this. It is the man who must answer for his actions.

Ms. Lyon enjoys a cooperative and mutually respectful relationship with the vice-president of personnel. Not only does she understand the implications of sexual harassment to women, but she is personally prepared to use what leverage she has to protect and support women in this situation. Ms. Lyon has no illusions about the difficulties involved in educating senior management about the seriousness of the problem. She understands quite clearly how threatening it is to men to speak openly about sexual harassment. Men, she has observed, can often imagine themselves soliciting sexual favors from female employees. For many men sexual harassment constitutes an integral part of their work life. They have sexually harassed women themselves or know a colleague who has. When someone in their midst speaks out against this abuse of authority, they become hostile, defensive, and angry.

Ms. Lyon's personal integrity, coupled with her attachment to real power, make her someone to contend with—a genuine advocate on behalf of women in her organization who are victims of sexual harassment. Unfortunately Ms. Lyon is a rare and distinct exception.

Conclusion

There were a number of companies who categorically refused to see us. It was revealing that Eaton's, an old, established retail outlet that has stores all across Canada and employs a vast army of female salesclerks, maintained that they had no problems in this area. The male spokesperson for the company finally came out and flatly stated, "We just feel we can't get involved at the moment."

Our contact at the Royal Trust Company was even more blatant. As he said, "I would be very reluctant to discuss this issue. I suspect, young ladies, that you will find that very few people are prepared to discuss it."

Shell of Canada was very friendly. The woman personnel manager did a little informal research among her colleagues and reported back that sexual harassment did not go on at Shell. It was her explanation that their evaluation system militated against this sort of behavior. "Also," she said, "the men at Shell are very square people and would not be the types to sexually harass women."

Out of this maze of comments, observations, experiences, and anecdotes it becomes clear that as things now stand, a woman who is being sexually harassed will not receive a particularly sympathetic audience with either personnel or management. On balance, it appears that in most circumstances she had best start looking for another job. Ignoring the situation, pretending naïveté, won't affect the harasser's behavior. Men are conditioned to think that there is no harm in trying even if they don't receive any encouragement. Speaking up doesn't guarantee success, either. It may simply speed up your exit from the company. What becomes apparent is that personnel perceives itself as powerless, and management closes ranks to protect its investment in the male employee. Women are truly expendable—easily fired and dismissed as troublemakers.

A common theme emerges on the part of most of the males interviewed. Sexual harassment doesn't occur without some encouragement. Heaven help us if we are perceived to be attractive! Almost no one has much sympathy for the attractive, "sexy" woman.

Very few of the people interviewed were prepared to admit that sexual harassment has very little to do with attractiveness or sexual desire. Sexual harassment is an expression of power. Working women have no power—either economically or politically. As yet, they cannot even marginally effect any changes within the corporate structure.

Mr. Kraft was right. If we had a critical mass of women in powerful positions in the workplace, they would collectively disapprove of sexual harassment. But we live in the now. The reality of the situation tells us that we are working in greater numbers, some 40 percent of the workplace, but the gap in wages, status, promotion, and training is ever widening.

And so for now there are few organizations where a woman could complain about sexual harassment to either personnel or management. As long as corporate entities do not recognize sexual harassment as a crime against their women employees, approach at your own peril!

2. WHAT YOU CAN EXPECT FROM THE UNION

The notion of a union intervening as an advocate on behalf of women suffering from sexual harassment is, on the surface, an appealing remedy. Unfortunately, only 25 percent of women are unionized in North America. If unionized, women have not traditionally been active in union hierarchies. Their numbers have never swelled the ranks of shop stewards, business representatives, or executive committees. They have been and are rank and file members.

Their disproportionate numbers in terms of membership and active participation is an understandable phenomenon, even though it operates in women's worst interests. Most working women are married, with children and homes. After work and in the early evening, when most unions conduct their business, debate policy, and form working committees, women are at home, madly attempting to make up the time lost while working. They are cooking, cleaning, and caring for children. In fact, these women are holding down two full-time jobs with little or no assistance from their spouses.

This deterrent is exacerbated by the union's general indifference and lack of support for its women members. Unions, like corporations, are guilty of ignoring and discriminating against their female members. The common union response to the question of how they are handling or would handle cases of sexual harassment is that they haven't given the subject any serious consideration. They explained to us that the hard money issues such as wages, overtime, and vacation pay are their major concerns. We asked union representatives, "What good are monetary concessions to women if their jobs are made miserable unless they come across sexually to their male bosses?" The general response was that unions are democratic institutions that can only respond to the issues that members present. As yet, they claim, women haven't made themselves heard on sexual harassment.

It was instructive to observe that trade union men, like businessmen, generally became defensive and attempted to turn the issue into a joke. Nevertheless, it became apparent, while interviewing a cross-section of union officials representing workers in manufacturing, transportation, and public service, and some organizers of embryonic employee associations in other industries, that women in a union or quasi-union environment felt more secure about their jobs. If the issue becomes better understood and incorporated into union collective agreements, unionized women would at least have access to a relatively cheap remedy. With the union as a woman's advocate in a grievance procedure, the woman would not stand alone, attempting to defend herself against an inquisition by management and personnel. The balance of power would be somewhat redressed. Management would be obliged to respond, and the women would be protected against being forced to quit or being dismissed outright. Unions pay for legal counsel at such hearings, removing a heavy cost burden from victims. A woman who belongs to a union must pay union dues, but these are minimal in comparison to potential legal fees.

The Grievance Procedure

Once the employees of an organization have decided to unionize and have joined a trade union that obtains certification to represent a particular bargaining unit under the applicable labor relations legislation, employer-employee relations are completely overhauled. Management can no longer set wage levels and other benefits on its own. Nor can it discharge or discipline employees at whim.

Instead, the trade union representatives bargain with management for a collective agreement commonly known as the contract, which sets out the terms of employment agreed to by both parties. In addition to dealing with wages and other benefits, most contracts stipulate that no employee can be discharged or disciplined without "just cause." In cases where an employee has been discharged or disciplined, for example by a sexual harasser because she failed to submit to sexual advances, she can take her case through the grievance procedure.

The grievance procedure will be set out in the contract and generally provides for several levels of review within the organization. The union represents the aggrieved employee at each level, and if it is not satisfied with the review, it can force the matter on to arbitration. At the arbitration stage the entire case is heard by an arbitrator. The arbitrator is an independent person, not employed by the company or the union, who has been chosen by both the union and the company to hear the case.

The arbitrator hears the evidence presented from both sides at an informal hearing. Management will try to prove that the reason for the discharge or discipline was justifiable—for sloppy work, absenteeism, and so on. The union will present evidence on behalf of the employee to show that the punishment was not just. The arbitrator makes a decision on the basis of this evidence, either to let the punishment stand, to reinstate the employee, or to alter the discipline originally meted out.

Unionized women obviously have an attractive remedy in the grievance procedure. To take a grievance through to arbitration costs the employee nothing, and she has her union to act as an advocate. There are two problems, however. Arbitrators theoretically should be impartial, unlike representatives of personnel and management. However, most of the people who sit as arbitrators with any frequency are men, and as such are likely to share some of the male biases endemic to our society. If the union is alert to this problem and consciously selects only truly impartial arbitrators to sit on sexual harassment cases, much of the danger will be alleviated.

The other problem is that only when there has been a breach of the contract can a woman seek redress through the grievance procedure. Although most contracts protect employees from unjust discharge or discipline, few contracts deal with sexual harassment specifically. Thus abusive conduct that falls short of discharge or discipline may provide no breach of the contract and allow for no remedy through the grievance procedure. As union women begin to voice their concerns about sexual harassment, it is possible that in successive renegotiations of contracts, clauses will be added to protect women more specifically.

Protecting Its Own

Our opening analysis of unions makes it abundantly clear that our male-dominated unions are guilty of the same attitudes about sexual harassment as male personnel and management. Male union officials and members are just as likely to be perpetrators of sexual harassment as their male personnel and management counterparts.

It is also important to remember that a union defines its role as both improving working conditions and protecting its members against the arbitrary actions of management. However, should a female union member lodge a complaint of sexual harassment against a male union member, the union is caught in a bind. It does not define its role as disciplining its own membership. In a rare instance where management would support the female union complainant, the union would support the male union harasser. Traditionally, regardless of the circumstances, the union defines management as its natural adversary.

A case that particularly exemplifies the position of the union faced with a perpetrator within its own ranks concerned the dismissal of a male teacher who had sexually harassed many of his eighteen- and nineteen-year-old female students. Mr. Handy, as we shall call him, was an associate professor at a small midwestern college and a member of his college teachers' union. The college had instituted extensive remedial testing and training in order to enable students to maintain acceptable progress in their chosen courses. Mr. Handy asked for and was assigned to the remedial reading section. This required working with one student at a time in a small room, the teacher and the student sitting side by side at a table.

Several months after Mr. Handy began teaching this program, the local authorities became alarmed at a report from one of the female teachers. She said that a student seeking her advice had told her that Mr. Handy had placed his hand on her leg while sitting beside her. Further inquiries revealed that other young women had had similar experiences and had been startled and embarrassed.

Mr. Handy was summoned and was said to have admitted in some degree the truth of the accusations. He was offered the opportunity to resign and to receive two months' salary, but he declined and was subsequently dismissed. Mr. Handy went to his union, which fully supported his claim of "wrongful dismissal" and acted on his behalf in the grievance hearing that ensued. At the hearing nine female students gave evidence under oath, each in the absence of the rest, with the result that their collective testimony was uniform and corroborative. Each young woman said that while she was sitting with Mr. Handy he had placed his hand on her knee or thigh for varying periods of time or had put his arm around her shoulder, massaging her back and arms. In some cases both actions had occurred. Some of the women were annoyed and some were alarmed. Some refused to take instruction from Mr. Handy again. All of the women were upset to a greater or lesser extent. None interpreted the actions as unconscious or as friendly or fatherly gestures. Each woman had reacted by objecting or by drawing away.

Although the arbitrator at the hearing did not construe Mr. Handy's actions to be gross sexual advances, he pointed out that Mr. Handy should have been aware that touching young female students in a fairly intimate manner was unacceptable behavior on the part of a man in his fifties, a virtual stranger to these female students, and a teacher. Although the arbitrator upheld the dismissal and disallowed the grievance, he did so with reluctance, pointing out,

The trivial hurt to any of the girls—or to all in total—can hardly be equated with the hurt already suffered by the grievor in terms of ostracism, mental distress, unemployability in his profession, and financial loss.

This particular case is an interesting insight into the attitudes of both the union and the arbitrator. In the first instance the union felt obliged to support Mr. Handy's action for wrongful dismissal, despite the overwhelming evidence that he was guilty of sexual harassment. Had the victims been members of the same union, the response would have been the same. What becomes apparent is that the union will not act in an intra-union dispute. It is contrary to its own self-definition to discipline one of its own members, even though another union member suffers as a result.

The arbitrator, on the other hand, despite the conclusive evidence that Mr. Handy had exploited his role as a teacher by using it as a means to sexually harass his female students, had reservations about upholding his dismissal. He refers to the women's treatment as trivial. There is no appreciation of the trauma, humiliation, and alienation that sexual harassment engenders. Once a woman has been a victim of sexual harassment, she may become extremely paranoid, constantly in fear of a repetition of her experience. The damage done to her self-esteem may have lifelong effects. It is obvious that the arbitrator's sympathies lie with the harasser. One wonders what would have been the outcome if one or two women had complained instead of nine.

Teachers' Unions

Elementary and high school teaching, which until the last twenty-five years has been a predominantly female profession, is unionized all across North America. We interviewed a representative of a state teachers' federation on the eastern seaboard. Ms. Blake, as we shall call her, was the director of this federation, herself a former high school math teacher, who had held her current position for the last ten years.

Ms. Blake conceded that teachers were historically very vulnerable to expressions of sexual harassment. "Men," she said,

have and currently hold nearly all the positions of power in the teaching hierarchy. The majority of department heads, vice-principals, principals, superintendents, inspectors, and senior administrators are men. Furthermore, men, for the most part, hold the most powerful positions on school boards. They hold local, state, and federally elected and administrative positions in the educational structure.

Historically, women who taught in one-room schools were open to sexual harassment by inspectors and superintendents. A woman could be denied a permanent teaching certificate unless she slept with these men. I suspect it goes on more than we know. Women rarely complain, even though they have a union behind them.

"Have you any cases?" we asked. She replied,

Yes, two that I think are representative of what women face in teaching. A male principal was simultaneously harassing two female teachers. He wanted to have sexual intimacy with both women. He was quite graphic about his demands. He threatened one with dismissal and the other with a denial of her permanent teaching certificate unless they complied with his demands. Both women, unaware of the other's situation, complained to the union at the same time. Our response was to protect the women. We confronted the male principal, who broke down and confessed and promised to stop this harassment. He was told that he would be watched. The women were asked to report any further incidents.

Our most current case concerns a woman probationary teacher who was dismissed by her principal. She claims that the principal continually pawed her, putting his hand on her knee, patting her bottom, grabbing at her and so on. He talked about how her perfume aroused him and how he fantasized about going to bed with her. She bluntly told the man to leave her alone.

"What happened?" we asked.

"Well," Ms. Blake paused, "this case is difficult. We only have one woman's testimony against a senior male principal. The man claims her work is unsatisfactory. We can't be sure. Unfortunately, the woman has left. But, I think," she said,

sexual harassment of teachers is not such a serious problem as it used to be. Today's women teachers are better educated, older when they enter teaching, and work in larger schools, where they can avoid too much contact with male harassers.

She hesitated and then added,

I admit that these are bad times for teachers. The profession isn't growing. It's hard to find a job, and you almost are forced to keep the one you have. Maybe I am naïve. Women may not be reporting incidents, since they are trying to hang on to their jobs. We still are ghettoized at the bottom, with very little real power in the hierarchy. But our union is prepared to act on behalf of women.

Ms. Blake is light-years ahead of many of the personnel managers and directors interviewed. She at least recognizes that the woman is a victim and not on trial. Her union's approach is based on goodwill and the empathy of one woman to another, but she doesn't appear to have any real clout in terms of reprisals and deterrents. Despite the support Ms. Blake offers, the issue of sexual harassment is such that not very many women feel confident enough to come forward. Ms. Blake does recognize that women are far from equal in the hierarchical structure and feel particularly vulnerable at times when teaching jobs are scarce.

No doubt unionized teachers are in a far better position to complain about sexual harassment than the vast majority of nonunionized women, but until teachers' unions institutionalize the issue, it is unlikely that their members will receive the support they require in fighting sexual harassment.

The Stewardesses' Union

Another profession that employs a majority of women and has succeeded in organizing itself into a strong women's union is that of flight attendant. We interviewed the woman president of flight attendants for a medium-sized charter airline that employs four hundred people. This woman, whom we shall call Ms. Stone, represents her members nationally. Her union is 70 percent female, with women holding the key union positions. Ms. Stone began her remarks by saying,

Let's face it, stewardesses are viewed as flying sex objects. Most men never take you seriously, assuming that you don't have a brain in your head. It's ironic, since most of the women I work with view flying as a part-time career. They often have other professions, such as law, accounting, and teaching. Unlike office workers and women in marginal jobs, stewardesses understand that the workplace is grossly unfair to women. We unionized, appreciating that collectively we could change working conditions for the better.

When asked about the specific issue of sexual harassment, she replied,

We train women about how to handle men who become sexually aggressive and abusive. They can complain to the attendant in charge. At times men become so totally obnoxious that we have to call the police to pick up the offender when the plane lands.

Women in our profession are very supportive of each other. We warn new women about which pilots to watch for, which male flight attendants get out of line, and so on. However, we are still vulnerable. If a male passenger complains about our service, that is, that we were rude, our airline conducts an investigation. If the rudeness is unjustified, we stand to be suspended. Being rude to a sexual harasser is justified, but our word isn't necessarily accepted over the passenger's. If we fail to report the incident to management at the time, it becomes more difficult to defend ourselves. You don't always complain. If you did, it would take up an inordinate amount of time. You start to think you can handle it. And then—you find yourself suspended. The next time you board that plane, you smile and smile and take more crap than you should. You find yourself reluctant to speak up when someone grabs your bum and tries to put their hand up your skirt. You're disgusted but frightened that the man will complain and you will be suspended.

"Ms. Stone," we asked, "what would your union do if a woman were sexually harassed by a superior in the airline who was not a member of your union?" Ms. Stone replied,

If a woman lodged a complaint of sexual harassment by an airline employee, we would force a confrontation with management. Our union doesn't require evidence, but management would insist on investigating. I believe that ultimately we could force the issue. The man in question would be moved, I suspect. We would take it very seriously. If the woman had lost her job, we would make sure she was reinstated.

Ms. Stone is an excellent example of the power that a woman's union can exercise. Still, the women in her union are open to sexual harassment and the reprisal of suspension. "The airlines," she said, "are in business to make money. The customers' complaints generally revolve around our taking issue with their unsolicited attempts at compromising us as women and professional workers."

At the very least, flight attendants recognize that they are open to abuse as sex objects. They face the issue of sexual harassment squarely. But in the end they can be rendered powerless by male perpetrators, who can adversely affect their livelihood.

Male Union Representatives

We interviewed a number of male union senior officials in a variety of public utilities and manufacturing industries to discuss both their recognition of sexual harassment and proposals for remedies to it. Many spoke of their awareness of the issues of equal opportunity and sex discrimination, but they had virtually no knowledge of sexual harassment. Never had one of them heard of a single incident. We cited statistics and real-life examples in their own areas, but they were sure that it wasn't a big problem. After all, they were approachable, and surely the women would have come forward with complaints. The definition of sexual harassment elicited laughter, disbelief, defensiveness, and hostility. However, they all agreed that women were not well represented in unions and that perhaps their own lack of awareness stemmed from this fact.

The Perspective of Female Union Leadership

Eventually we did encounter a woman who had been a union organizer for twenty-five years. Ms. Peel, as we shall call her, had had various degrees of success in organizing nonunionized women in those industries where women work as cheap labor, such as bank clerks, textile workers, office workers, domestics, and waitresses. On the issue of sexual harassment, about which Ms. Peel was very conversant, it was her observation that union and nonunion women, if they complain at all, approach women's organizations first.

The case that she remembered most vividly concerned a young immigrant woman who was working as an office building cleaner at night. She worked alone but was under the supervision of a middle-aged, married man. The man began to harass this woman nightly, pawing her and attempting to coerce her into physical intimacy. The woman was terrified of losing her job, her future options being severely limited by language difficulties and very little formal education. Her sister, with whom she lived, became alarmed when she noticed that the woman ate very little, lost over twenty-five pounds in a short period of time, and began to withdraw from contact with other people. As a result the sister pressured the woman to tell her what was wrong. Eventually the woman broke down and confided about her work situation.

The sister's immediate response was to call the Women's Bureau, who advised her to take the case to the State Commission Against Discrimination. They, in turn, agreed to investigate the incident under the auspices of their sex discrimination jurisdiction. The investigating officer informed the owner of the cleaning company that a complaint of sexual harassment had been lodged against his supervisor. The owner was horrified, admitting that this was the second time such a complaint had come to his attention.His solution was to move the woman to a new location and to have a talk with his supervisor. But he had no intention of firing the man.

Ms. Peel had, over the years, spoken to many union officials about the problem of sexual harassment. "Their response," she said, "was to become defensive, to feel very threatened, to claim that women provoked men to acts of sexual harassment. On many occasions," Ms. Peel said,

I suggested we put the subject of sexual harassment on the agenda. The union men refused, arguing that it would become a joke. But you know, I think that when men recognize the issue of sexual harassment as a serious threat—since so many are guilty of this behavior themselves—they attempt to make a joke out of it. The real solution is for women to take collective action on this issue. It could be a potential tool and a starting point in attracting women into unions. But existing unions should make it clear to their membership that they are prepared to deal with the problem. If the contract language is not clear enough to protect women, the union in question should press for a contract variation in the next round of negotiations.

Ms. Peel recognizes both the weaknesses and the strengths of existing unions. As long as women are so unconnected with real power within the union and are unable to make sexual harassment a broad concern, it will be difficult to demand action. Union people, she has observed, consolidate their support on issues that they perceive to be "immediate." Sexual harassment, she concluded, is a nonmonetary issue and, as such, will be just as difficult to negotiate with union men as with management.

Ms. Peel is currently engaged in a campaign to educate union officials about the dimensions of the problems of sexual harassment. She intends to conduct a survey of salaried union representatives to determine whether the problem of sexual harassment is understood and recognized and how it is generally handled in a union context. She said,

I plan also to prepare an article requesting that union women let us hear about their problems with sexual harassment on the job. It's a difficult subject, but public education is a beginning. However, should the issue receive the recognition, understanding, and support it deserves, union women will be at a great advantage compared to their nonunion women counterparts. The union shop creates an atmosphere where employees feel less vulnerable. They are, in fact, protected from the reprisals for speaking up or entering a complaint that nonunion women are more likely to incur.

Sexual Harassment as an Impetus to Women's Unionization

The issue of sexual harassment has the potential of crossing the social, economic, political, and racial barriers that militate against collective action. No woman is immune from sexual harassment. Most working women can identify with a victim's embarrassment, humiliation, frustration, and sense of helplessness.

There is a union in existence that received its impetus from the issue of sexual harassment. In California there is a network of what are regarded as highly progressive legal-assistance offices, as a result of their support of the United Farm Workers' grape boycott.

A woman who worked as a legal secretary in one of these offices experienced a gross expression of sexual harassment on the part of one of the lawyers in her office. The lawyer grabbed her breasts in full view of the rest of the office staff and refused to let go when she vehemently objected.

The woman was so incensed by the lawyer's behavior that she discussed the incident with other women in the legal-assistance offices' network, only to discover that many other women had endured similar treatment. Ultimately the women formed a union known as the California Legal Workers, which addressed itself to the problem of sexual harassment along with other employment problems that legal secretaries confront as workers and women. Their first contract included a clause stipulating that the employer has an affirmative duty to investigate complaints of sexual harassment.

Our research indicates that the California Legal Workers' Union is the first union in North America to receive its impetus from the issue of sexual harassment. Office workers have traditionally been extremely hard to organize, especially secretaries, whose identity is often bound up with that of management—namely, their bosses. The issue of sexual harassment in this instance was able to mobilize these women into collective action—into the realization that they were the victims of coercive sexual behavior. Once the demystification process began, namely that their best interests did not lie with the benevolence of their particular bosses, they began to assess the myriad of other problems inherent in the workplace, such as salaries, promotion, and training.

The Role of an Association

The office workers in the administrative branch of a West Coast community college, although not unionized, had managed to form an association. They did not have a contract with management that specified terms and conditions of work, but rather the possibility of raising mutually contentious issues as a collective body. Admittedly their success in securing major improvements in their working environment was marginal at best without the power to demand a collective agreement.

Ms. Taiman, as we shall call her, the association president and office manager, spoke of sexual harassment as one small problem concurrent with a host of other larger issues. The subject of sexual harassment had come to her attention during lunch-hour conversations with her female co-workers. Upon reflection, she could recall numerous incidents of varying degrees of seriousness. In fact Ms. Taiman, of all the people interviewed in both the personnel and the union functions, was personally aware of more current cases of sexual harassment in her work environment than anyone else interviewed. As she related,

There was a twenty-year-old female, newly hired in the department of biochemistry, whose middle-aged, married supervisor told her to go to the washroom and remove her bra. When she refused, he attempted to back her into a corner. After several weeks of this harassment the supervisor informed her that if she didn't agree to an affair with him, she would be fired. The woman marched off to the chairman's office to complain of her situation. The chairman responded by telling her she was lying. The woman then approached a woman in the personnel department, who was sympathetic but told her that that is the way men behave and she would have to understand and to accept. At this point the woman applied for another position in the department, but the chairman refused, saying that he had heard that she was boy crazy. And so the woman resigned.

"I have heard of other incidents," she continued.

A supervisor who was a young single man made obscene phone calls to his secretary. For example, he would phone to say that he had his zipper down and was thinking of her.

One professor in our history department has nothing but attractive female staff and graduate students. His behavior toward these women consists of a continual stream of abusive remarks and sexual advances. The situation is such that no one wants to work for him, and he is having difficulty in attracting any female students.

Another incident involves a young woman who lives with her parents. Her married supervisor was coming on to her sexually at work and calling her for dates at her parents' home. When she refused to respond, he began to exhibit nasty behavior toward her at work by refusing to cooperate, by denying her interesting work assignments, by questioning her every move, and by becoming very critical of all her work. Although the woman has discussed this with her co-workers, she is terrified that she will lose her job if she makes a formal complaint.

Ms. Taiman at this point appeared perplexed, as she realized that sexual harassment was definitely a serious problem. She paused for a moment, but continued,

There was a young, very attractive woman who worked for our senior administrator—a man in his late fifties, a grandfather of four. This man pursued this woman to the extent of driving up and down her street and making late-night calls to her home. The woman finally resigned. Most women who work for this man rarely last longer than a month or two.

Ms. Taiman stopped her recital by remarking,

I guess I could write a book too. Until this moment I had no idea how vulnerable all women are to sexual harassment. You know, none of these women ever came forward to lodge a formal complaint with our association. I realize that our association mainly exists as an educational body, but we should assist in handling grievances of this kind. It is our responsibility to bring sexual harassment out of the woodwork, to nip it in the bud before it becomes too serious. Most men, I suspect, have no idea how much their behavior bothers and intimidates women.

Ms. Taiman is limited by the fact that she heads a voluntary association of salaried employees, an association whose objectives are the same as a union's, namely, to improve the salaries and working conditions of its membership, but whose actual power is extremely limited. Nevertheless, members of an association have a distinct advantage over the totally isolated women in a corporate structure, in that they have some person or group of persons to whom they can turn for support.

Ms. Taiman informed us that her association was very much concerned that association members had not as yet come forward with complaints of sexual harassment, despite the fact that the subject was of grave concern. In order to encourage the association membership to come forward on the issue, Ms. Taiman and her executive committee were planning to run a series of articles in their newsletter, requesting that women write or call the association with their specific cases. Furthermore, Ms. Taiman was organizing a seminar on sexual harassment that she hoped would give her members a feeling of commonality and dispel the pervading attitudes of helplessness and frustration.

Ms. Taiman, like Ms. Peel, is sufficiently concerned about sexual harassment to mobilize what authority her association has in order to begin the necessary process of educating the victims of sexual harassment that they have strength in collective action and that their association is aware of sexual harassment and is prepared to act on their behalf.

Conclusion

In February 1978 a landmark strike occurred, solely involving the issue of sexual harassment. In protest against the sexual harassment of two female workers who had been fired for resisting, members of the International Woodworkers of America shut down a sawmill in Campbell River, British Columbia. The strike lasted six days. One hundred and eighteen workers, both male and female, refused to cross a citizens' picket set up in front of Raven Lumber by local women.

The dispute concerned two part-time women workers who had been doing relief work at the mill on weekends. One of the women charged in a written statement that the supervisor had offered her Scotch, kissed her, and grabbed at her breasts. The supervisor allegedly propositioned the other woman repeatedly, even following her to her home to do so. The strikers demanded the dismissal of the supervisor and the immediate reinstatement of the two women.

This was one of the first strikes centered on the issue of sexual harassment. Although the women actually organized the strike, male workers were supportive by refusing to cross the picket line.

Despite the fundamental problems that male union officials and male members have around the issue of sexual harassment, a partial remedy exists for women in this context. Unions negotiate contracts, utilize grievance procedures, and hold the powerful weapon of the strike. All of these mechanisms can be employed in protecting women against sexual harassment. Admittedly the unions, as we have previously pointed out, will not discipline their own members.

Unlike legal actions, union action and support do not require an outlay of possibly large sums of money on the part of the women. Women in unions where women hold office and are instrumental in affecting policy have a great advantage over women in male-dominated unions. Women in the process of organizing their own unions, such as secretaries and bank workers, are in the best position to include the issue of sexual harassment in negotiating their first contracts.

At the very least, women within established unions can pressure for educationals to inform their membership that sexual harassment is an issue that women intend to address.

5

The law: outside the organization
(The Courts, Human Rights Commissions, and the Equal Employment Opportunity Commission)

When personnel departments, higher management, and trade unions fail to provide remedies inside the organization, where can victims of sexual harassment turn? Faced with betrayal and resistance inside the work environment, women are increasingly turning to outside agencies for help. Relying upon legislation and common-law principles, they are seeking assistance from the criminal courts, human rights agencies, and the civil courts.

Obviously there are problems facing women who are courageous enough to take their complaints of sexual harassment to an outside institution. The organization will, in most cases, react with horror and outrage that any employee would dare to attack it from the outside, in the public realm. Most women who lodge complaints with outside institutions can expect that their employer will act quickly to oust them from their jobs. As a result this is rarely a useful remedy for any sexually harassed woman unless she has already been fired or has quit, or unless she feels confident that the outside entity to which she is turning can protect her job at the same time as it investigates and seeks to resolve her complaint—a tall order.

Furthermore, taking legal action can be expensive, time-consuming, and emotionally draining for all concerned. There is some indication that women will receive the fairest treatment in legal cases when they bring their actions in groups. Where an individual woman can be beaten down by the legal system, women who take their cases collectively stand a much better chance for success. In addition, the courts are imbued with discriminatory attitudes that beset society at large. Sexist justice is by no means a relic of the past. In fact, an examination of the legal cases on sexual harassment provides a fascinating insight into the thinking of men who sit as judges in the courts. It is unsettling to learn how completely the male perspective has dominated the law. The distortions evident in their decisions must be given public scrutiny. Knowledge is the first step toward change in the future.

But this is not intended to discourage women from using legal tactics. The law is a powerful tool and not always prohibitive in terms of cost. There are significant benefits to be gained from legal action. First, there is a matter of principle at stake. Many organizations will not take complaints seriously until they are made in a legal forum. If a victim of sexual harassment cannot obtain justice at the hands of her organization, she may wish to make her stand in front of the courts to seek redress from the wrong she has suffered.

Secondly, there is the matter of monetary compensation. Traditionally women have been led to believe that to display an interest in money is "unladylike," that money is the root of all evil. In fact many victims of sexual harassment today disclaim any desire to sue for money. Their wish, they reiterate, is to obtain only an apology and some assurance from the organization that the incident will not be repeated.

Yet this is rather shortsighted. Sexually harassed women suffer serious financial loss—lost wages, vacation pay, pension benefits, medical care, dental care, and life insurance. Some lose out on promotions and transfers for which they have worked long and hard. Many become psychologically and physically ill from sexual harassment and incur medical costs in treating such illness. These are measurable costs, which should be recovered from the harasser or his organization. Selfless sentiments ought to have no place here, and litigation is an excellent tool with which to fight for financial compensation.

During the course of our research, we came across a number of feminist lawyers in both the United States and Canada who are becoming well versed in the area of sexual harassment law. They are sensitive to the issue and are willing to deal with such cases for small fees, and in some cases at no charge. They, too, are gravely offended by the phenomenon of sexual harassment, and are committed to doing their part to fight back as attorneys for female victims.

In the final analysis, the decision of whether to take legal action rests with the woman herself. The important thing is that women make this decision fully conversant with the facts. It is critical that they understand, at least in a general sense, how the law applies to sexual harassment on the job. In this chapter we have attempted to demystify the law, to provide an overview of the different areas of the law, how the law works for you and against you, and how the courts function. This is not a legal treatise with laborious, detailed legal analysis, but a short guide, written in general terms, to indicate what you're up against in a legal action.

There are three outside avenues open to women at the present time. They are criminal proceedings, a complaint to a human rights organization, and civil litigation in the courts.

1. THE CRIMINAL COURTS

The criminal law has moved some distance from the historic days of Carrie Davies's trial for murder on a charge of shooting her employer out of fear of sexual harassment. At that time the criminal system took no notice of the criminality of her employer's actions. It contented itself with examining the sole question of Carrie's guilt or innocence.

A Landmark Case

A recent rape trial in Vancouver, British Columbia, marked a milestone in Canadian criminal law and provided some insight into modern North American criminal law. In August 1977, the trial of a wealthy Vancouver businessman, on charges of raping a real estate saleswoman, became one of the most hotly discussed issues in Vancouver. The case was an example of an extreme form of sexual harassment. The real estate saleswoman was raped in the course of trying to close a real estate deal with her client.

The accused, George Pappajohn, a thirty-eight-year-old man, was a wealthy businessman with interests in two fashionable Vancouver restaurants. He was in the market to sell his house in Shaughnessy, one of Vancouver's most exclusive residential neighborhoods. He invited the complainant, a thirty-seven-year-old real estate saleswoman, to his house one evening to discuss the sale. According to her, he had behaved very pleasantly as they drank sherry and discussed the proposed deal. Accordingly, she was pleased when he telephoned her a month later and asked her to meet him for lunch at a restaurant to discuss retaining her to sell his house. The saleswoman had formerly been a flight attendant and was just launching her career as a real estate saleswoman. She was extremely anxious to close this house deal for such a prestigious client.

During the rather lengthy lunch a fair amount of alcohol was consumed. The saleswoman was shocked and offended when Pappajohn asked her what she would do to get a three-million-dollar listing of a property owned by another landlord. However, she thought Pappajohn had meant a bribe and did not remotely anticipate that anything physical was being suggested. When the lunch ended, Pappajohn suggested she accompany him back to his house. She agreed, telling him that she would return to discuss the sale. She also wanted to change the For Sale sign in front of the house and to help him decide what furniture should be removed. Once back in his home, he poured another drink for her.

The evidence given in the case disclosed that he suddenly pushed her into a bedroom, tore off her clothes, and tied her hands and legs. He told her he wanted to keep her prisoner for several days. Then he raped her repeatedly over a three-hour period. The woman was finally able to escape from the bedroom. She ran naked out into the back lane, with her hands still tied behind her. The panic-stricken woman managed to reach a nearby house, where she was taken in by a neighbor.

Charges of rape were laid against Pappajohn. The saleswoman agreed to testify during the criminal trial. Not only was she suffering from the trauma most women feel when they have been attacked by a rapist, but the adverse influence on her career had been substantial. Due to her reaction to her attack, she felt unable to continue her work. She felt she could no longer go into a client's home alone and that she could not make herself vulnerable again. Furthermore, with the glare of publicity focused on her rape complaint, her sales business had dried up completely. Few clients were seeking her out.

During the trial, Pappajohn contended that the complainant had voluntarily agreed to go to bed with him, but "underwent a personality change and began objecting to sex after she was tied up."[1] This was the reason she laid the complaint, the accused rather lamely asserted. The courtroom in Vancouver, where the case was tried, was jam-packed with an audience that was largely composed of members of various women's groups.

The controversial trial ended on August 22, 1977. The accused man sat white-faced and near collapse in the prisoner's dock as the nine men and three women of the jury announced that they had ended two days of deliberation with a guilty verdict.

Since this conviction was appealed, we would be hesitant to mark it as a landmark in criminal jurisprudence too quickly, although in May 1980 the Canadian Supreme Court upheld the rape conviction of Pappajohn. In examining how the legal system operates, it becomes obvious that sexual harassment cases comprise a new phenomenon. As such, the law surrounding this issue is very fluid, with dramatic decisions being handed down only to be overturned in a court of appeal. Until the case law has developed sufficiently, it is difficult to speak with authority on legal trends.

However, the Vancouver case is one good example where there was a conviction for rape in a sexual harassment context. There are few other successful cases reported in North American jurisprudence. While there are other rape convictions, most cases do not disclose whether the rape occurred in a work setting. Clearly this points out how economic coercion is considered irrelevant. The courts persist in looking for physical coercion, completely overlooking the fact that rapists often operate with impunity in the workplace.

Sexual Intercourse with an Employee

In the Canadian legal system, the criminal code retains an anachronistic provision dealing with sexual intercourse with a female employee.[2] This prohibits a male employer from having "illicit sexual intercourse" with a female employee. However, to be covered by this provision, the female employee must be under the age of twenty-one and of "previously chaste character." Furthermore, where an accused is charged under this provision, the criminal code states that the court may find him not guilty if the evidence does not show that the accused is more to blame than the female person.

The scope of this rather limited provision is tightened even further by other sections of the criminal code. They provide that no criminal proceeding can be commenced on this charge after the passage of one year from the date the offense was committed. In addition the code has retained the explicit need for corroboration. It specifically states that no accused shall be convicted upon the evidence of only one witness unless that evidence is corroborated. Finally a rather horrifying additional provision announces that the accused cannot be convicted of this offense where he marries the woman after the date of the offense.

Even in the rather unlikely event that a woman who is being sexually harassed can fit herself into all of the stipulations of this provision, further hurdles await her due to the interpretation that the courts have given the phrase "of previously chaste character." Courts have held that chastity and virginity are not synonymous. In fact, they state it is quite possible for a woman to be unchaste although she is physically a virgin. "An unmarried woman may have a vile and lewd character and yet stop short of sexual intercourse," stated one judge in a 1948 case.[3] "Chaste character means the possession of the qualities and traits of pureness and decency of thought and conduct. It is moral cleanliness in the sense that reasonable, right-thinking people would say there is an absence of impurity or indecency," he concluded.

Of the three reported cases we found under this provision, all of the women were employed as live-in housemaids.[4] One case stands out. As recently as 1966, at Val St.-Michel in the province of Quebec, Napoleon St.-Hilaire had been found guilty of illicit sexual intercourse with Nicole Plante, age sixteen, of previously chaste character, who was employed by him as a housemaid. He was sentenced to twelve months' imprisonment but successfully appealed his conviction. The appeal court determined that there had been no corroboration of the girl's evidence. The only corroborating evidence that had been produced at trial had been the testimony of a Dr. Boilard. He stated that Nicole Plante's hymen was broken and that 95 percent of the cases he had seen where the hymen was broken, it had been due to sexual intercourse with a male. The appeal court concluded that this was not corroborating evidence, not only because of the 5 percent margin for error, but also because they felt Nicole Plante could have lost her virginity for many other reasons than that mentioned by the doctor. As a result the conviction was overturned.

Statistics Canada, which keeps records on many criminal charges and convictions, had no information as to the number of cases under this provision, although the gentleman we spoke to there did comment, rather gratuitously, "That's a dandy of a section, now, isn't it?" The attitude of the police is also one of amused chuckling, and they, too, frankly concede that the section has long outlived its usefulness. However, they appear to have given little consideration to whether any other sections of the criminal code adequately cover the coercive assaults working women often receive from male sexual harassers.

Other Criminal Offenses

In all criminal action, there can be no conviction unless the Canadian crown attorney or the American district attorney proves the case beyond a reasonable doubt. This is a very difficult burden of proof in all cases, but especially in cases of sexual harassment. The discriminatory attitudes that pervade society often label sexually abused women as probable enticers. The situation is further exacerbated by the fact that acts of sexual harassment often occur behind closed doors. Even when sexual harassment occurs in full view of co-workers, few people are prepared to come forward to testify in a court of law.

Both rape and the prohibition against sexual intercourse with a female employee in Canada deal with extreme manifestations of sexual harassment. However, we are not suggesting that both offenses are a rare occurrence. Our research suggests that a surprising number of working women have experienced rape on the job.

Nevertheless, less extreme forms of criminal behavior are more common. To find protection from these less virulent actions, women must look to other provisions in North American criminal statutes.

These include indecent assault, common assault, assault causing bodily harm, threats, intimidation, and soliciting. In Canada, the criminal law is set out in the federal criminal code. In the United States the criminal law is found state by state in various different pieces of legislation, although there are few substantial differences.

The Odds against Winning

So where does this leave us in terms of criminal sanctions for sexual harassment on the job? Suppose that a woman victim of sexual harassment has been subject to treatment that falls within the confines of criminal behavior. She may then phone the police to lay a complaint. In a typical case the police would then meet with the complainant and take her story. Initially they would ask her if she would agree to testify in court should they turn up sufficient evidence to proceed. Unless the woman agrees, the police will refuse to investigate.

As one supervisor of criminal investigations for a regional police office stated, "We're not in the scare business. Unless the woman will agree to press charges, we will not even consider speaking to the alleged offender."

In their investigation the police will ask for details concerning where, when, and how the sexual harassment took place. They will ask if there were any witnesses and, if so, will take statements from them also. At this point they will speak to the accused, confront him with the complaint, and get his side of the story, which will most likely be a denial. The police will then decide whether they feel there is enough evidence to proceed and whether they have "reasonable and probable grounds" to believe an offense has been committed.

Several adjournments in the case will be likely. In the more serious offenses the accused has the right to have a preliminary hearing before trial. In those cases the woman will have to appear in court twice (once at the preliminary hearing and again at trial) to give her evidence on the stand. The length of time the entire process will take depends on the size of the judicial jurisdiction and the court backlog, but ranges from a number of months to several years. Even after completion of the trial there is no guarantee that the process is over. Appeals are a distinct possibility. Where the accused is convicted, with the exception of rape, most of the other offenses we have considered give rise only to small fines. Sentences of imprisonment and larger fines are almost nonexistent. Typical games lawyers play drag out criminal proceedings until complainants become so weary they want out of the entire business.

There is also the glare of publicity. Only rape and indecent assault victims can be screened from the press. All others can find their names, their evidence, and the conflicting evidence of the defense reported and commented on by the press, radio, and television media, unless the court gives orders otherwise (an extremely unusual move). Furthermore, the woman will probably find her continued employment by the firm in which she was sexually harassed in jeopardy. If she loses that job, her chances of finding another position will dwindle dramatically. No one wants to hire a troublemaker. If she succeeds in finding a new job, she may be able to hide from her new employer that she is involved in a criminal battle with a former employer. However, she will have to appear continually in court, and this will arouse the suspicions of a new employer and may result in his impatience with an absentee employee.

Despite all of the pitfalls of the criminal process, most women do not get a chance to make the decision of whether or not to go forward with their cases. Police officers will rarely lay charges and pursue a case where there are not witnesses besides the complainant. By their very nature, acts of sexual harassment almost always take place in the absence of witnesses. Yet one police officer had this to say:

If a girl came to us and told us her boss had called her into the office, put his arm around her, and grabbed her breast, we would first investigate to see if there was some additional evidence. No judge would convict without further evidence. Our practice is that we will not deal with complaints of this kind without some corroborating evidence. It's just too easy for her employer, an upstanding man in the community, to testify that she had asked him for a raise, that he had turned her down, and that this false cry of assault was her ploy to get even.

The police conclude that a case is "founded" when they think there is a real likelihood that there would be a conviction at trial. They are usually unwilling to push a case to prosecution if they know an acquittal is likely, because a great deal of time, energy, and public money is put into the preparation of each case. Furthermore, the police know how reluctant crown and district attorneys are to prosecute problematical cases. They are therefore reluctant to bring forward to court cases where they think a judge or jury would be unlikely to convict. Like the police, they prefer to work on cases where the attacker is a stranger to his victim, where overt signs of the woman's resistance can be found, and where other witnesses are available to back up the woman's story. This vicious circle means that the biases of the judges and case law from the past prevent the type of sexual harassment cases we are discussing from getting to court at all. But unless such cases are brought, and brought often, it is unlikely that the jurisprudence and attitudes of the judges will be sensitized to the real coercion focused on working women in our society.

In the absence of corroborating evidence, the police may refuse to proceed themselves but allow the complainant to proceed by way of private prosecution. Instead of having the police officer lay the charges, the woman herself will do so. Most cases of common assault where there is no evidence apart from the victim's testimony get to court only by way of private prosecution. In most of these cases, however, the complainant does not have the assistance of a crown or district attorney in arguing her case. She is forced to hire her own lawyer or argue it herself. It is common knowledge that the judges who hear private prosecutions treat them with much less concern than they do police-laid charges. In fact very short shrift is given to such cases unless the complainant retains private counsel to act as prosecutor and to force the judge to deal seriously with the case.

Although most instances of sexual harassment happen behind closed doors and in private without witnesses, the victim can create a much stronger case if she can find other women who have been similarly harassed by the particular man involved. The police will be much more likely to get involved if there is a pattern of harassment that extends to a number of women, all of whom are prepared to corroborate each other's stories and give evidence in court.

The other possibility to obtain evidence for use in court is to have the female complainant use a body pack. A body pack is a tape-recording device often used in police undercover work. The tiny "bug" is a piece of equipment that is strapped onto the woman, which would fit under her arm. The receiver, which actually records the conversation, is located in a police car. The police must wait in their car outside the building the complainant is in, to intercept the conversation she has with the sexual harasser. If the sexual harasser is caught in the act and the conversation is taped with this body pack, the recording can be introduced into court. (So long as one party to the conversation agrees to tape-record it, it is perfectly admissible in a court of law.) There would be no danger that the complainant would be "entrapping" the man (a common law defense in the United States to a criminal charge), unless she actually induced the man to commit a crime he had not contemplated.

Since this would be an ideal way to get evidence of sexual harassment, body packs hold out a great deal of promise for future successful criminal prosecution of sexual harassment cases. First, however, the police will have to recognize their usefulness and advise women to gather evidence through such units. At present police forces do not have a large supply of these fairly costly units, and so far as we were able to determine they have never yet been used in a case of sexual harassment.

In conclusion, the criminal law appears to be a rather blunt instrument, ill designed to deal with the problems of sexual harassment on the job. Initially all charges must be proved beyond a reasonable doubt—a strict test and one that is difficult to meet without an abundance of corroborating witnesses and other evidence. Most rape and assault cases that get to court involve strangers. At the present time police precincts and most courts of law still operate from the assumption that a woman who has been raped by a man she knows is a woman "who changed her mind afterward." Sexual harassers who operate through a dependent relationship such as the employment setting, with its hierarchical, authoritarian structure, have been relatively immune from prosecution. Coercion can take many forms—economic and emotional as well as brute force. Yet the criminal law holds a distinct preference for violent, physical actions, failing to recognize that the imposition of sex by an authority figure is hardly consensual or a relationship between equals.

Finally there remains the critical question of who interprets and enforces the criminal law. At present female victims of sexual crimes who seek legal protection must rely on a series of male authority figures—from the police, through the crown and district attorneys, to the judges. The masculine orientation of these men means that their values and fears place them squarely in the offender's camp. The surprising findings of our research were that the attitudes of policemen, crown and district attorneys, and judges paralleled very closely the frightening attitudes of the personnel, management, and trade union figures we interviewed.

Police forces, crown and district attorneys, and the judiciary are all male-dominated groups. Like the other male opinion makers we interviewed, these men react with disbelief to discussion of pervasive, serious sexual harassment. Unable to recognize the economic coercion inherent in sexual harassment, they, too, grasped immediately at the argument of mutuality. The commonly voiced opinion of police officers and supervisors was that most of these cases must be based on situations where "a guy and a gal are together—she's prepared to go along for a few months—after that she wants to cut it off and he doesn't." Not only does it appear that the criminal law itself (with the exception of a few, to date undeveloped sections) is stacked against women, but the men enforcing and administering it are also virtually insensitive to the realities of sexual harassment facing working women.

2. THE CANADIAN HUMAN RIGHTS COMMISSIONS AND THE AMERICAN EQUAL EMPLOYMENT OPPORTUNITY COMMISSION

In Canada legislation prohibiting sex discrimination is found in human rights statutes, administered by various human rights commissions across the country. They alone have the authority to take a complaint as far as adjudication. The ultimate step in the process is a hearing before a board of inquiry, not before courts of law.

In the United States the federal Civil Rights Act of 1964 is the statute that prohibits sex discrimination. The Equal Employment Opportunity Commission has been set up to investigate complaints brought under this act. There is no system for boards of inquiry. Instead cases are ultimately taken before the courts by the complainant or the Equal Employment Opportunity Commission (EEOC).

It is important to note that both the Canadian human rights commissions and the American EEOC attempt in the first instance to conciliate a settlement between the two parties. Conciliation means to reconcile the two disparate parties to a mutually acceptable resolution. This could take the form of severance pay, reinstatement, a letter of apology, a letter of recommendation, and so on. The foregoing is what conciliation is ideally meant to accomplish. In reality women in sex discrimination cases are frequently persuaded to drop their complaint.

The conciliation process, although similar in result in both Canada and the United States, differs in methodology. In Canada the conciliation process begins and ends before there is ever any finding made that the legislation has been breached. In the United States an investigation officer must first find that there is "probable cause" that the legislation has been violated. Only then can the conciliation process begin. Theoretically the American system should give the EEOC greater powers to conciliate a more equitable settlement.

The Equal Employment Opportunity Commission

Apart from equal pay laws, there was no law in the United States prohibiting discrimination against women in employment until the Civil Rights Act of 1964. Largely riding on the coattails of the black civil rights movement, sex was written into Title VII of that act. It was made an unlawful employment practice to discriminate against any individual with respect to conditions or privileges of employment on the basis of sex.

Women who wish to file a charge under this act must present a written complaint to the Equal Employment Opportunity Commission (EEOC). All complaints must be filed within 180 days of the alleged violation. The complaint must identify the parties and clearly describe the discriminatory acts. If there is a state or local fair-employment-practices agency or human rights commission, the EEOC must give this state agency first crack at solving the complaint. The state agency has sixty days to act on the charge (120 days if the agency has been operating less than a year). In localities where there is no state agency, the EEOC assumes immediate responsibility for processing the charge.

The complaint will be investigated by a field officer. The officer will take a statement from the complainant and speak to the alleged harasser and co-workers to get their stories. Based on the evidence that he or she uncovers, the field officer will decide whether there is reasonable cause to believe there has been a violation. If there is such a finding, the EEOC will try to negotiate a settlement informally. The time required for the investigation and conciliation process varies throughout the country, depending on the nature of the complaint, the size of the EEOC office, and so on.

If a successful conciliation cannot be reached, the complainant may file a civil court suit on her own. The EEOC also has the right to file suit on behalf of the woman, but does so rarely. The complainant's right to sue on her own is fairly broad. Even where the evidence from the investigation does not indicate a violation of the law, and the EEOC will take no further action, the woman has a right to sue. She can also request a right-to-sue letter if the EEOC has not brought suit within 180 days from the official filing of the charge.

The EEOC has the authority to commence investigation on its own without a complaint. These "pattern of practice" charges, as they are called, are utilized to expedite enforcement. Instead of dealing with a large number of complaints on a piecemeal basis, the organization is systematically examined for evidence of sex discrimination, and large awards are possible. As yet the EEOC has not seen fit to initiate such an investigation for evidence of sexual harassment, and none appears likely in the foreseeable future.

Since the EEOC rarely goes to court itself, unless a victim can obtain a satisfactory settlement at the conciliation level, the only option is to pursue a legal remedy in the courts. There are distinct benefits to be gained through court action based on the Civil Rights Act, 1964, Title VII.

If a civil action is brought, the violation will have to be proved in court. Then the judge may issue an order requiring the employer to rehire an employee he has discharged wrongfully. Other remedies can provide financial compensation to the victim, including up to two years of back pay. The actual civil cases that have been adjudicated thus far will be examined in the following section.

Does Sex Discrimination Include Sexual Harassment?

All of this legislation, in both Canada and the United States, prohibits "sex discrimination." It does not specifically prohibit sexual harassment on the job. In Canada there has not yet been a case brought to a human rights board of inquiry for a legal ruling on whether sexual harassment fits within sex discrimination. In the United States to date only certain forms of sexual harassment have been held to be a violation of human rights legislation. The harasser must be the woman's supervisor or someone who can make sexual activity a condition of a promotion or job retention. Sexual advances that are not accompanied by job-related sanctions are not covered.

Harassment that makes the work environment objectionable and unpleasant but yet doesn't jeopardize the woman's job has not as yet been construed as a violation. However, it is anticipated that in the future the courts will begin to include this type of harassment, finding it equally reprehensible.

Canadian Human Rights Commissions

In Canada labor legislation is primarily a provincial matter. All of the provinces have enacted provincial human rights codes, which in most cases cover all of the employees of that province. However, approximately 10 percent of the workforce falls under federal jurisdiction. This group includes employees who are involved in interprovincial transportation, interprovincial trade and commerce, atomic industries, banking, federal government employees, and other groups specifically designated as coming within federal jurisdiction by the British North America Act. These employees must look to the federal Canadian Human Rights Act for protection.

How the Human Rights Commissions
View Sexual Harassment

Until recently none of the human rights commissions was interpreting its legislation to cover sexual harassment. Women who lodged complaints of sexual harassment were told that the legislation did not prohibit this behavior. Most human rights bodies had unwritten policies that no written record should be kept of such complaints and that only "informal" efforts should be made to assist women with such problems. Why this was so is not clear. To some extent it may have been wrapped up with rather disconcerting notions that sexual harassment was embarrassing, that to deal with such issues would "sully" the reputation of the human rights commissions. Far better the commissions should concentrate on "real" sex discrimination cases—such as equal pay and failure to promote women on an equal basis with men.

Some of the commissions even developed "legal" reasoning to back up their contention that sexual harassment was not covered. The Manitoba commission made the argument that when the legislation said no discrimination on the basis of sex, *sex* meant biological status, not sexual intercourse. Where a man was harassing only one woman, it might have been a result of her personality, rather than sex itself, it was argued. A man who harassed only one woman would not necessarily harass all women. It is obvious here that the commission is completely misinterpreting its own legislation. Even if *sex* is confined to a meaning of biological status, the man is harassing the woman precisely because she is a woman—a female sex object in his eyes. It is her very "femaleness" that is causing him to harass. He certainly would not be harassing her if she were male. And the fact that only one woman may be the object of sexual harassment should be totally irrelevant. If almost all of the women working in an office were receiving pay equal to pay given to men for the same work, but one woman was paid less for doing the same work, would that be grounds to deny her a remedy under human rights legislation? The parallel argument is not made in other cases of sexual discrimination—only in sexual harassment cases.

Even more absurdly, the chairman of the Alberta human rights commission, Max Wyman, has decided that in his province sexual harassment is not covered by the human rights legislation, based on American cases that have since been overruled by the American higher courts. In a recent letter to the Calgary Status of Women Action Committee, Wyman defended his position that sexual harassment should not be covered, with the flawed logic of the following statement: "Sexual harassment does not necessarily involve discrimination. In a one-man, one-woman office, either could be guilty of sexual harassment, but it is difficult to see how a discriminatory practice is involved."

Most of the human rights acts in Canada provide an anomalous exclusion for domestic servants. A domestic who lives at her employer's place of residence or is employed at a single-family dwelling has no protection from discrimination on the basis of sex. This is particularly shocking in view of the fact that historically some of the harshest, most pathetic instances of sexual harassment have involved female housemaids. There is absolutely no reasonable excuse for such legislative irresponsibility, and the exemptions should be wiped out.

Very recently, as women have become more vocal about the pervasiveness and seriousness of sexual harassment, some of the commissions have begun to change their minds. (Alberta, it should be noted, at the date of writing, continued to hold with its position that sexual harassment was *not* covered.) Although the Manitoba commission felt it was still questionable whether sexual harassment was covered, it decided to take formal complaints and proceed on the basis that sexual harassment was covered until a board of inquiry or court ruled otherwise.

The human rights commissions that are now taking formal complaints on sexual harassment find that the only women who come forward are those who are no longer employed with the harassing organization. They have either been fired or have been forced to quit by intolerable working conditions. Apparently many women who are still on the job telephone the various commissions about sexual harassment problems. The commissions generally ask them to come in in person and lay formal complaints. With rare exceptions, however, women only feel brave enough to complain when they no longer have anything to lose. Their fears of on-the-job reprisals appear to be justified. Most organizations insist that their employees deal with personnel matters inside the company. Despite their poor record of solving sexual harassment cases, they want at all costs to contain the situation within the organization and are outraged when employees "hang out the dirty linen for the public to see." When a woman seeks an outside remedy, she can expect the organization to close ranks behind her and provide solid support for her male harasser in the face of any outside investigation. Furthermore, most organizations perceive any woman who files a complaint with an outside agency as disloyal, and often steps are taken to have her fired.

In one case we learned of, two women who were being sexually harassed by the same male supervisor had complained to their personnel manager. After he failed to assist them, they filed complaints with their provincial human rights commission. Several days after they did this, one of the women was fired and the other was suspended. Although most human rights legislation states that no employee shall be fired or disciplined for lodging a complaint or testifying to the commission, these sections are rarely enforced. In addition, it is very easy for employers to allege that the employees were fired for something other than their human rights complaints. Few employees have a completely un-blemished work record. To prove that your human rights complaint was the cause of discipline is often difficult.

The Complaints Procedure

Once a human rights commission receives a complaint, the procedure will be as follows: The woman will be interviewed and asked to give her story. The obvious problem is that there are few witnesses to sexual harassment, and outside of the woman's own testimony there are few sources of confirmation. The commission's investigators will interview any witnesses the woman may have and find out if they would be prepared to testify on the woman's behalf. Then they will interview the employer and other supervisory and co-workers who deal with the com-plainant. If there is any indication that the harasser may fall within the "relentless repeater" category, the investigators may try to follow up with other female victims who have been subjected to sexual harassment and persuade them to testify or file additional complaints.

Based on the nature of the evidence that is turned up or how strong the woman's case appears to be, the investigators will try to negotiate or conciliate a settlement between the woman and her organization. Of course, if the harasser or his organization denies that sexual harassment took place, there is not much chance of "settlement." At that point the commission will assess how strong a case they could make in the face of the employer's denial. In most situations where there is no further evi-dence apart from the woman's own testimony, they will abandon the case. Where more than one woman is prepared to testify or there are witnesses prepared to testify, the commission will have more bargaining leverage in a conciliation. The types of conciliated settlements they go after include the following: assurances that the human rights legislation will not be breached in the future, the posting of human rights legislation at the place of employment, letters of apology, and in some cases money compensation and/or reinstatement of the complainant. If the commis-sion is unable to negotiate what they consider to be a reasonable settle-ment in the circumstances, they may decide to take the matter before a formal board of inquiry.

At a board of inquiry an impartial, independent person is appointed to hear the evidence and argument of both sides. The commission may hire a lawyer at its expense to represent the complainant. The organiza-tion accused of discrimination may also retain a lawyer to defend it. All of the witnesses, including the complainant (and also usually the alleged harasser), give testimony under oath and are subject to cross-ex-amination by the lawyers of the other side. The board of inquiry then makes its decision, which is binding on all the parties, just as a court decision would be. The board can dismiss the complaint as unsubstantiated or find that it has been proved and award money compensation to the woman for any loss of income and expenses resulting from the sexual harassment. It can also order the employer to do anything it finds to be necessary to end the discrimination, including forcing the employer to reinstate the woman in her job. The board's decision can be appealed to the courts in most jurisdictions. All board-of-inquiry proceedings are public and are often covered extensively by the media.

Very few boards of inquiry are ever set up by Canadian human rights commissions. They are viewed as expensive, time-consuming, and an arena of last resort for only the strongest of cases, where employers refuse to come to a reasonable settlement. As stated earlier, no sexual harassment case has yet gone to a board of inquiry in Canada.

Although it costs a woman nothing to have her case dealt with by a human rights commission, the procedure can be extremely cumbersome and in many cases drags on for a long period of time. The months can stretch into years before a case is ultimately resolved, and in many instances a resolution is never reached that is truly acceptable to the woman.

Actual Cases

Due to the discouraging attitude of the various human rights bodies on the issue of sexual harassment until very recently, it is not surprising that they have dealt with few cases. However, the manner in which these few cases was handled is instructive in understanding current Canadian human rights thinking on sexual harassment.

CASE 1

A young female office worker had lost her job because of sexual advances from her boss. Her boss had driven her home from work one day and propositioned her. There were no witnesses, and when the commission interviewed the employer and other employees and supervisors at the woman's place of work, they were told the woman had "personality problems." The commission decided that the complaint was "unsubstantiated" and proceeded no further.

CASE 2

A divorced mother of two was fired from her job because she failed to go along with her boss's sexual come-ons. On investigation, the commission found no witnesses who were prepared to come forward to support the woman's complaint. The employer told the commission that the woman lost her job because of a change in requirements for her position that made her unqualified to fill it. The woman had previously stated that she was told when she was dismissed that her firing had nothing to do with her work. The commission also found this case to be "unsubstantiated." The woman took her case to the newspapers, stating that the reason none of the other employees would come forward to support her story was fear. "There's no way any other woman there is going to put her head on the chopping block and substantiate my story. They are afraid for their jobs," she told the media. She explained to a newspaperman that she was looking for another job and felt she must eliminate the circumstances of her last employment situation from her résumé to prevent reprisals. Despite the commission's failure to assist her, she was determined to hire a lawyer if she could get legal aid and take her case to the courts. "I don't back down from something I believe in," she said. "If I had one person who could stand up for me. . . . Right now the boss can say whatever the devil he likes."

CASE 3

A seventeen-year-old woman who was working as a salesclerk in a small bakery had been sexually assaulted by her boss, the owner of the business. She quit and lodged her complaint. The commission was able to get the employer to compensate the woman for the money she had lost while between jobs and to give a serious commitment that there would be no further violations.

CASE 4

A thirty-one-year-old divorced woman had been employed as a receptionist by a small professional organization for two years. She had been acquainted with her employer's son, a man in his late twenties who also worked for the organization, before she started to work there. The son asked her out, and she did attend a sports event with him but decided she did not wish to continue the relationship further. According to the woman, her employer's son was not prepared to let it go at that, but continually harassed her at her place of employment. He verbally abused her, was constantly touching her, and pinched her. He persistently telephoned her at home, insisting they go out, and when she would hang up on him, he would drive over to her home and grab and kiss her. She was so frightened that she phoned the police, but did not lay criminal charges. She complained to her employer, who responded defensively with the accusation, "You give it away." She was very disturbed by this treatment and eventually quit her job. The commission interviewed the employer, who admitted he knew of his son's behavior and had warned him about it, but claimed his son's behavior was an understandable case of "boy chasing girl." The son, when interviewed, stated his only objective was "friendship" and that he was justified in making the remarks he had made to the complainant "because she had many boyfriends." The commission did not take this case to a board of inquiry, but settled for a cash payment to the woman of two weeks' severance pay and an assurance from the employer that no further incidents would occur.

CASE 5

A twenty-nine-year-old married woman had been working as a waitress for fifteen years. She had held her current position with a small restaurant for only four months. She complained that her employer was making numerous crude remarks and constantly touching her, often in front of customers. She had also had to put up with sexual abuse from male customers. She was upset by this behavior, and fearing dismissal for failure to come across, she resigned. When the commission interviewed her employer, he accused her of discussing personal matters with the customers and using abusive language toward them. The commission found the complaint "unsubstantiated."

CASE 6

A thirty-six-year-old divorced woman, who had been working as a salesclerk for seventeen years, took a job in a small retail shop. Her employer, a married man in his late sixties, asked her personal questions about her relationships with men, made physical and verbal advances, and treated her this way in front of customers. When she objected to this treatment, she was laid off. Suspicious when she learned that the female staff had a very high turnover rate, she filed a complaint with the commission. Her employer countered with the argument that she was let go because of her poor attendance record and job performance. (In the face of such treatment, it shouldn't have been particularly surprising that her productivity was slightly off. It would be a rare woman who could withstand constant sexual importuning from her boss without suffering a decline in her work performance.) Although the employer offered her her job back, she declined the offer. The commission concluded that the complaint was "unsubstantiated."

CASE 7

A nineteen-year-old single woman took a job as a secretary with a small manufacturing company. During her employment interview her supervisor asked her personal questions. Once she was hired, he made verbal propositions and physical advances. When she objected, he dismissed her. The woman related to the commission that certain medical problems she had, had been exacerbated by the anxiety and tension she had suffered in trying to deal with her supervisor's passes. She had been so distraught that she had even been driven to consult with the police about the criminal consequences of harassment, although she had laid no charges. Her supervisor denied her allegations and told the commission that the basis of her complaint was that she had discussed her problems with her boyfriends with him on occasion and that she must be embarrassed now. The commission settled this complaint when the employer agreed to pay three hundred dollars in severance pay to the woman, post copies of the human rights legislation in the office, and give assurances that there would be no future violations.

CASE 8

A twenty-four-year-old single clerical employee, who had been working with her employer for one year, complained to her supervisor about the sexual remarks, gestures, and practical jokes with sexual overtones of her male co-workers. She told the commission that the staff was largely male and that women clerical employees before her had had similar problems. After her complaint to her supervisor, the company fired her. The company told the commission she was fired because she was "nervous and excitable." The commission concluded that the complaint was "unsubstantiated."

CASE 9

A twenty-four-year-old single woman worked as a part-time waitress in a large modern hotel. Two of her male supervisors harassed all of the female staff both verbally and physically, but when the women complained, management took no action. On one occasion one of the men grabbed the woman's breast in the public area of the restaurant. The woman, supported by friends who were in the restaurant at the time, called the police and laid a charge of common assault. Her employer then fired her on the spot. The employer told the commission she had been fired because she had been drinking on the job. The commission did not take this case to a board of inquiry, but settled for a payment of $250 to the woman, posting of the human rights legislation in the hotel, and a memo to the staff assuring them that this behavior would not be countenanced by management. In a most unusual result, one of the male employees involved (the one who had been charged with assault) was dismissed, and the other male employee resigned.

CASE 10

A single seventeen-year-old woman took a position as an apprentice in a small service company. She stated that sexually derogatory remarks had been made to her and that she had been lectured that her clothing was not "revealing" enough for the job—for a mainly male clientele. When she refused to follow this advice, she was fired. The employer admitted to the commission that he had suggested the woman wear more revealing clothing, but stated she had been fired because of poor work performance, too many personal phone calls, and a poor reference from her previous employer. The commission concluded that the complaint was "unsubstantiated." They did not press further when the employer was persuaded to apologize to the woman and post copies of the human rights legislation in the office.

CASE 11

A thirty-two-year-old married woman was employed as a kitchen helper in a large restaurant. A male co-worker, aged fifty, made physical advances and invited her to come to his home. When the woman resisted these advances, her male co-worker accused her of interfering with his work and he quit. The employer was so upset at losing the male employee, whom he felt was a good worker, that he fired the woman. When interviewed by the commission, the employer charged that she was fired for "poor work relations." The commission found the complaint "unsubstantiated." Although the employer offered the woman another job in a branch restaurant, the woman refused to accept the offer.

CASE 12

A nineteen-year-old woman reported for work in a small service company on the date of hire. After closing on her first day of work she was subjected to sexual advances from her manager. She complained to the commission. When they interviewed her manager, he denied that a firm offer of employment had ever been made to the woman and stated that any advances he might have made to the woman were carried on in his home, not at work. The commission found the complaint to be "unsubstantiated."

CASE 13

A forty-five-year-old married woman had worked for her employer as a factory worker in a large manufacturing plant for two years. Nearly a year after she began to work for the company her foreman, a married man in his late twenties, made sexual advances. When the woman's husband phoned her boss to ask him to stop the foreman's unsolicited behavior, management refused to take any action. She was fired several months later for "inability to get along with co-workers." The commission concluded the complaint was "unsubstantiated."

The Pros and Cons of Human Rights Complaints

While these are just some of the cases dealt with by the various human rights commissions, a pattern is very evident. In the most extreme cases the woman is offered several weeks' severance pay. In most other sexual harassment cases the complaint is not held to be "substantiated," or the employer is merely asked to post copies of the human rights legislation and give assurances that no further incidents will occur. In only one case were the male offenders disciplined, and this was largely as a result of the fact that criminal charges were pending against them for their sexually coercive behavior. In virtually none of the cases was action taken to prevent these harassers from harassing other women, such as removing them from situations where they could be in direct contact with female employees on a one-to-one basis.

In the face of all this evidence of unsatisfactory disposition of sexual harassment cases, women continue to resort to human rights bodies, seeking assistance. They may view the human rights complaints procedure as preferable to court action because it is free of charge. Also, making a complaint to a public agency can be less frightening than engaging a lawyer and undertaking a court action.

Yet there are very serious weaknesses with our present human rights legislation and its enforcement. Underlying these acts is the principle that discrimination is a problem of faulty attitudes, best solved by education, a proposition that is highly questionable. The Canadian human rights agencies regard the complaints procedure as only one weapon in their arsenal—a weapon far less important than public education. In practice, prosecutions and boards of inquiry based on violations of human rights legislation are extremely rare. From the commencement of the complaints investigation process the goal of conciliation overshadows a determination of guilt. As a matter of policy, investigators judge their success by their ability to foist "settlements" on the parties.

The conciliatory, negotiating practice of complaints investigation is not well suited to dealing with sexual harassment cases. Women are sexually harassed because men perceive them as vulnerable and because power positions allow men to coerce sexual favors from subordinate women. To redress this act of aggression and prevent its repetition, male sexual harassers must be confronted with evidence of their unsavory practices by a commission prepared to act as a staunch and tough advocate of the vulnerable victim. To begin the discussion with talk of settlement and negotiation immediately renders the commission a less than effective agent.

This approach ensures that the commission will remain an agency relegated to restoring equilibrium to the employment system at its main stress points. By pursuing a policy of quiet containment and resolution of conflict, the commission displaces and frustrates the growing recognition of the need for more drastic measures to deal with such abusive employment situations as sexual harassment.

3. CIVIL LITIGATION

Pros and Cons of Civil Litigation

The third option open to women is to sue their employers in court for the damages they have suffered as a result of sexual harassment. The major advantage of this method over the use of criminal proceedings or human rights commission complaints is that you retain control over the action. You are not at the mercy of the police, criminal prosecutors, or human rights investigators, nor subject to their biases or conciliatory bents. You have hired your own lawyer, who conducts the action subject to your direction.

In addition, in a civil suit, you would in most cases be suing both the sexual harasser and the organization. This is an obvious advantage over a criminal proceeding, since in the latter only the sexual harasser is on trial. Since organizations to date have not tried to stop sexual harassment of their women employees, and in some cases have actively aided and abetted male supervisors in such activities, it is only just that they also be the object of litigation. As well in a criminal action, the goal of the proceeding is to punish the offender. Rarely is compensation of the victim considered. In a civil trial the goal is to obtain enough money to compensate the aggrieved party completely. Sexually harassed women would sue for all financial loss suffered from the loss of employment, expenses incurred in finding another job, any differential in salary if the new job pays less than the last one, and compensation for any medical expenses and pain and suffering that may have been caused by the harassment. Employers view civil lawsuits as more serious, more potentially harmful, than human rights proceedings, because there is a possibility that a much more comprehensive and larger award may be given to women victims.

There are, however, some disadvantages with civil lawsuits. For one thing, if the sexually harassed woman wants her job back, she is better advised to seek a remedy from a human rights organization. There is more wide-ranging power under human rights legislation to reinstate employees who are dismissed for discriminatory reasons. The civil courts have historically felt that the only remedy they could provide was to award financial compensation, that it would be too precarious to order an unwilling employer to take back a dismissed employee. It is an open question whether a reinstated employee has any job security or a decent working environment. Nevertheless, the courts have held that they are unable to provide this type of remedy. (Cases brought under Title VII in the United States are exceptions to this rule. There, because of the specific wording of the Civil Rights Act, the court has the authority to reinstate victims of discrimination.)

The major drawback of civil litigation is that women must hire a lawyer. Many people—both men and women—feel uncomfortable with the idea of seeking legal advice. In part this feeling arises from a widespread view that lawyers overcharge for their services. Also, unless one deals with a lawyer regularly or knows numerous people in the legal community, most people do not know how to go about choosing a lawyer. This problem is further complicated when a woman is seeking legal advice on the issue of sexual harassment: This is a new legal issue, and most lawyers have little or no expertise in the area. An obvious solution would be for the legal profession to advertise its services—both costs and areas of expertise. Legal advertising is being advocated in many quarters today, and sweeping changes are certainly possible for the near future. Until that time, however, the best alternative is to have women's organizations and groups build up some familiarity with the cost and quality of legal services offered by lawyers in the area. They can then act as referral agencies by providing this type of information to women seeking legal advice.

Women who do hire lawyers must recognize that they have the same rights all consumers do and should feel free to demand that their lawyers give them, over the telephone or at the first reasonable opportunity, a reasonable estimate of the cost of their services. Most lawyers are willing to meet with a potential client for an initial assessment for a modest fee, one that is within the range of most women's ability to pay. At that interview the lawyer should be able to provide the woman with an estimate of the probable costs of the lawsuit and an initial opinion as to the advisability of going ahead.

The ultimate costs of the lawsuit will depend upon the employer's response and how complicated the case is. If the employer defends the action vigorously, the length of the trial will be extended, and the costs will go up accordingly. If the case is a complex one, more legal research may be required and more time may be needed to set forth the facts before the court. The length of time required to conclude a civil suit depends, as does a criminal case, upon the facts of the case and the backlog of cases in the jurisdiction in which the litigation is brought. It can range anywhere from a number of months to a number of years. It is important to recognize, though, that as the plaintiff in the action the woman has a great deal of control over the litigation. She can do things to speed up the process or slow it down. She can also decide to stop at any point and withdraw her case from the litigation process. Depending upon how far the litigation has progressed, she may, however, be penalized for withdrawing by being forced to pay the costs incurred by the other side in defending the action.

It should not be overlooked that most civil cases are settled before they ever get to court. Because court proceedings are expensive and time-consuming, both parties prefer to settle on an agreeable sum to be paid from the defendant to the plaintiff long before the trial begins. In many cases the plaintiff can also extract from the defendant money to pay her lawyer's costs. This is obviously an ideal solution, and the settlement-inducing value of commencing legal proceedings is something to be borne in mind by all sexually harassed women.

It should also be noted that the situation with respect to legal costs differs quite dramatically in Canada from the United States. In Canada the general rule is that the party that loses the lawsuit has to pay the legal costs incurred by the successful party. This is meant to be a deterrent against unnecessary litigation. While this is obviously helpful to women who win their suits, it is a matter of some concern to those who are not so fortunate and is an active deterrent to pursuing a case through to trial.

This is not the general rule in the United States. In most cases there, regardless of the outcome of the lawsuit, each party absorbs its own costs. Another difference between the two countries is that in the United States lawyers can and often do charge contingency fees. In this type of arrangement the lawyer demands no payment from the client directly, but stipulates that if the case is successful, a portion of the money received must be paid over to the lawyer as a fee (usually one-third of the award). This type of arrangement is generally quite useful to plaintiffs who have no money at their disposal initially but who have a good case with a decent chance of winning. In most Canadian provinces contingency fees have been made illegal, again largely out of the desire to prevent litigation.

In cases where women cannot afford to hire lawyers or contingency fees are not available, another resort may be to consider legal aid or the services of law student programs or public interest lawyers. Many of these services are available only to people who can meet the financial criteria in force. However, this is an avenue that should definitely be explored by women seeking to pursue lawsuits against sexual harassers. Further, if the amount being sued for falls within the limits of small claims courts in the jurisdiction, women can bring their own actions without needing the assistance of a lawyer at all.

The Grounds for a Lawsuit

A. Title VII

While many of the grounds for civil lawsuits are the same in Canada and the United States (because both legal systems spring from the same British common law), some are different. The most striking difference is that in the United States most civil cases on sexual harassment have been based on Title VII of the Civil Rights Act, 1964.

Since the jurisprudence is so new in this field, cases are constantly being overturned in courts of appeal, and new cases are appearing every day. For this reason, we have not attempted to undertake a comprehensive examination of all sexual harassment cases. The ones we have chosen should illuminate the types of reasoning prevalent in the American court system.

While some of the cases have been successful, others have not, and it is helpful at the outset to examine the reasoning of the judges in the cases that were not won by women. In a 1975 Arizona case, *Corne v. Bausch and Lomb, Inc.*,[5] two women, both clerical workers employed by the same company, sued for a violation of their civil rights based on sex discrimination under Title VII. Their male supervisor, Leon Price, had taken unsolicited and unwelcome sexual liberties with both women. He repeatedly subjected them to verbal and physical advances. He was notorious among all the women employees of the company for harassing on a daily basis all the women he supervised. These two women found his activities so offensive that they were forced to resign.

The court dismissed the complaint on a number of grounds, all of which deserve examination. First, the court stated that Title VII outlawed discrimination where such discrimination arose out of company policies that had been designed and implemented by the organization. Leon Price, on the other hand, was merely satisfying a "personal urge." This activity was nothing more than a "personal proclivity, peculiarity or mannerism." The court failed to recognize that an organization should be legally responsible for the actions of supervisors. Whether these actions were a personal proclivity of Leon Price should have been irrelevant. Second, the court stated that nothing in the act could be applied to prohibit "verbal and physical sexual advances" by another employee, even a supervisory employee, where such conduct had no relationship to the nature of employment. But that, of course, was precisely the issue. The court should have examined whether the supervisor's sexual advance was a nonemployment-related encounter or whether sexual consideration was being exacted as a condition of employment. These two women, after all, had been forced to quit their jobs because of the intolerable behavior of their supervisor. Clearly sexual favors were being demanded as a condition of employment.

Third, the court stated that "it would be ludicrous to hold that the sort of activity involved here was contemplated by the act, because to do so would mean that if the conduct complained of was directed equally to males, there would be no basis for suit." Obviously the court was concerned about women harassing men. But if the court was disallowing the claim for discrimination on the ground that someday somewhere the roles may be reversed, that is ludicrous. The present issue before the court was whether there had been discrimination in the present case, not the future of the sexes. If the court meant that there could be no suit if the male supervisor was equally harassing men and women, it was probably right. By its very definition such harassment would not be discriminatory, since all groups would be subjected equally to it. But there was no evidence of this in the present case, and without such evidence (which we expect would be difficult to produce) there should have been no problem.

Finally, the court made a statement that illustrated the real reason behind its decision. The court stated,

An outgrowth of holding such activity to be actionable under Title VII would be a potential federal lawsuit every time an employee made amorous or sexually oriented advances toward another. The only sure way an employer could avoid such charges would be to have employees who were asexual.

Humorously, the judge has in fact come to the conclusion that some of the most advanced thinkers on sexual harassment have reached: In order to avoid sexual harassment on the job, men and women must treat each other as individuals and not as potential sex partners. But the judge thinks the idea is so farfetched that he uses it as a basis for his decision that legislation couldn't possibly cover such behavior. The judgment seems to us to be obviously wrong both on legal and on ethical grounds, and since an appeal is underway, it is to be hoped that the two women will have a fairer hearing from a higher appeal court.

In another case, *Miller* v. *Bank of America*,[6] a California court dealt with a complaint of sexual harassment from a black woman bank worker. Her white male supervisor had promised her a better job if she would be "sexually co-operative." When she refused, he had her fired. She sued for reinstatement, back pay, and her attorney's fees.

The court in this case also dismissed the woman's argument. The court penalized the woman for failing to bring the matter to her employer's attention. It was stated that she should have filed a complaint with the employee relations department, which would have conducted "an appropriate investigation." One can only imagine how helpful such investigation would have been in light of the typical reaction of organizations to individual sexual harassment complaints.

The court went on to say,

It is conceivable that flirtations of the smallest order would give rise to liability. In addition, it would not be difficult to foresee a federal challenge based on alleged sex-motivated considerations of the complainant's superior in every case of a lost promotion, transfer, demotion, or dismissal. And who is to say what degree of sexual cooperation would found a Title VII claim?

There are two strains of thought running through this paragraph. Initially the court is concerned about the degree of sexual harassment required. The court obviously feels that some degree of personal flirtation is to be tolerated as a normal situation in any environment where men and women work together. Many people would likely agree with this sentiment, although some would argue that all sexual harassment, however minor, is offensive—and threatening to the economically dependent— and should be prohibited. Nevertheless, it is a matter to be determined by the courts in each case whether the conduct was so minimal that no remedy should be provided. It is extremely unjust to deny all persons a remedy because conceivably some of the cases in the future might be considered unwarranted. The other strain visible in this paragraph is the fear of false accusation that so permeates judicial interpretation of rape and indecent assault laws.

The court concluded by saying,

The attraction of males to females and females to males is a natural sex phenomenon and it is probable that this attraction plays at least a subtle part in most personnel decisions. Such being the case, it would seem wise for the courts to refrain from delving into these matters short of specific factual allegations describing an employer policy which in its application poses or permits a consistent, as distinguished from isolated, sex-based discrimination on a definable employee group.

In this appalling conclusion the court has admitted rather circuitously that sexual lust plays a part in all personnel decisions and implies that for courts to entertain sexual harassment cases would thus be unwise. This is like saying that all men are rapists and thus the laws on rape should be withdrawn. The fact that unlawful behavior is extremely widespread is certainly no justification for withdrawing laws against it. It merely indicates how critical it is to provide strong legal remedies for the vast number of victims.

Furthermore, the court is requiring that women who bring sexual harassment cases prove to the court that the organization has a policy of endorsement of sexual harassment, something that would be quite a feat to prove in even the more blatant of cases. While almost all organizations do in fact endorse sexual harassment, they do not do so openly, but rather they do so through their failure to stop or punish offenders in the numerous instances that occur. To prove an endorsement of such a policy would be almost impossible.

In another case, *Tomkins* v. *Public Service Electric & Gas Co.*,[7] a New Jersey woman sued her former supervisor and the company for sexual harassment. Adrienne Tomkins had been working for a public utility company for two years as an office worker when her supervisor invited her to lunch to discuss her prospects of promotion within the company. Over lunch he made physical sexual advances, told her a sexual relationship was essential to a satisfactory working relationship, threatened her with work-related reprisals when she resisted, and ultimately restrained her physically from leaving the restaurant. Upon her return to the office she made a complaint about the lunchtime incident and sought a job transfer. So anxious was she to get away from the clutches of her boss that she even accepted a demotion when a lateral transfer proved unobtainable. This was not a productive solution, however, because for a number of months after her complaint to the company she was subjected to disciplinary layoffs, threats of demotion, and salary cuts, all attributable to her complaint. Fifteen months after having made the complaint she was fired.

In a decision that can only be categorized as more appalling than the *Miller* case, the New Jersey District Court dismissed her case. In an amazing statement, the court commented,

[Title VII] is not intended to provide a federal tort remedy for what amounts to a physical attack motivated by sexual desire on the part of a supervisor, and which happened to occur in a corporate corridor rather than in a back alley.

The court continued that although "the abuse of authority by supervisors of either sex for personal purposes is an unhappy and recurrent feature of our social experience," and though that conduct might be criminal or subject to a civil tort action, it was not discrimination within the meaning of Title VII.

The court in this case used the "floodgates" argument, that to allow recovery in a suit of this nature would encourage a flood of litigants, so many that the court system would be swamped and unable to administer justice. In a revealing statement the court said,

An invitation to dinner could become an invitation to a federal lawsuit, if some harmonious relationship turned sour at a later time. And if an inebriated approach by a supervisor to a subordinate at the office Christmas party could form the basis of a federal lawsuit for sex discrimination if a promotion or a raise is later denied to the subordinate, we would need 4,000 federal trial judges instead of some 400.

We see here vestiges of that inability to believe that sexual harassment can occur uninvited. Complaints of sexual harassment are not made by frustrated, vindictive women who are angry that an affair has "gone sour." The fact that the judge acknowledged the pervasiveness of sexual harassment is surprising. That he does so only to point out that it is so pervasive that the judicial system could not handle litigation, and then to use that as an argument for denying a remedy to a victim of sexual harassment, is positively shocking.

In a more interesting analysis, the decision continued with an examination of power in a hierarchical structure. The court reasoned that Adrienne Tomkins's theory rested on the proposition that the power inherent in a position of authority was necessarily coercive and that every sexual advance by a supervisor is made under the apparent cloak of that authority. The court commented with the pithy statement that "any subordinate knows that the boss is the boss whether a file folder or a dinner is at issue. If the plaintiff's views were to prevail, no supervisor could, prudently, attempt to open a social dialogue with any subordinate of either sex."

Here the court has in fact stumbled upon a correct analysis of sexual harassment, but instead of using that reasoning to provide a remedy for the victim, the court finds its conclusions to be so absurd that it sees this reasoning as a basis to deny a remedy. Fortunately, the appeal court that heard the appeal of this decision also disagreed with the trial decision and reversed this ruling at the level of the Third Circuit Court of Appeals. The parties agreed to a tentative settlement at this point. Adrienne Tomkins was to receive twenty thousand dollars compensation and her attorney's fees. The employer would notify all of its employees that sexual harassment was against the law and that supervisors engaging in sexual harassment would be disciplined. Personnel manuals would be changed to reflect this policy, and a film was to be shown to all employees explaining their right under Title VII.

Several other cases have provided a successful remedy for women victims of sexual harassment.[8] For example, the case of *Barnes* v. *Costle*[9] dealt with a woman who had been hired by the director of the Environmental Protection Agency's Equal Employment Opportunities Division to be his administrative assistant. Shortly after she began to work for this man, he began to solicit her repeatedly to join him for special activities after office hours, despite her continued refusals to do so. He made repeated remarks to her that were sexual in nature and constantly suggested to her that if she had an affair with him, her employment status would be enhanced. She resisted these overtures and finally advised him that notwithstanding his stated belief that "many executives have affairs with their personnel," she preferred that their relationship remain a strictly professional one. At this point the director began a conscious campaign to belittle her, to harass her, and to strip her of her job duties. Ultimately her job was abolished in retaliation for her refusal to grant her boss sexual favors.

The district court that heard the case decided that it should be dismissed because the woman was discriminated against not because she was a woman but because she refused to engage in a sexual affair with her supervisor. The appeal court reversed this decision and held that Title VII did prohibit such behavior. The fact that only one woman was being harassed was irrelevant, the court held, because the protections afforded against sex discrimination were extended to the individual, and a single instance of discrimination was sufficient. The argument that the discrimination was based on the refusal of a sexual relationship and not on the fact that the victim was a woman was dismissed summarily, with the court stating as follows,

We think that the discrimination as portrayed was plainly based on the appellant's gender. Retention of her job was conditioned upon submission to sexual relations—an exaction which the supervisor would not have sought from any male. To say, then, that she was victimized in her employment simply because she declined the invitation is to ignore the asserted fact that she was invited only because she was a woman subordinate to the inviter in the hierarchy of agency personnel.

The fact that the courts are looking to whether the harasser harasses only women or whether women and men are harassed equally is somewhat humorous and results from the fact that at present we are trying to deal with sexual harassment within the framework of existing legislation.

None of the legislation specifically prohibits the sexual harassment itself, so with rather awkward arguments, lawyers and judges are forced to deal with sexual harassment as a form of sex discrimination, rather than as coercive behavior punishable in itself.

In the *Barnes* case, after this decision was handed down, the Environmental Protection Agency agreed to settle the case rather than go on to a full trial. Paulette Barnes was paid eighteen thousand dollars in back pay as damages for lost promotions in the settlement.

B. Wrongful Dismissal

In Canada, although there is no parallel legislation to the Civil Rights Act, 1964, Title VII, there is one area of litigation that holds a great deal of promise for women who lose their jobs because of sexual harassment: an action for wrongful dismissal. Although the courts generally cannot provide a remedy of reinstatement, financial compensation can be ordered.

The action is based on the contract of employment, whether written or oral. Once you work for an employer, you have entered into a contract of employment, whether it is a written contract or not. You contract to work for the employer, and he contracts to pay you. Although at common law an employer could fire an employee whenever he liked and for whatever reason, if the dismissal was not based on "just cause," he was obliged to provide the employee with a reasonable period of notice prior to the firing or money payment for the wages the employee would have earned during such a period of notice.

All crown employees in Canada (government employees and employees of crown corporations) have been denied the right to wrongful dismissal actions by the common law, unless legislation or the terms of their employment contract provide for reasonable notice. Similarly, union employees who work under collective agreements may be forced to pursue their cases under the collective agreement through to arbitration, rather than through the courts with wrongful dismissal actions.

Although it was stated at the outset that Canadian law is much more favorable than American law to wrongful dismissal actions, there has been one successful wrongful dismissal action in the United States that actually dealt with sexual harassment: *Monge* v. *Beebe Rubber Co.* [10]

In that case the plaintiff, a married woman with three children, was a recent immigrant to the state of New Hampshire. She had been a school teacher in Costa Rica before she came to the United States in 1964. She was attending night school five nights a week to qualify to teach in the United States and had taken a job as a machinery worker in a factory to earn enough money to pay her college expenses. She began work at the factory on a conversion machine and then applied for a job on a press machine, which paid more. The foreman told her that if she wanted the promotion, she would have to be "nice." When she got the job, he asked her to go out with him. She refused, and found that her machine was shut down and that she was demoted to working on a greaser machine at less pay. Her overtime was also taken away. When she pleaded with the foreman that she needed the overtime, he told her that she could sweep floors. She agreed and took on these tasks, but the foreman also made her clean the washrooms and subjected her to ridicule. The personnel manager visited her at her home and told her he knew that her foreman used his position to force his attentions on the female employees under his authority, but he asked her "not to make trouble." Tormented by daily abusive treatment at the hands of her foreman, she became ill to the point that she required hospitalization. The company deemed her absence to be a "voluntary quit."

She sued for wrongful dismissal to recover compensation for a breach of her oral contract of employment, and the court upheld her claim, stating,

In all employment contracts, whether at will or for a definite term, the employer's interest in running his business as he sees fit must be balanced against the interests of the employee in maintaining his employment, and the public's interest in maintaining a proper balance between the two. We hold that a termination by the employer of a contract of employment at will which is motivated by bad faith or malice or based on retaliation is not in the best interest of the economic system or the public good and constitutes a breach of the employment contract. The foreman's overtures and the capricious firing, the seeming manipulation of job assignments, and the apparent connivance of the personnel manager in this course of events all support the jury's conclusion that the dismissal was maliciously motivated.

The employee was awarded the pay she would have received over a twenty-week period. This decision is very unusual, and it may be some time before American courts decide to follow its lead in awarding damages for wrongful dismissal. The general rule of American case law, despite the *Monge* decision, is that most employers are not required to give employees reasonable notice. Employers and employees are free to make such agreements between themselves, but where an employment agreement does not specifically set out the length of employment envisioned or the length of notice required, none is judicially required. Such hirings are viewed as terminable at will, and no notice is required upon dismissal.

C. Torts

Apart from contractual remedies, there are also a number of tort actions available to sexually harassed women. These are very similar in both

Canada and the United States because of our shared British common-law heritage. The word *tort* derives from the Latin *tortus,* meaning "twisted" or "crooked," and early found its way into the English language as a general synonym for *wrong.* Later the word disappeared from common usage, but retained its hold on the law.

While there is no satisfactory definition for the word *tort,* it is best explained by comparing it to a crime. A crime is wrongful activity that is an offense against the state. A criminal prosecution is a state-initiated proceeding that is not concerned with repairing an injury that may have been done to an individual, but rather with exacting a penalty in order to protect society as a whole. Tort liability, on the other hand, exists primarily to compensate the injured person by compelling the wrongdoer to pay for the damage he has done. The action is brought privately by the aggrieved individual, not by the state. There are some activities that are subject to both criminal and civil actions. One example is assault. Generally in these cases, the wrongdoer can be both punished criminally and forced to make good the losses of the injured person in a civil tort action.

A whole range of common-law torts might prove helpful to victims of sexual harassment. These include assault and battery, the intentional interference with contractual relations, and the intentional infliction of nervous shock. This last tort holds out great promise, and it is interesting to examine it more closely.

The tort of intentional infliction of nervous shock is concerned only with intentional infliction of harm. The sexual harasser must have either desired to cause alarm or fright or have known that it was substantially certain to follow from his action, and proceeded recklessly. This tort does not cover all unsavory conduct or every trivial indignity, but provides for liability only for conduct of a nature especially calculated to cause mental damage of a very serious kind. Thus there must be proof that the alleged misconduct was reasonably likely to cause terror in a normal person, unless indeed the sexual harasser was aware of his victim's peculiar susceptibility to emotional shock. Secondly, the victim's emotional distress must be accompanied by objective and substantially harmful physical or psychopathological consequences, such as actual illness. Mere anguish or fright is not sufficient.

To outline the parameters of this tort indicates how well sexual harassment will fit within its criteria. Sexual harassers often employ a pattern of verbal abuse and solicitation that is intentionally directed toward breaking down a woman's will to oppose sexual encounters. The fact that the sexual harasser is in a position of authority or power over his victim almost certainly causes serious mental suffering in the victim. The development of "sexual harassment syndrome," the physical and psychological anxiety symptoms of sexual harassment, occurs in a large number of cases.

In fact, a 1961 case decided by the Supreme Court of Utah, *Samms* v.

Eccles, [11] concluded that sexual harassment had resulted in the commission of the tort of intentional infliction of nervous shock. Although the facts of the case do not indicate that it arose in an employment situation, the case is certainly helpful authority for future employment sexual harassment cases.

The plaintiff, Marcia Samms, had been persistently implored with indecent proposals by David Eccles. For a period of eight months Eccles had repeatedly and persistently telephoned her at various hours including late at night, soliciting her to have sexual relations with him. On one occasion he had even come to her house and indecently exposed himself. Marcia Samms claimed that she was a respectable married woman, that she had never encouraged Eccles's attentions in any way, and that she had repulsed them at every opportunity. She claimed that she had suffered great anxiety and fear for her personal safety, along with severe emotional distress, and claimed three thousand dollars in damages.

On the preliminary question of whether the plaintiff had shown a cause of action, the court answered yes and gave the following reasons:

We quite agree with the idea that under usual circumstances, the solicitation to sexual intercourse would not be actionable even though it may be offensive to the offeree. It seems to be a custom of long standing and one which in all likelihood will continue. The assumption is usually indulged that most solicitations occur under such conditions as to fall within the well known phrase of Chief Judge Magruder that "there is no harm in asking." The Supreme Court of Kentucky has observed that an action will not lie in favour of a woman against a man who, without trespass or assault, makes such a request; and that the reverse is also true: that a man would have no right of action against a woman for such a solicitation. But the situation just described, where tolerance for the conduct referred to is indulged, is clearly distinguishable from the aggravated circumstances the plaintiff claimed existed here. Trial court erred in dismissing the action.

This case is quite exciting, for it holds out much promise for future sexual harassment cases where the solicitation is both aggravated and severely disturbing to the female victim.

In conclusion, the civil remedies available have, with the exception of the Title VII cases, been used very few times as yet to deal with sexual harassment situations. Despite some of the backward attitudes evidenced by the courts, the potential exists for some very fruitful and financially rewarding litigation on the part of sexually harassed plaintiffs.

Some New Trends

Another possibility is to deal with sexual harassment as an occupational hazard. This would be covered under occupational health and safety legislation in both Canada and the United States. Sexual harassment is indeed an occupational hazard that often causes mental and physical breakdown on the part of the victim. Legislation is two-pronged in that it generally provides for financial compensation (under the auspices of workmen's compensation) and for the removal of hazardous conditions. Compensation could include temporary disability payments, permanent disability payments, rehabilitation programs, and retraining. Admittedly this avenue has been used infrequently. But depending on the actual wording of the applicable legislation, future actions are clearly possible.

An exciting new trend is the enactment of statutes specifically outlawing sexual harassment on the job. Lobbied by women's groups, various state legislatures in the United States are beginning to pass laws that ban all sexual harassment in employment as unfair labor practices. In February 1978, Wisconsin became the first state to enact such legislation. Similar bills are pending before the legislatures of California, Virginia, Florida, Pennsylvania, Michigan, and Minnesota. Depending on how comprehensively such acts define sexual harassment and how effective the remedies provided prove to be, such legislation will definitely improve the position of working women.

In the Final Analysis

The law has distinct limitations in providing remedies to victims of sexual harassment. Nevertheless, it is extremely crucial that women pursue their legal options. Without a body of case law supporting the contention that sexual harassment is indeed a serious crime, little progress can be made. Litigation is an invaluable tool in educating the public. On the one hand, sexual harassers will be forced to recognize that their actions furnish grounds for lawsuits. On the other, female victims will be made aware that it is not necessary to stand by helplessly and allow themselves to be rendered powerless.

It is our contention that the best method of pursuing legal remedies is to sue collectively. As an individual, the case obviously becomes more difficult to prove. In addition, one individual is open to ridicule, humiliation, and future employment reprisals. Where women sue in groups, no one woman can be singled out, and the possibility of reprisals diminishes.

We do not believe that any single woman should become a sacrificial lamb in fighting court battles from which all women benefit. The remedy of collective legal action can be pursued in two ways. Initially the possibility of class action may be open where one or more women sue on behalf of a larger class who have all suffered from sexual harassment. Alternatively several individuals who have all been harassed by one man, or by several men in one organization, can sue as a group.

A heartening example of collective legal action is currently underway at Yale University in New Haven, Connecticut. In 1977 five female undergraduate students and one male professor began a class action against Yale University charging that the university condoned sexual harassment of its students by the professors. The students alleged that sexual harassment was so widespread that Yale should have set up a grievance procedure to deal with the various incidents that arose. When the university refused, the students went to court. Since this was not an employment-related sex discrimination case, the suit was brought under Title ix of the Civil Rights Act, which deals with discrimination in education. The parallels, however, are obvious between sexual harassment in the educational setting and sexual harassment in the workplace.

This case has received widespread publicity in the North American and European press. The prospect of women suing organizations in groups to stop sexual harassment is little short of revolutionary. This particular action holds out hope that women no longer need suffer as victims of sexual harassment in isolation, frustrated and helpless.

6

The women's movement

"The issue of sexual harassment, like all women's issues, will come kicking and screaming out of the closet," says one of the leading Canadian women's advocates. This comment is extremely indicative of the status of sexual harassment as an issue within the Canadian women's movement. Concern about the issue is in an embryonic state, about to emerge, as did the issue of rape five years ago. No one is quite sure how to proceed. At the present time Canadian women's organizations are simply referring women who complain to them to government agencies, such as the women's bureau and the human rights commission. As yet, no one in the Canadian women's movement has come up with specific guidelines and policy statements. There is definitely an innate realization that the movement, however loosely connected, will have to take a public stand and actively search for and promote solutions. In order to stimulate discussion and action on sexual harassment issues, we have drafted a policy statement, which is on page 131.

In the United States the issue of sexual harassment has gained national prominence and serious consideration under the auspices of two national nonprofit organizations—the Working Women United Institute, in New York City, and the Alliance Against Sexual Coercion, in Boston. Both were specifically formed to provide forums for thought, action, and assistance. At the present time both organizations are inundated with appeals for help from women from every conceivable job category, age group, racial origin, and social and economic class.

Redbook and *Ms.* Magazine—two widely read American women's publications—have both devoted extensive coverage to the issue, with the result that they were flooded with an avalanche of letters to the editor.

The educative process has begun in earnest in the United States. Unlike Canadian women, American women have grown up in a tradition where individual civil liberties are extremely important. The Canadian

SEXUAL HARASSMENT IN THE WORKPLACE

Sexual harassment can be defined as "any sexually oriented practice that endangers a woman's job, that undermines her job performance, and threatens her economic livelihood." It is one of the most serious occupational health hazards facing working women today. North American surveys indicate that 70 percent of all working women have experienced sexual harassment at least once in their working lives from bosses, co-workers, clients, or customers. Sexual harassment takes its toll physically and psychologically as victims suffer trauma in attempting to fend off coercive sexual advances.

Recommendations

1. Further research must be undertaken to document sexual harassment and to provide further information on its various manifestations, consequences, and solutions.
2. A program of public education must be undertaken to demonstrate that sexual harassment is a heinous crime against women and to raise public awareness of the problem.
3. New legislation must be enacted that will outlaw sexual harassment and provide speedy, effective, and inexpensive legal remedies for victims of sexual harassment.
4. Sexual harassment crisis centers must be established to provide counseling and advocacy for sexual harassment victims and to act as a lobbying agency to promote societal change.

political tradition focuses on a respect for institutions and the legislative process. Canadian women are not as well versed in the art of lobbying as a special interest group. While American women have fought for an affirmative-action approach that incorporates the principle of quotas and special assistance to redress discrimination against women in the workplace, Canadian women have generally accepted the notion of "moral persuasion," hoping to change discriminatory attitudes and practices by engaging in low-key educationals. The American women's movement, both within and outside the government, has adopted the stance that if one can legislate behaviorial changes, then discriminatory attitudes will ultimately be eradicated. In Canada women are patiently and not so patiently plugging away at those discriminatory attitudes, which they hope will one day alter abusive, repressive behavior. It is a moderate approach, which somewhat explains the time lag in Canada on the issue of sexual harassment.

In Canada there is a groping for definition and direction. No one woman's organization is ready to claim the issue. Perhaps the solution, as in the United States, lies in setting up an independent center or institute outside of government that addresses itself solely to sexual harassment.

In this chapter we intend to explore the status of sexual harassment within the context of government agencies devoted to women's issues and outside, volunteer women's groups. The focus will be on an analysis of the internal and external responses in terms of their impact in appreciably assisting women victims and educating the public.

THE AFFIRMATIVE-ACTION SPECIALISTS

In both Canada and the United States exists a new breed of affirmative-action specialists, who are often referred to as special women's consultants, women's advisors, and managers of female resources. In most cases these specialists are in-house employees, but on occasion an organization will hire outside, independent consultants. Organizationally they appear to be an extension of the personnel function, although in some instances they have direct access to senior management on an informal basis.

The role of these affirmative-action specialists is to demarcate problem areas, to suggest new policy initiatives, to design training programs, and to undertake the task of sensitizing and educating employees about sex stereotyping and discrimination. Their mandates are rather broad and all-encompassing. However, in actual fact their power to effect any significant changes is highly dependent on how serious a commitment their particular organization has made.

In the United States the quota system, with its attendant affirmative-action plan, places considerable pressure on private industry and government to comply. Despite this legislative imperative, affirmative-action specialists can be sabotaged and subverted if the opposition is strong enough.

The Canadian affirmative-action programs are almost entirely voluntary and as such often act as token gestures to the notion of equal opportunity.

Affirmative-action specialists, unlike the personnel function and management, are supposedly a part of and yet outside the organizational structure. In theory these specialists are to act as "change agents," bypassing normal bureaucratic red tape to ensure that discriminatory attitudes and practices are exposed and ultimately eliminated. Each specialist faces a different set of circumstances, which determine both the relevance and the success of his or her programs.

It is interesting to examine two case studies, one in government and one in private industry, to assess how worthwhile and successful these programs are.

A GOVERNMENT WOMEN'S ADVISOR

Ms. Davis, as we shall call her, works as a women's advisor in a government department that employs a vast army of female support staff, such as clerks and secretaries. "I'm unique," Ms. Davis says. "Myself and a handful of other women hold professional jobs in this department."

"Ms. Davis," we asked, "do you receive complaints of sexual harassment?" "Yes, all the time," she replied:

I am so concerned about the problem that I have designed a questionnaire, which I took to personnel. They laughed and treated it as one big joke. I got the feeling that they were thinking, 'Hasn't she anything better to do?'

"Why do you think it's treated so lightly?" we questioned. "Well," she continued, "all women's issues are threatening to men, but sexual harassment strikes a special nerve. It occurs at every level in government. So many men are guilty of this behavior in some degree that it engenders a collective and pervasive fear of exposure."

When we asked Ms. Davis what she thought women's advisors should be doing, she replied,

It's a difficult question. Women's advisors are not very popular with personnel. They would like to eliminate our function. I've been here longer than most of the other women's advisors, since the turnover is very high. It's a frustrating, going-nowhere job. But I think it's our job at least to educate women about sexual harassment. The only way I feel it can be handled is directly, bluntly. The harasser should be talked to and warned of the legal implications. If he continues, he should be fired. Realistically, my senior management would rarely fire a man for sexual harassment. At the most they would warn the offender, and only in serious, blatant cases.

As a women's advisor Ms. Davis is the recipient of many complaints, but like her counterparts in private industry and the unions, she does not appear to have much power to take action. She, as did all the women interviewed, understands what sexual harassment is. Her influence and authority are contingent, however, on her relationship with senior management. Personnel treated her questionnaire as a joke. Her influence with senior management is obviously limited. They may warn a serious offender but are not prepared to move or fire him.

Ms. Davis has what she terms a "career going nowhere." In some respects she is a repository for women's dissatisfactions. She listens; she is sympathetic; but she can't effectively alter prevailing policy and ingrained attitudes. Her legislative base is so vague as to be ineffectual. In the end her only strength lies in her access to and influence on senior management. Ms. Davis unfortunately has neither.

A WOMEN'S CONSULTANT IN PRIVATE INDUSTRY

We did meet one special women's consultant in the private sector who was amazingly influential. She had direct access to the vice-president of personnel, a senior exeuctive, who had enormous respect for her judgment and an unusual commitment to women's issues. Ms. Christie, as we shall call her, required no explanation about the issue of sexual harassment. She had some very definite observations and insights.

"As a women's consultant, are you able to respond to complaints of sexual harassment?" we asked. She replied,

Women's consultants, women's advisors—whatever—we are like psychiatrists. We listen and even diffuse a woman's anger. Our function is not designed to be action oriented. Most of us are good listeners, but we really can't do very much. I think that men generally draw together when sexual harassment becomes an open problem.

My situation is very unusual, since my boss recognizes that sexual harassment is a serious problem. He has three daughters—all feminists—whose goals and ambitions he encourages. You could say he has a unique and sympathetic approach. I have never met any man in private industry or elsewhere who is so completely committed to affirmative action. So I am able to act as an advocate for the women in complaints of sexual harassment.

"What specifically do you advise women victims to do?" we asked. She answered,

My first instinct is to tell them to document everything, to find witnesses among their co-workers, and to determine if they are the only one being harassed. I have seen many women at the point where they are starting to fall apart both physically and psychologically. They haven't the energy or the self-confidence left to respond to my advice. But you must compile a case. Even with such a receptive boss, I must have some proof of sexual harassment. The system demands that. I appreciate that this is not always possible. Somehow we must instill in men that it is simple justice to stop sexual harassment. I consider sexual harassment to be a definite crime against women.

"Do you hear of many cases?" we questioned.

All the time and of varying degrees of seriousness. In many cases, I only hear about it later, after the woman has resigned. It takes courage to come forward. We don't exactly broadcast that we are waiting to hear cases. That would bring the house down. My boss must answer to his peers. So we keep a low profile. But there was one case that was exceptional.

We had a secretary to a senior manager who was actually assaulted. Her manager was a very aggressive middle-aged Romeo. She was very young and quite naïve. His comments were crude, and he was "all hands." I noticed her becoming very tense, nervous, and weepy. When he finally hit her, she hired a lawyer, who sent a letter to personnel. The whole place was in an uproar. She was eventually promoted, and he was actually demoted, with a warning that he was being watched. This is the only real success story that I know. Usually the woman is moved—that's about the best we can do.

Ms. Christie, although well connected to power, must deal with the peer pressure her supportive boss experiences. It is instructive to note that Ms. Christie hears about many instances of sexual harassment after the woman has resigned. Her advice about compiling a case is excellent, but she admits that the women who complain are generally transferred and the men get off with a reprimand.

So even sympathy, understanding, and the support of senior management is only a partial solution. Ms. Christie and her boss are only two people in a vast bureaucracy that is generally unsympathetic and almost hostile to the issue of sexual harassment.

The foregoing are two clear examples of how affirmative action specialists are stymied in their attempts to assist victims of sexual harassment. These women operate in isolation, separated from the mainstream of bureaucratic power. Although the senior administrator was receptive to Ms. Christie, he could not fight the entire system and often buckled under the united pressure of his staff.

In a sense, affirmative-action specialists are deflectors. They cool off an issue by providing a space where women can come and talk over their situations. Very few can do more than offer sympathy. They know that if they take too strong a stand, they themselves are open to reprimands. As yet there is no mechanism to deter a harasser. Usually, at the very worst, he has his knuckles rapped and is told to behave. But even this rarely happens. If women do complain to affirmative-action specialists and they take it to either personnel or senior management, the familiar scenario repeats itself: The woman may find herself in the position of defending her innocence; she may be fired; or she may be demoted on some pretext; and she faces the distinct possibility of having her working life made intolerable by the harasser, who is angered by her public complaint.

VOLUNTARY ASSOCIATIONS AND ORGANIZATIONS

1. An Overview of the Canadian Women's Movement's Position

The Canadian women's movement perceives sexual harassment as a fledgling issue. Since, unlike the United States, there are no centers established in Canada to deal specifically with sexual harassment, we canvassed the opinions of numerous representatives of women's organizations. At the time of writing no one organization had developed a comprehensive analysis, and therefore we can only attempt to outline some of their views in a general way. Their attitudes and opinions range from cynicism to shock and indignation.

One predominant attitude that recurred with disconcerting frequency was that sexual harssment was a lower-class phenomenon; that factory workers, secretaries, clerks, and waitresses were indeed the unfortunate victims of coercive sexuality, but that middle- and upper-class women were not subject to such behavior.

As one woman professional put it, "Professional women are fully capable of handling unsolicited sexual come-ons without serious repercussions. After all, if a woman achieves a certain status in the workplace, she is not open to victimization. We are mature, capable, and self-confident women, and it would never occur to men to try to force their attentions on us. It's all part of our training."

This is a comforting fantasy in which professional women often indulge. In some ways it leaves professional women in greater jeopardy than their working-class counterparts. They have greater difficulty in openly acknowledging sexual harassment when it occurs precisely because of this kind of myth. They have convinced themselves that they should be able to handle unsolicited attentions.

Their inability to acknowledge sexual harassment creates a conspiracy of silence, behind which professional women are left as vulnerable as other women. It is exactly for this reason that there are so few public complaints from professional women. Should they be able to come to grips with the fact that all women suffer under a similar oppression, they could become powerful allies in the battle to eradicate sexual harassment.

At the bottom of the economic scale, women who work as waitresses, factory workers, maids, salesclerks, and so on sincerely believe that if they could earn a decent wage, their problems in the workforce would be solved. It is an understandable illusion. These women, like all female workers, are caught in the double bind that sexual harassment implies. Regardless of what you earn, your job security is tenuous if you are constantly in danger of sexual harassment. For example, being a rich woman protects you from neither rape nor sexual harassment. Large paychecks do nothing to shield a woman from unsolicited and coercive sexual advances from a superior.

Obviously the battle must be fought concurrently—a decent wage and a right to work in an environment free from sexual coercion. As yet most of these low-income workers do not think in terms of collective action. They do not appreciate that individually we are isolated and profoundly vulnerable to all forms of economic and sexual injustice.

Another attitude expressed is one of reluctance and fear to tackle the problems presented by sexual harassment. As one feminist trade union activist said, "It's an explosive issue, and a lot of people won't touch it. It's an issue that separates men and women. To take up the issue of sexual harassment in the trade union movement, you need support and confidence from the men. The women are certainly aware of sexual harassment. They are constantly coming forward with stories about their experiences. Let's face it, you can't work for long and not be sexually harassed. I suspect that there are a million stories in Canada, but as yet there is no articulation."

Quite accurately, this trade union representative recognizes that sexual harassment is a potentially divisive issue between men and women. But this does not justify its avoidance. The pursuit of equal opportunity by working women ultimately necessitates acknowledging the nature of sexual harassment and its attendant consequences. It is incumbent on organizations of working women to take issue with all manifestations of sexual harassment.

Another recurring theme expressed by many women's advocates was that in any discussion of sexual harassment one must be very careful not to put down the possibility of romantic liaisons at the office. They were concerned that women have very few opportunities to meet men socially and that the workplace was a legitimate environment in which to pursue one's romantic inclinations.

It became quite evident that these women were confusing unsolicited and coercive sexual advances with relationships that result from mutual attraction and desire. They seemed unable to make this distinction and were attempting to lump sexual harassment in with a mild form of what is commonly referred to as "the chase." It seemed incomprehensible to many of these women that rampant forms of sexual coercion exist independently of "the office romance" and cause untold misery and suffering.

Another common misunderstanding was a failure to comprehend the scope of the term *sexual harassment*. One leading Canadian spokeswoman, when interviewed about sexual harassment, stated at the outset of the meeting that she herself had never experienced it. Twenty minutes later she proceeded to tell us about both her own incredible encounter with sexual harassment as a young woman and her daughter's recent brush with the same syndrome.

This is indicative of women's amazing ability to tune out incidents of sexual harassment because they find them so humiliating and utterly frustrating. Without open discussion and a full understanding of what sexual harassment really is, the problem will continue to be a pervasive feature of all working women's experience. It is incumbent on the Canadian women's movement to acknowledge its leadership responsibilities and to declare its position emphatically.

2. The American Approach to Sexual Harassment

(i) *Working Women United Institute (wwui)*[1]

In the early part of 1975, two feminist activists, Susan Meyer and Karen Sauvigne, were working at Cornell University on a Human Affairs program designed to provide resources to the surrounding community. They received an appeal for assistance from a woman who had been a victim of a severe form of sexual harassment. The woman in question, Carmita Wood, is a forty-five-year-old mother of five who is sole support for her family. "Ms. Wood had lived in the Ithaca area all her life and had worked since she was seventeen. She is a self-taught bookkeeper and accountant. After a series of waitress, cashier, and other types of service jobs, she was hired as a head account clerk by Cornell University, where, after eight years, her outstanding work resulted in her becoming the first woman administrative assistant in one of the laboratories. She was earning more money than she had ever earned before. At the same time, she became the second woman to be admitted to the Ithaca Management Club, and she took out a large loan to remodel her home in Ludlowville. Nine months later Ms. Wood had quit her job because of sexual harassment."[2]

Ms. Wood's supervisor had made repeated unsolicited sexual advances. In an effort to dissuade him, Ms. Wood avoided the elevators, where he had repeatedly accosted her, and altered her mode of dress, exchanging her customary habit of wearing skirts and dresses for pants. The situation did not improve, but worsened to the extent where the supervisor attempted to undress her at the annual Christmas party. Ms. Wood developed excruciating physical pain in her neck and her right arm. Unable to endure either the emotional pressure of the situation or her physical pain, she resigned from her position. A week after her resignation her arm and neck pains completely disappeared.

Ms. Wood approached the Human Affairs office after her application for unemployment insurance was turned down. Ms. Meyer and Ms. Sauvigne were shocked and outraged by Ms. Wood's story and agreed to help her in any way they could. Not understanding the explosive nature of the issue, they secured Ms. Wood's permission to generate publicity around her case. The response was "virulent." Ms. Wood's story was treated with skepticism, and her credibility was called into question.

Deeply disturbed by the response, Ms. Meyer and Ms. Sauvigne decided to investigate the issue of sexual harassment more fully. They sent out a search letter to approximately three hundred women's organizations in the United States asking for case studies and any other pertinent information.

They then held a speak-out in the small town of Ithaca, New York, where Cornell University is located. As far as they know, this was the first time women had come together to hold a public forum on the issue of sexual harassment. Some 275 women showed up, an enormous turnout for a population the size of Ithaca. The speak-out was a clear indication to Ms. Meyer and Ms. Sauvigne that sexual harassment was indeed a very serious and pervasive problem for working women.

With this incentive, in June 1975, along with Carmita Wood and Lin Farley, a writer and teacher at the university, they incorporated themselves as Working Women United, an organization created to deal with the specific problems of working women. At this point they were not solely concerned with sexual harassment. It was their ultimate goal to encourage women to act collectively by unionizing their places of work.

After a year of attempting to organize women in the southern tier of New York State, the women decided to alter their focus. They incorporated once again, changing their name from Working Women United to Working Women United Institute (WWUI). Unionization, they realized, was a premature and difficult goal. Instead they devoted their energies to research and educationals on the issue of sexual harassment, which they assessed as one of the most compelling problems of working women.

In June 1977 they decided to move WWUI to New York City because they realized it was an infinitely better location from which to run a national organization. Since New York houses most of the granting foundations, they wanted to be where they could maximize their options. Like most voluntary feminist organizations they found themselves struggling from grant to grant.

A month after they had established themselves in a church basement on Park Avenue, *Ms.* magazine ran a cover story on the issue of sexual harassment, listing WWUI as an agency to contact. This gave the issue national attention, so that most of the major women's publications and newspapers picked it up and did feature stories. WWUI began to receive as many as two hundred letters and phone calls a week from women seeking advice on how to cope with sexual harassment at work. Ms. Meyer and Ms. Sauvigne were stunned at the range of women who contacted them. As they said, "They were all ages, all races, and all job categories."

Initially WWUI began a research program that involved a survey of the role of human rights commissions in dealing with sexual harassment across the United States and a national survey that they hoped would provide a sense of the dynamics of sexual harassment. WWUI is also engaged in building a network of referrals for the victims of sexual harassment, be it legal advice or job counseling services. "Our role," Ms. Sauvigne told us, "as a crisis intervention center is a very critical aspect of our service. It is important to encourage women to talk openly about their experiences in a sympathetic and supportive environment. Most women do not realize that they are not alone, somehow singled out, but rather that it is a common experience of large numbers of working women."

The undertakings of WWUI also involve a content analysis of the letters they receive, from which they are extrapolating a sense of what women in crisis want and need. Since a part of WWUI's focus is educational, they have developed elementary workshops on sexual harassment for private corporations, foundations, unions, government, and voluntary organizations. The educative objective is also pursued by means of brochures, which define sexual harassment and suggest remedies. WWUI is currently collecting a legal-brief bank and building a resource library.

And finally, WWUI has engaged itself in lobbying for legislative change. Along with a number of other groups and individuals, including Carol Bellamy, New York City Council president, they sponsored a bill that would modify the terms and conditions of unemployment insurance to incorporate sexual harassment as a "good cause" for resigning from a job. Although the bill was approved by the New York State Assembly Labor Committee, it died in the Ways and Means Committee.

In the future, WWUI plans to develop a newsletter that will be circulated to concerned agencies to keep them abreast of changes, to provide a forum for analysis, and to exchange tactics.

Ms. Meyer and Ms. Sauvigne, who are respectively the executive director and program director of WWUI, believe that the major achievement of WWUI is that "it helped to bring both official and unofficial recognition to the problem of sexual harassment. Previously it had been considered trivial and amusing by many who had not experienced it and humiliating and confusing by those who had."

(ii) The Alliance Against Sexual Coercion (AASC)[3]

Unlike WWUI, the Alliance Against Sexual Coercion (AASC) is a collective of nine women, situated in the Boston area. It has been in existence since June 1976 and began as an outgrowth of the Rape Crisis Network. Three of the women in the collective, Freada Klein, Elizabeth Cohn-Stuntz, and Lynn Wehrli, were originally working for the Rape Crisis Center in Washington, D.C. Although they were not engaged in any outreach program on sexual harassment, women came on their own, seeking assistance from the Rape Crisis Center. Their contact with these women convinced the founders of AASC that the issue of sexual harassment was as yet so poorly understood and virtually ignored that there was a real need to establish a specific program. In an effort to link sexual harassment as a subset of rape, they approached the American Rape Crisis Network to incorporate the issue into their programs. The response was that they were aware of the problem of sexual harassment but that they were overloaded with cases of rape and could not undertake yet another issue, even one so closely related.

As a result, the three women decided to set up a separate organization as a collective, whereby all the members earned their livelihood separately but placed their major energies and commitment into what they called the Alliance Against Sexual Coercion. They did not want to deplete their energies by worrying about grant money to cover their own salaries. Within a short while their collective grew to nine members.

Freada Klein, one of the founding members of AASC, spoke of the first year as "an intensive research period that resulted in a brochure that describes the whole range of behavior constituting sexual harassment and offers a variety of personal, legal, and societal remedies. We also provided crisis intervention counseling. But during that time we were essentially educating ourselves about how to deal with the victims of sexual harassment, what were the legal and personal remedies, and who were the best referrals."

AASC is currently undertaking a number of innovative programs. They are in the process of producing a brochure that will be a practical guide to victims of sexual harassment. It will include advice on how to solicit support from women co-workers without placing yourself in jeopardy, how to survey your own workplace, how to utilize the grievance procedure, and how to affect personnel policy.

Another project involves the production of a documentary film on sexual harassment in conjunction with WWUI. The focus of the film will be women who have successfully fought sexual harassment, especially those who have taken collective action.

AASC is also planning to do a number of scientifically valid surveys on sexual harassment. They are concerned that all the existing surveys are based on a self-selection process, that is, that the results are compiled from women who voluntarily chose to respond. AASC fears that by approaching women at their place of work, the women may be placed in jeopardy. Therefore, it is their intention to conduct a household survey in the greater Boston area. As well, they have approached women working in local hospitals, introducing the subjects of rape and battering, which are generally accepted issues, and then discussing sexual harassment by making parallels.

Freada Klein of AASC is a contributor to a Washington-based bimonthly publication, *Aegis: A Magazine on Organizing to Stop Violence against Women*, which covers all issues of violence against women. She will be providing an analysis of case studies, bills pending, and strategies in an effort to sensitize other groups to the seriousness of sexual harassment.

Ms. Klein is concerned about the low level of public consciousness. As she said, "Sexual harassment happens in all industries across the board. It is my perception that sexual harassment can manifest itself anywhere. Men are conditioned to take out their frustration on women, often resulting in coercive sexual harassment. They discover it makes them feel powerful and that many other men admire their actions. As yet there are no real penalties."

CONCLUSION

Canadian and American women's advocates are beginning to recognize that sexual harassment is a major occupational hazard, although the Canadian women's movement lags far behind its American counterpart. The American experience suggests that women are effective when they organize themselves as self-help units. There is enough evidence to indicate that there is strength in numbers. In both countries the politicization process has begun.

Since no other institution in society will take responsibility for sexual harassment, the women's movement has a critical role to play. They must be the major thrust in raising the general level of consciousness and in evolving effective solutions. Although the problem of sexual harassment presents a grim picture of female oppression, women are living in exciting times. They are participants in a major social revolution that is continually exploding myths about the feminine condition and destiny.

7

Role reversal:
Can Women Sexually Harass Men?

In any discussion with men about sexual harassment, inevitably the question arises of whether women sexually harass men. Men frequently voice concerns that a thorough analysis of sexual harassment would be incomplete unless it addressed this issue. In an effort to explore fully all aspects of sexual harassment, we took this question seriously. In most of the interviews we conducted, whether with men or women, we sought their views on how significant a problem this role reversal really was.

Men invariably had stories to tell. One of our most surprising findings was that many male personnel and managerial representatives, who could not recall any incidents of men sexually harassing women, were eager to relate anecdotes about women sexually harassing men.

We discerned one consistent critical fact in their stories: The women were rarely in a position to mete out job reprisals for noncompliance. The sexual harassment they spoke of amounted to an irritant, a joke, and at times an embarrassment. There is a world of difference between embarrassment, however severe, and outright coercion.

It became evident by interviewing a cross-section of men that they tend to find even minor forms of female sexual advances disconcerting. This is likely because it represents such a departure from what they view as traditional sex roles. In their socialization process, they come to expect that men should always take the initiative and that women should wait to be approached.

What follows are three interviews that we believe are fairly representative of the range of sexual harassment that men experience.

PINCH AGAIN, HONEY

So many of the men we interviewed seemed to fantasize about women sexually harassing them. Mr. Ramsay, a thirty-two-year-old bachelor who works as a salesman at a large multinational corporation, was highly amused when we first contacted him to seek his views on whether or not women sexually harass men. "I only wish I were so lucky," was his initial comment. He laughed, and continued, "I'll take anything I can get; bring them on."

Mr. Ramsay could not conceive of a situation where he would find a woman's sexual advances unpleasant. "Hell, I'd be flattered by any female attention. As far as I'm concerned, there just isn't enough of it," he told us.

Mr. Ramsay perceives that any sexual contact with a woman enhances his virility. The attitude he presents to the world is that he would welcome any sexual advance on the part of a woman. He literally cannot conceive of an instance in which he would be reluctant to comply. The notion of sexual harassment is completely foreign to Mr. Ramsay's philosophy of male-female relations.

I DIDN'T PUT UP WITH SEXUAL HARASSMENT: I FIRED HER

Mr. Sampson was a paunchy, balding, fiftyish, middle-level civil servant. When he learned we were conducting an interview with some of the women in his office about sexual harassment, he knocked on the door and demanded to be heard. "I have a case, too," he said. "If you're writing a book on sexual harassment, you wouldn't be covering the subject unless you included my story.

"I want you to know that there are women who come on to men very aggressively. I had a secretary not too long ago whom I was forced to fire because she was so sexually explicit," he told us. "What did she do?" we asked. He lowered his voice and confided, "She was a black woman, you know. She dressed in very suggestive clothing. She didn't button up all of the buttons on her blouse, and wore tight, short skirts. She used to bump into me all the time. I'm sure she did it deliberately. She was always staring at me."

"Is that all?" we asked. "Well, isn't that enough? I'm sure she was after me," he replied. "After a couple of months of this kind of behavior, I had her fired. I'm not going to put up with that." "Did you fire her specifically for the sexual harassment?" we inquired. "Well, I didn't phrase it that way. I said she was unsuitable for the job."

In our opinion it is very doubtful whether this case constitutes a valid example of sexual harassment. It appears more closely related to racism or fantasy. The sexual behavior on the part of Mr. Sampson's secretary, if that is what it was, was not combined with any possibility of coercion. At the most it was an irritant to Mr. Sampson. His secretary had no real power or authority over his future career in the civil service. But

Mr. Sampson chose to take drastic action in firing her. In effect the secretary suffered the ultimate reprisal for what Mr. Sampson termed sexually explicit behavior.

HER ADVANCES MADE ME UNCOMFORTABLE

Dr. Morgan is a thirty-eight-year-old surgeon with a very busy practice. He is married, with two small sons. He had some reservations about being interviewed but consented because he felt that what he had experienced was a good example of what men are up against. Dr. Morgan's case involved what he termed "blatant and relentless advances" from his receptionist, Ms. Grant.

Ms. Grant was a twenty-four-year-old single woman, whom Dr. Morgan believed was "desperately" looking for a husband. "There are so many women like that," he told us. "They reach their midtwenties and suddenly a bell goes off in their heads and they want to marry upwardly mobile, financially successful, professional men. I guess I fit the bill.

"I admit," he said, "that I found Ms. Grant, at least in the beginning, an extremely personable and attractive young woman. On occasion I would take her out for an afterwork drink, and sometimes we would go on to dinner. But that is all part of good employer-employee relations. I guess she assumed that there was more to it than mere friendship.

"I realized things were getting out of hand," he continued, "when I started to receive love notes from her, which she attached to some of the patients' charts. She was always trying to engage me in personal conversation at her desk, suggesting that I come to her apartment for dinner. I often overheard her talking on the phone to friends, describing our relationship as something much more than it actually was."

Dr. Morgan told us that all of these things annoyed and embarrassed him, but he had hopes that if he maintained his distance and behaved in a cool and reserved manner, she would ultimately give up. "But," he told us, "the night I discovered she had followed me home and was sitting in her car on the street in front of the house, I became quite apprehensive. A doctor's reputation must be above reproach. Any kind of scandal could be very detrimental."

"Well, what did you do?" we asked. "I have another office in the west end of the city," he replied, "which I share with my partner. It is much busier and more impersonal than the one I maintain in the north end. I transferred Ms. Grant to the west-end office, in the hopes that she would realize that I wasn't interested and wanted her out of the way. I replaced her with a grandmotherly-type woman," he laughed, "and so far she hasn't come on to me. I suspect that Ms. Grant got my message, for shortly after the transfer she resigned."

Dr. Morgan, like female victims of sexual harassment, expressed some of the same feelings, namely, embarrassment, discomfort, and apprehension. However, unlike the female victims of sexual harassment, he was in a position to take direct action. The offending Ms. Grant was transferred out of his office and into an environment where she could not cause any further embarrassment. The fundamental difference between Dr. Morgan's case and the cases of most women victims is that his harasser was not in a position to bring down economic reprisals, to demote or fire him, or to deny him job-related benefits.

PATTERNS OF RESPONSE

By far the overwhelming number of men interviewed fell into the "pinch again, honey" category. The initial response of most men was to laugh and proclaim that they would welcome all would-be sexual harassers. An excellent illustration of this type of response was the worldwide surprise and interest generated by the recent trial of an American beauty queen, Joyce McKinney. She was charged with tying a Mormon man to a bed and raping him. The criminal proceedings were seen as such an anomaly that media coverage was extraordinarily widespread. In private many men professed skepticism and disbelief.

The men who admitted to being sexually harassed almost without exception conceded that their harassers were not in a position to place their jobs in jeopardy for failing to go along with the advances. The harassers in virtually all instances were lower-level female employees often subordinate to the man in question. If the sexual harasser's actions made the man uncomfortable, steps were taken in very short order to fire or transfer the offender.

This clearly points out the distinction between female sexual harassers and male sexual harassers. When male sexual harassers make advances to working women, their actions are seen as a joke, a mere fact of life. When women make sexual advances to men on the job and their behavior causes discomfort and apprehension, the situation is treated as serious. Steps are immediately taken to bring a halt to the behavior.

TRADITIONAL SEX ROLES

The apparently low incidence of sexual harassment of men by women is likely due in large part to traditional sex roles and patterns. From early childhood men are conditioned to take the role of sexual aggressor. Traditional notions of female sexuality are rooted in the image of women as passive seductresses. Women are encouraged to direct their energies toward making themselves attractive; men are the pursuers.

As a result of this social conditioning women are much less likely to act as the initiators in sexual relationships. Women are not conditioned to physically paw and ogle men against their will. Therefore there is much less scope for sexual harassment. And not surprisingly the incidents of sexual harassment perpetrated by women on men are few.

However, attitudes are changing, and some would argue that in our modern, sexually liberated society, women operate under less burdensome restraints. Since women feel freer to initiate sexual advances, the argument goes, the odds will increase that women will become sexual harassers in greater numbers.

Furthermore, jobs that have come to be recognized as heavily laden with sexual overtones, such as the position of the stewardess, are increasingly being filled by men. For example, male flight attendants have become quite common since a 1971 United States Supreme Court ruling that men could no longer be denied jobs as flight attendants on the basis of their sex. Men who are taking these jobs frequently find themselves treated as sex objects, in much the same manner as their female co-workers. United Airlines Steward Cliff Cooley provides explicit evidence of this when he relates how he was asked out by a member of the Roller Derby team and took her up on the offer. He also says he has been the victim of a classic role reversal—he has been pinched on his way down the aisles.[1]

It is not clear whether Mr. Cooley perceived his experiences as serious incidents of sexual harassment, but the potential is clearly there. As men move into job categories that have traditionally been classified as female, it may be that these role reversals will become more common. Perhaps these men will develop some empathy for women as they themselves are exposed to sexual harassment.

WOMEN SEXUAL HARASSERS FACE GRAVE RISKS

It is unlikely, however, even with changing societal notions about sexuality, that there will be a dramatic increase in the phenomenon of the female sexual harasser. Initially a sexual harasser must be able to utilize job-related sanctions to coerce an unwilling victim. In a workforce where women hold less than 20 percent of all managerial positions and approximately 4 percent sit in the executive suite, there is little opportunity for them to exercise any authority or power over men. Despite numerous, much-touted affirmative-action programs, few women have succeeded in "making it" in a male-dominated job market. As a result few women are in positions of authority over men, and their power to enforce economic reprisals against male employees is extremely limited.

Secondly, the few women who have been fortunate enough to make it into positions of authority are, in most cases, working at excess capacity. They must work harder than the men around them to continue to be successful against almost insuperable odds. They have little time or energy to devote to the task of sexually harassing male employees. Furthermore, they are politically astute enough to recognize that to be discovered sexually harassing male subordinates would be disastrous for their careers. They are unlikely to risk hard-earned promotions for such minor stakes.

These women recognize intuitively that there is a double standard for sexual harassers. Men who sexually harass successfully are generally viewed as virile, victorious studs. At worst, their behavior is joked about. Men in groups reinforce sexual harassers in their midst. Women who try to behave as men do, who make sexist jokes, and who come on to male co-workers and subordinates, are the butt of ridicule. They are seen as crude, ridiculous creatures by both men and women. They will find no peer support from other women. In large measure all women react contemptuously towards sexual harassers, whether they are male or female.

In the final analysis the few women who do reach positions of power and authority are not about to court disaster by sexually harassing male subordinates. As women they know it is political suicide to engage in such behavior. They would never have achieved their hard-earned status unless they were wellversed in the games played around them. Of all women they are probably most aware of the consequences inherent in such sexually explicit behavior.

8

The other side of the coin:
Women Who Exploit
Their Sexuality for Gain

THE WIDESPREAD VIEW

At a recent Ontario government conference on sexual harassment, the first question raised by a member of the audience was, "What about women who exploit their sexuality?" The answer given by one of the panelists was, "I don't think women gain from trading on their sexuality in the workplace." A small chorus of obviously angry women in the audience retorted, "Oh, come on!"

After an American newspaper covered the results of a study in San Antonio, Texas, on sexual harassment, an irate male reader shot back the following in a letter to the editor:

Why protect only working women from sexual harassment? Should not all women be protected from the harassment of flowers, dinners, theatre tickets, trips and such like? And what about the silent majority of women harassed by being neglected and ignored by the men who chase the resident blonde, and totally ignore the plump pulchritude of brunettes? Why should the inconsiderate brutes not be thrown in jail for discrimination? After all, scorn is much more annoying to women than unsolicited advances.

It is only too clear that in most sectors of our society there is a widespread view that women can and frequently do exploit their sexuality for gain in the workplace.

At the outset we should point out that we are not speaking of office romances, which are mutual affairs. Both parties have willingly decided to enter into a liaison, and no element of coercion is present. Such relationships are not instances of sexual harassment. However, in any discussion of sexual harassment the question of whether women are trading on their sexuality for unfair job advantages is inevitably raised.

Certainly, if you took office gossip at face value, you would be forced to admit that successful women owed most of their promotions to the liberality with which they dispense their sexual favors. One high-ranking corporate manager we interviewed openly voiced his firmly held conviction that any woman who has achieved success in business has used sexual relations to get to her position of power.

To some extent such attitudes are a smokescreen that serves to obfuscate what is, in reality, a reluctance to attribute competence to women. Many men and women are uncomfortable with the notion of an able, powerful, economically independent woman. They assume she has been sleeping with powerful men. After all, they reason, what other way could she have done it? Women really don't have anything else to offer.

WHY DO WOMEN USE THESE TACTICS?

To be fair, however, one must admit that some women in our society do try to exploit their sexuality for gain.

Some do so out of anger. They recognize that the workplace is saturated with discriminatory attitudes and policies. For women who have assessed that hard work and competence are not enough to break into the upper echelons of the work world, the notion of trading on one's sexuality becomes an alluring option.

Many women build up a tremendous internal rage when they realize that the odds are stacked against them in the workplace. This rage translates into an attitude of "I'll get even"—namely by exploiting my sexuality. Unconsciously or consciously these women decide to reap whatever advantages they can from their sexuality. One powerful and well-known Canadian trade unionist freely admits that she has to be seductive in order to get what she wants. "It's all fair in this game," she says.

Other women try to trade on their sexuality because of financial need. In Victorian times women's wages were set so low that many were forced to supplement their incomes through prostitution to survive. Today, although their situations may be less desperate, the vast majority of women have to come to an accommodation with a husband or a boss in order to maintain their economic livelihood. One American female sociologist sees it as the inevitable extension of low wages. She told us,

In a society where the male is the fundamental breadwinner, you're going to have office romances, and some women will try to use their sexuality. But women who exploit their sexuality, in some cases, are looking for sexual attention as a means of income-supplement. One woman I know had to ensure she was asked out for dinner every night, just in order to make ends meet.

SOCIAL CONDITIONING

Still other women try to curry favor in the workplace with sexual attention because they have accepted the role forced upon them by a society that defines a woman as nurturer, mother, wife, and the helpmate of men. Magazines such as *Cosmopolitan* openly counsel women to adopt a strategy of sexual manipulation, advising them to use this technique for their own advantage. It is difficult to place the blame on individual women, who are merely acting out the patterns of behavior they are encouraged by society and the media to utilize.

MARRY THE BOSS

The peculiarities of North American life prepared the social-psychological ground for the mass sex market, and the mass competition among females.

Just as the Horatio Alger stories became the handbook for men on how to rise from rags to riches, so the romance stories for women told them how to get and marry the boss's son or even the boss himself.[1]

The majority of working women quickly learn that the possibility of rising on their own to a position of prominence that would afford them both power and financial independence is extremely unlikely. Rather than remain a marginal worker in a dead-end, low-paying job, the prospect of marriage, especially to a man who by comparison has the trappings of power and money, becomes an obvious way out.

In effect women who aspire to marry the boss are only complying with the social mores of our society. They are encouraged from childhood on to cultivate their physical attributes with the objective of "catching" a man. Most of society does not condemn this type of trading on one's sexuality. If anything it is considered perfectly legitimate, particularly when it leads to marriage.

With all of this outright encouragement of sexual interplay in the workplace, it is not surprising that some women do attempt to gain promotions, pay raises, and other benefits by virtue of their sexual attractions. The obvious question becomes whether they find this tactic successful in the long run.

THE UNWRITTEN RULES OF THE CORPORATION

Although you will never find company policies on office affairs written in personnel manuals, a comprehensive code of ethics exists in all organizations. These rules are patterned after the customs and standards of a male-dominated society, where male-female relationships are viewed as a male conquest, an indication of power, virility, and domination.

Michael Korda, in *Male Chauvinism: How It Works*, acknowledges this:

> On a basic male chauvinist level an office affair is a badge of status, always provided that it's handled well; that is, with the minimal amount of emotional disturbance and with its course and direction firmly controlled (or thought to be firmly controlled) by the male partner. Any display of emotion on the part of the man, or suggestion that the woman either initiated the affair or decides when and how it will end, loses the man his status in his peer group.[2]

While all organizations will strenuously disclaim in public that they have corporate policy on male-female sexual relationships, in fact, office affairs are a male assertion of superiority in corporate gamesmanship. A man who sleeps with an employee or co-worker is instantly superior in game terms, while the woman is downgraded to inferior status. As a general rule, a woman augments the status of any and every man she sleeps with in the office, while lowering her own. Betty Lehan Harragan, author of *Games Mother Never Taught You*, cautions women as follows:

> What this unwritten and unverbalized canon of male ethics adds up to for women is clear: any corporate woman employee who engages in intercourse has jeopardized her chances of significant advancement within that particular corporate structure. She is irrevocably labeled "inferior" and must go elsewhere to move upward with a clear path.
>
> Women can't win this game. They must not play the game with any male member of their particular business community if they want to remain viable activists in the impersonal master game of corporate politics where the goal is money, success, and independent power.[3]

The double standard stands out clearly in any discussion of whether women derive unfair gains based on their sexuality. Even presuming that a woman has made substantial job gains from an office liaison, the anger and hostility from fellow employees and the world at large focus exclusively on her. The role of the male partner in granting promotions or job benefits for sexual favors he has been bribed with is surely just as reprehensible. Yet his actions are rarely scrutinized, and reprisals against such men are vitually unheard of.

Robert E. Quinn, a thirty-two-year-old professor of public administration at the State University of New York, recently completed a comprehensive study of the office affair. His study entitled *Coping with Cupid: The Formation, Impact and Management of Romantic Relationships in Organizations*, revealed that "women who put their sexuality to work for them in the workplace are playing a dangerous game that, statistically, leads them to be fired for fooling around twice as often as men." Professor Quinn observed that "because the male is usually in a higher position, he is seen as less dispensable than the female, if superiors feel an affair is getting out of hand." As he said, "If people are stepping out of line, sexually, there seems to be a compulsion on the part of the upper hierarchy to do something about it. Unfortunately, it's the woman who has to go."

Despite this deterrent, women, according to Professor Quinn, do "use their sexuality to attempt to accomplish organizational ends." In 74 percent of the affairs that he studied, the male held a higher position in the office than the female partner. Co-workers, he discovered, reacted with disapproval, cynicism, and hostility—all of which are particularly directed at the woman, whom they perceived as engaging in sexual exchange for career advantage and favoritism. The women who evoked these negative responses from their co-workers became depressed and defensive.[4]

MALE GOSSIP

Talking about one's conquests—real or imagined—is a favorite male pastime. Harragan cautions working women that "as long as sexual conquests of female employees are male status symbols, the trophies must be publicized." She estimates that 80 percent of conversation in all-male groups is about sex, specifically the availability of women and the sexual prowess of men in "making" those women. Furthermore, she points out that "male-initiated propositions and consummations would have no status value if nobody knew about them, so office affairs are the most public personal relationships there are."

Successful women are particularly the butt of male gossip, be they subordinates, peers, or superiors. With so many men threatened by the notion of job equality, lewd insinuations about women achievers offer an easy, but vicious, way of discharging anxiety. Whether a woman is engaging in office romances or not, she may become the target of this insidious male gossip, which is often a gross exaggeration or a fantasy. Harragan strongly urges women "to refuse to talk about other women disparagingly." When they engage in this, she concludes, "they play right into men's hands and help reduce all women (including themselves) to the contemptible level of cunts."[5]

EXCEPTIONS TO THE RULE

There are two kinds of office affairs that generally do not result in reprisals to the woman. You can marry the man in question or be his secretary.

Marriage legitimizes you as part of a couple and places you outside the realm of office politics. You survive and may even thrive, since you have conformed to society's notion of an upstanding, moral member of the community. You are a wife, not a temptress or a seductress. As a wife, other men are loath to pursue you or gossip about you, since your husband may be a co-worker or a superior. Furthermore, territorial imperatives are involved. As another man's wife in the same workplace, you are viewed as his exclusive property, his conquest.

The only other instance in which a woman's office affair does not place her in job jeopardy is the long-term affair between a secretary and her boss. As Harragan points out, this exemption only applies to those secretaries "who remain in their subservient, noncomplaining role of the dutiful doormat." These sexual relationships, she continues, are only possible because secretarial jobs have no place in the hierarchy as presently constituted. They are extraneous servant positions. A secretary has no upward mobility. A secretary-boss sexual liaison is degrading to the woman, but it affects nobody else in the hierarchy, so nobody really cares—as long as she "behaves herself" and is completely under the man's controlling thumb.[6]

HOW HIGH ARE THE STAKES?

With such obvious risks facing any woman who enters into an office affair, it becomes important to examine how lucrative the potential gains may be. Do women gain in a significant way from sexual liaisons on the job?

What we are asking, essentially, is whether women who exploit their sexuality receive substantial payoffs. Since these women are, in effect, selling sex indirectly, it is helpful to look to the example of women who are selling sex directly: the prostitutes. Prostitutes are women who are exploiting their sexuality in a forthright manner. Consequently one would assume they would derive greater financial rewards than women who merely exploit indirectly.

However, the vast majority of the most elegant call-girls find themselves old at thirty, bitter, and broke. Prostitution is not a profession in which one moves up through the ranks. Experience is no asset, and it is all downhill as one gets older. Although the top call-girls earn between $30,000 and $100,000 a year, taxfree, their expenses are monumental. They require costly clothes and plush apartments in the most exclusive districts. A large proportion of their income goes to pay off pimps, madams, building superintendents, landlords, doormen, prostitution lawyers, politicians, the police, and in some cases even the Mafia. In two thousand interviews conducted over ten years, Charles Winick and Paul

Kinsie found no more than one hundred older prostitutes who had any money left.[7]

With such a dismal picture facing prostitutes, it should not be surprising to discover that women who try to use sex indirectly, for job-related gains, have little success. These women may be able to improve their job title or pay *over other women*, but they are never able to compete with men on such a basis.

SERIOUS PITFALLS

Women who do "buy" promotions, raises, and so forth, with sexual payoffs almost always find they are left with nagging doubts about their abilities and job skills. Whether or not they are in fact competent to handle the work they are doing, their crises of self-confidence often jeopardize their job performance.

Furthermore, they are faced with a complete absence of job security. Office affairs, like all male-female relationships, have a disturbing propensity to shift with the winds of time. When the relationship goes on the rocks or another, more tantalizing woman comes along, the cozy setup could be called off in a hurry.

The "love 'em and leave 'em" routine can quickly turn to "love 'em and fire 'em" in the work setting. One clear-cut example of the devious lengths to which this scenario can be taken was related to us by an affirmative-action specialist from a multinational manufacturing concern.

"The executive director of our all-male marketing department did everything he could to forestall the introduction of our affirmative-action program in his department," she told us. "When he realized he would have to bow to the inevitable," she continued,

In keeping with his childish personality, he devised a sneaky plan to subvert the program. He agreed to hire women, all right. But he hired them not on the basis of their ability to do the job, but because he found them sexually appealing. He would have a short and swift affair with each of them, and when it was over, he would try to fire them. He would point out, quite correctly, that they were not qualified to fill the positions and that their work was not up to standard. He used this to create an outcry about the affirmative-action program, arguing that it was forcing him to hire unacceptable women. I was left in the intolerable position of trying to defend these poor women, trying to protect them from losing their jobs. After all, they certainly were qualified for the jobs they were really hired for—to be the sexual playthings of the executive director. Unfortunately, the president of the company did not believe me, and all the women were fired. The affirmative-action program was effectively scuttled by these outrageous tactics.

Another critical obstacle facing women who try to trade on their sexuality is the hostility and frustration felt by other employees, who inevitably react against what they perceive to be an unfair advantage. A woman who is handed a promotion as a return for sexual favors will find her work so sabotaged by her fellow workers that she will rarely be able to function. Subordinates and superiors of both sexes will undermine her work and belittle her authority. They will all assume that she holds her position not on an independent basis, but only so long as her male paramour can protect her. She will never be able to take control or build up satisfactory working relationships with her fellow workers. Inevitably the performance of the operation will suffer, and no matter how powerful her male protector is, she will be removed because of her inability to get the job done in an acceptable manner.

The prevailing mythology is that women can sell sex to men and receive adequate or spectacular financial, professional, or emotional rewards. In fact, upon closer examination, it becomes clear that most women do not receive adequate or spectacular financial, professional, or emotional rewards whether they sell sexual services or refuse to do so.

9

Lowering the odds:
Are There Any Personal Solutions?

Sexual harassment is not a personal problem. It is a personnel problem. A sexual harasser chooses his victim because of her vulnerability, because he has authority over her. Women of all shapes, sizes, and personalities are victims of sexual harassment.

The problem of sexual harassment of working women is not truly solvable by personal solutions related to behavior and dress. To imply that the woman incites sexual harassment on the part of male harassers by virtue of what she wears or what she says places the responsibility squarely on the woman's shoulders. That is not the intent of this book nor the reality of women's predicament. Women are not guilty of incitement; they are the *victims* of morally and ethically reprehensible male behavior.

It is our conclusion that once a woman finds herself enmeshed in a situation involving any of the range of acts constituting sexual harassment, there is very little that she can personally do. She is dealing with a power play in which she is generally a minor and dispensable player.

Understandably, countless women have asked us how they can personally lower the odds to avoid victimization, and if that fails, what steps they can take to minimize the reprisals and repercussions that flow from sexual harassment. With this in mind we have compiled a list of suggestions gleaned from discussions with victims, sympathetic male and female personnel directors, managers, and union representatives, the Boston-based Alliance Against Sexual Harassment, and the New York-based Working Women United Institute.

The danger is always present that although a woman who follows special cautionary advice may diminish her chances slightly, the sexual harasser remains at large. He will merely shift his efforts to another less difficult target. Furthermore, there is a price to be paid by women adopting a special burden of caution. Their freedom of behavior is restricted, and they may find that the personality alterations required are too high a price to pay for the questionable security they afford. Having stated all this, it is interesting to explore the various options and strategies that have been suggested. However, one should bear in mind that experience indicates that nothing will stop a determined harasser.

PREVENTION—DO'S AND DON'TS

1. A Dress Code

John T. Molloy, the author of *The Woman's Dress for Success Book*, believes that "there is one firm and dramatic step women can take toward professional equality with men. *They can adopt a business uniform.*" He is very specific about what this uniform should be. As he advises, "beyond any doubt, the uniform should be a *skirted suit and blouse*. In most cases the suit should be dark and the blouse should contrast with the skirt and jacket."[1]

Mr. Molloy has designed this uniform based on in-depth interviews with male business representatives and extensive surveys. He provides a very detailed analysis of accessories and makeup. The idea is to convey an image of professionalism and authority. He suggests a basic plain pump; neutral color pantyhose; slightly below the knee, straight, tailored skirt; a man-tailored blouse; contrasting scarf; an attaché case without purse; shoulder-length hair; and what he calls a feminine fedora.[2] He is very specific about advising women to use clear nail polish and the minimum amount of makeup.

For the few executive women Mr. Molloy's suggestion may be appropriate, but the waitress, the salesclerk, and the factory worker all work in environments that preclude such attire. There is also the question of cost. The soft, feminine clothing for social occasions, according to Mr. Molloy, should never be worn to places of business. But the average working woman has a limited budget for clothes and so attempts to build an integrated wardrobe that will serve for both business and social occasions.

It is obvious that provocative attire—that is, plunging necklines; sundresses; short, short skirts; and masses of glittery makeup—*do not* belong in the workplace. Our research indicates that personnel and management are terribly biased against a woman whom they describe as provocatively dressed. Your chances of creating a professional image are vastly improved if you do choose to dress unspectacularly.

2. Professional Behavior

It is very important, when trying to avoid the possibility of encountering sexual harassment, to learn to distinguish between behavior that is friendly and behavior that is too friendly. We are not suggesting that women become aloof and overly guarded. Such a stance can only serve to make work unpleasant and lonely. Being too friendly involves divulging one's personal problems. Unfortunately a potential sexual harasser could misconstrue the confidence as an invitation to "comfort" you. You should also be careful not to relate details of your personal social life. Such personal data, whether you are single or married, may stimulate his fantasies about you. Despite your best efforts to keep your personal life out of the conversation, the potential sexual harasser may ask you pointed sexual questions. Counter with the assertion that you are concentrating on your career and attempt to steer the conversation to the work at hand.

3. Don't Drink Alone with Him

Numerous women have told us that bosses who had always behaved with perfect decorum become aggressive when the two were "having a drink" together alone. It is their observation that a woman should never allow a situation to develop where she is having an afterhours drink alone with her boss. These women claim that they were forced out of their jobs after this one isolated incident, despite years of service and what they had believed to be a mutually cooperative and respectful relationship. Obviously the harasser cannot tolerate having the woman he has harassed and who has rejected him in the same office. We are dealing with the full wrath of the offended male ego. Perhaps "hell hath no fury like a woman scorned," but a scorned man often has the power to make a woman's life intolerable.

4. Create a Male Protector

Many of the women we interviewed were of the opinion that a husband or boyfriend, real or imaginary, would serve as a deterrent. You are signaling that you are another man's exclusive property. They suggest that you find occasions to bring up your husband's or boyfriend's name in conversation with a potential harasser and allude to his violent jealousy. Some even go so far as to suggest that you subtly warn the potential harasser that this protector of yours has been known to "punch out other men" on the slightest provocation.

Perhaps this strategy may have some marginal success with a fledgling harasser, but we suspect that unless your protector actually works in the same environment, it is not an effective deterrent. It may even present a challenge to the man and further excite his interest. You must also consider the possibility that a woman who talks incessantly about her husband or boyfriend will not be taken seriously in the workplace. It may effectively bar you from career advancements, since you run the risk of being labeled "the little housewife working for pin money," or "the typical young woman prepared to give it all up for marriage."

5. Talk about His Family

One very enterprising businesswoman told us she managed to avoid victimization on one occasion by deliberately arranging to meet and befriend her boss's wife. She knew that her boss was on the verge of "coming on to her." At every opportunity she made reference to his wife and children—inquiring about their health, activities, and so on and commenting on how impressed she was by his loyal and stable familial relationship. She would often ask to speak to his wife when she telephoned the office, and arranged to have lunch. Very soon the potential harasser gave up all thoughts of pursuing the woman.

This technique has potential where the wife is open to these friendly overtures. It may, in some instances, raise suspicions in the mind of the wife. On balance, each woman must assess whether or not this tactic would be advisable in her particular circumstances.

6. Distinguish between Business and Pleasure

Business lunches and working dinners are part of the way work is conducted in our society. To further one's career it may be crucial to participate in these events. It is often the opportunity, in a more relaxed environment, to learn about critical aspects of your job and the hierarchy in which you work. It may also be a way for your boss and co-workers to learn how serious you are about your work.

But ultimately you must discern which lunches and dinners are for business and which ones may lead to sexual harassment. It is helpful if you can arrange to have other co-workers or supervisors present. Of course this is not always possible. In the end, once again, you must assess what is the real purpose of the meal—business or pleasure. If you are confident that the objective is "pleasure"—not yours—do not accept the invitation. Over time the potential sexual harasser will be forced to acknowledge that you are deliberately avoiding socializing with him.

7. Don't Ask for or Offer to Do Special Favors

Try never to become indebted to a potential sexual harasser by asking for special favors. You may find that the man in question will come to collect what he believes to be his due for having indulged you. You also run the risk of incurring co-workers' jealousy and animosity. When and if you find yourself being harassed by this man, you will find little support among your peers. In fact, the office gossip may have escalated to the point where all and sundry have concluded that the two of you are having an affair.

By the same token do not agree to do personal favors for your boss. You will be labeled "the office wife," content to do your boss's bidding, without any personal ambitions of your own. The boss himself may conclude that your eagerness to run personal errands is a sign of interest. The situation could quickly escalate to the point where you find yourself fending off his unsolicited advances. Again, your co-workers and management will be less than sympathetic. They will assume that the sexual innuendo is mutual, not coercive.

TACTICS AND STRATEGIES ONCE HARASSMENT BEGINS

When all these tactics fail and the harasser makes his intentions clear, there are a number of reactions with which women can respond. At the outset, it must be understood that a sexual harassment victim will recognize immediately how precarious her position is. Most women see their economic livelihood jeopardized and plunge into a natural reaction of utter terror. It goes without saying that such a frame of mind makes it extremely difficult to strategize or to plan rational responses. It is to the tribute of any sexual harassment victim if she can master the courage necessary to fight back.

1. The Emperior Has No Clothes

At least in the initial stages, the overwhelming majority of women try to ignore the sexual advances. They pretend not to see them, hear them, or understand them. In fact, Margaret Hennig and Anne Jardim in *The Managerial Woman* recommend this as the first and best strategy. They suggest that women respond to a come-on with "How much is your area going to be over budget this month?" and advise women to pretend to be totally preoccupied with the job.[3]

The lengths to which some women go to ignore sexual harassment almost defies belief. One high-ranking civil servant tells this story. She had been working for her boss for a number of years without incident when one night, after working late together, he offered to drive her home. She was grateful for the ride and asked him in for a cup of coffee. She left him in the living room and went out to the kitchen. When she returned several minutes later, he was sitting on the sofa, stark naked.

She faltered momentarily, but quickly concluded that the only way to proceed was to act as if he were fully clothed. She fought to remain calm outwardly, and served the coffee while chattering away about mundane matters. After they had finished, she stood up, telling her boss that she was exhausted and was sure he was too and thought they should wind up for the day. She said goodnight, adding that she was sure he would be able to show himself out. She walked upstairs to her bedroom and locked the door.

Despite this and other equally valiant attempts to ignore sexual harassment, research indicates that sticking one's head in the sand and pretending that sexual advances are not being made offers no solution. Ignoring a sexual harasser's overtures merely encourages him to adopt more direct methods. The obvious risk that this approach creates is that rather than discourage unsolicited sexual attention, feigning ignorance will escalate the problem.

2. Direct Confrontation

Another approach is to deal with the harasser directly, telling him you are not willing to go along with the sexual come-on. Women can reject sexual harassers' advances in a number of ways—ranging from a disarming, joking response to a blunt no. The many excuses that have been given by recalcitrant sexual harassment victims in the past encompass the following:

- I'm sorry, but I make it a rule never to mix business and pleasure.
- My husband and I have a wonderful relationship, and we intend to keep it that way.
- I hate to admit it, but my 6-foot-6-inch quarterback boyfriend is notorious for his jealousy.
- I really respect you, and I like you very much. I'm not interested in a relationship with you, but I hope we can be friends.
- You've got to be kidding!
- I'm flattered by your interest, and if it weren't for the fact that I have a number of virulent social diseases, I'd love to take you up on your offer.

Most women find it easier to use a low-key, diplomatic approach in turning down these advances. They are more familiar with evasive ruses than blunt rejections, since the former more closely resemble the dating patterns they have been using all their lives. Cautioned not to injure the male ego, they never turned down a date with a curt "I don't want to go out with you." They used a variety of other pretexts—they had to baby-sit, they had to go bowling, and so on. Now faced with an advance from a figure of authority, these patterns are reinforced with the recognition that the man's ego must not be bruised if the woman wishes to continue working with him. However, the problem with the polite response is that the no may be misinterpreted as a maybe.

The tougher tactic—the blunt no—is also problematical. Most women find it upsetting to use this method in a normal social setting between equals. In a hierarchical work structure, telling your boss in no uncertain terms that you object to the sexual advance puts you in a precarious position. Furthermore, the stern rebuff only stops fledgling harassers, amateurs in the sport. No full-fledged harasser worth his salt will be deterred. The struggle, after all, is half the fun. A reluctant victim only presents a more interesting challenge.

When both of these confrontation methods fail, the next step is to threaten your harasser. You can threaten to expose him publicly to his superiors in the organization. You can tell him that sexual harassment is against the law, and that you are prepared to engage a lawyer and take legal action. You can threaten to tell his wife. You may have no intention of carrying out these threats, but you can use them for their shock value. While the first two threats may carry some weight, the last suggestion—threatening to tell his wife—is generally of little value. Most wives have little bargaining power, and for a variety of reasons they tend to disbelieve your story and side with their husband.

It is also important to recognize that if the situation has deteriorated to the point where threats are necessary, the possibility of a productive, supportive working relationship in the future is quite remote. A woman in this position is best advised to start looking for a new job or a transfer away from the clutches of the sexual harasser. While this is clearly not a just solution—the harasser is causing the problem, and in any fair analysis he should be moved—sexual harassment victims can expect little justice and should take immediate steps to protect themselves.

3. Taking It Over His Head

If a new job is not available and a transfer within the organization to another department is impracticable, the woman in question may wish to dig in her heels and fight. As a word of caution, since most organizations and society at large have yet to recognize sexual harassment as a crime against women, the way will be tortuous, and the final result may be less than satisfactory.

For this reason the woman is well advised to prepare her case as thoroughly as possible. She should keep a written record of the sexual harassment, listing details of when, where, how, and under what circumstances the harasser has made his moves. She should look for witnesses who have seen the sexual harassment and remind them of the implications of what they have witnessed. She should ask them if they would be prepared to support her case and testify in her behalf. If there are no witnesses, she could consider making use of hidden tape recorders to collect evidence.

Since most harassers are repeaters, she should do some investigative work to see if she can determine who the previous victims were. She should talk to these women and ask them to support her complaint. Finally, she should talk to other women in her workplace, seeking their support. After all, this is a common problem for all working women, and the most effective way of dealing with it will be collective action. A harasser and his organization will be threatened much more by a group complaint than by an individual whose objection can be laughed off and easily dismissed.

Once prepared, the woman can consider whether to take the complaint to personnel, management, or if the workplace is unionized, to her union representative. She should approach whoever in personnel, management or the union is most likely to be sympathetic. Our research has indicated that women are far more likely to be supportive of a sexual harassment victim than men, but this is not always the case, and the victim should trust her own sense of who will give her a fair hearing.

No sexual harassment victim, however, should expect justice at the hands of an organization. While it would be nice to believe that the managers in most business and government offices are by and large decent people, when it comes to the question of sexual harassment, this is not the case. As do rape victims, a sexual harassment victim falls prey to a host of sexist assumptions, which cause her to be treated with disbelief, unfairly categorize her as a provocateur, and attribute blame to her. To force an organization to behave responsibly, she should present it with a written complaint and make it clear that unless her problem is dealt with expeditiously and fairly, she will seek outside legal remedies.

A woman who takes her complaint over her harasser's head is waging war. She is overstepping the hierarchical structure and risks incurring the wrath of other sexual harassers in the organization. The old-boys network is likely to close ranks and take swift action to expel her from the organization. A group complaint, however, cannot be so easily disposed of, and the chances of a fair hearing increase with the number of women willing to speak up.

4. Legal Reprisals

This option is always open to victims of sexual harassment, although it may be time-consuming, costly, and ultimately less than satisfactory. Women can take their carefully documented complaints to human rights commissions, the Equal Employment Opportunity Commission, or a private lawyer. The organization will most certainly respond with hostility to any outside action such as this, however, and the woman can expect serious repercussions.

Despite these drawbacks, there is one critical advantage to legal action. A woman who is being sexually harassed is being harassed because she is not seen as an equal. It is obviously difficult for a person who is not seen as an equal to fight back a sexual harasser's advances on her own. By engaging a lawyer she retains an advocate who can stand in an equal position with the harasser and the organization and fight on equal terms. It is precisely because of this that the organization will respond so viciously to any outside legal activity.

There is the chance, however, that by engaging a lawyer, a sexual harassment victim can nip the harassment in the bud. She can have her lawyer make it clear to the harasser in no uncertain terms that legal action will flow from any reprisals and unless the behavior ceases. This discussion can take place on a confidential basis, and if the harasser is frightened off, no one else in the organization need know.

The state of the law and the past practices of courts and human rights organizations in handling sexual harassment complaints leave much to be desired, although the situation seems to be improving. Nevertheless, the stakes can be high, and the woman, if successful, can receive relatively comprehensive compensation. The best way to approach legal solutions, as with complaints inside the organization, is where there is more than one complainant. Clearly there is greater safety in numbers.

5. A Parting Shot

If you do not decide to take a complaint higher within the organization or to an outside legal agency or the courts, you may well find yourself forced out of your job. Rather than go without leaving any imprint, you may consider taking these steps, hoping they may work to improve the situation for the women who come after you.

You can talk to the women you work with in the organization and be frank about why you are leaving. They deserve to know the score, and your speaking up may encourage them to act collectively in the future. You may also consider sending a letter after you leave to the chief executive officer of the organization, explaining the situation and noting your concern that this harasser may bother other women in the future. Although he may laugh off your letter as a crank, he is at least put on notice, and a second female victim who complains may cause him to consider taking action.

6. Don't Allow Yourself to Feel Guilty

The most important consideration in dealing with sexual harassment is to protect yourself, to refuse to feel guilty or in any way responsible for your problems. By all rights you should be angry. You are a victim and are in no way to blame for being the target of this heinous behavior.

If you have sympathetic family and friends you can trust, tell them of your problem and get their support. Women's groups of all descriptions are springing up, and they are starting to develop a keen appreciation of the problems of the sexual harassment victim. You may solicit their support and assistance in coping with your trauma and in securing a new position in the workforce.

10

Action plans for management and unions

A. MANAGEMENT AND SEXUAL HARASSMENT

A Case for Action

Most male managers we interviewed either denied that sexual harassment was a problem or were aware of only a few isolated incidents. All of the female managers acknowledged that sexual harassment was a definite occupational hazard for women in the workplace. Most of the female managers had had firsthand experience with sexual harassment during their careers. Their success in dealing with it was uniformly limited, since their senior management was not prepared to take any action, unless it involved transferring or firing the female victim. With a few exceptions they concluded that a female victim of sexual harassment was in a "no-win" situation. Her only real option, they believed, was to look for another job at the first signs.

Since female managers are few and far between in most organizational structures, it is understandable that their influence is marginal. There is also an element of fear—fear that if they push too hard, their own jobs may be in jeopardy.

What we are left with is male indifference and female sympathy mingled with justifiable fear. However, management as a whole has a definite vested interest in addressing itself to the problem of sexual harassment. Women are and will increasingly become an integral part of the workplace. They are irrevocably in the workplace as full-fledged participants. Their own perceptions of how they are victimized and discriminated against will become crystallized in the next while.

In order to achieve the overall organizational objectives of high productivity and continual expansion, a stable, relatively contented workforce is a prime prerequisite. If sexual harassment is a rampant feature within a hierarchy, the result is a high female turnover and a poisoned working environment. Office morale as a whole suffers, and with it follows a definite plunge in productivity.

Even if the victims of sexual harassment do not have the option of quitting their jobs, our research indicates that they lose a considerable amount of time due to sickness. Sexual harassment syndrome, as we have mentioned previously, manifests itself in a variety of physical and psychological ailments. Nervous, unhappy employees eventually lose interest in their jobs and may ultimately grow to hate work itself.

Most institutions today are aware that they have an obligation to promote what is commonly called "corporate responsibility." The public and the media are constantly scrutinizing corporate practices and have been known to switch products and services when a business enterprise is exposed as a perpetrator of unfair practices. But on a more immediate level, a good corporate policy demands the promotion of amiable employer-employee relations.

Employees must trust that their organization will administer corporate justice. If not, the victims of sexual harassment may choose a legal remedy outside the corporation. Then the corporation is almost assuredly open to the glare of publicity. The press will paint a picture of corporate complicity in female exploitation. Once a corporation is labeled with this image, it will become difficult to attract female employees who seek long-term careers.

If female employees are so dispensable that this is hardly an organizational concern, consider the cost to the corporation in key male employees. As women begin to speak up about sexual harassment, the male perpetrators' careers become at risk. The organizational investment in male harassers can be considerable. Management would be wise, for this reason alone, to take issue with sexual harassment.

Sexual harassment is an incendiary issue, smoldering beneath the surface. Avoidance is always a disastrous approach. There are a number of definite steps that management can take to ensure that the incidence of sexual harassment is dramatically reduced. Coupled with this is the need to devise tactical measures to deal effectively with perpetrators of sexual harassment. We have prepared a ten-point plan for management. This plan incorporates the principles of both prevention and positive intervention.

TEN-POINT PLAN FOR MANAGEMENT

1. Corporate Blue Letter

As with all corporate policies, a corporate statement condemning the practice of sexual harassment must have the strong endorsement of *all* the chief officers. The corporate blue letter should define sexual harassment and clearly state that such behavior is *unacceptable*. This letter should be posted on all bulletin boards, reprinted in any in-house publications, and placed in the manager's manual.

2. Management Training Sessions

Companies are beginning to respond to occupational hazards such as alcoholism and drug addiction with educational programs. Sexual harassment is a problem of the same magnitude. A special educational program should be designed for the benefit of management to explain more fully the corporation's stance on sexual harassment. The emphasis should be that sexual harassment is disastrous behavior for managers, constituting a case of coercion that could cost the manager his career.

3. Branch Meetings

To supplement the special training sessions and to demonstrate the seriousness with which the corporation views acts of sexual harssment, special branch meetings should be held where the branch director or supervisor issues the corporate directive in more precise terms and invites a dialogue to avoid any misconceptions.

4. Conduct an Employee Survey

Since sexual harassment is such a secretive and potentially explosive issue, consider conducting a survey among your employees. Promise employees anonymity and confidentiality. Be careful to word the survey in such a way that you cover the whole range of behavior and the consequences that flow from sexual harassment to the victim. The results of the survey should be posted and printed for distribution.

5. Orientation Sessions for New Employees

New employees should be advised of company policy on sexual harassment at their orientation session. They should also be made aware that their complaints will be treated seriously.

6. Establish an Investigative Procedure

The first step in dealing with a complaint of sexual harassment is to assure the victim that her job is not in jeopardy and that she is not on trial.

Advise the victim to document all incidents relating to the sexual harassment. Encourage her to enlist the support of witnesses, if she has any. Search for other victims, particularly if the harasser has a history of firing female subordinates or his female subordinates regularly resign.

The moment you approach the harasser, the victim is in greater jeopardy. So if you choose to proceed this way, warn the harasser that a complaint has been lodged and that he is under surveillance. Make it very clear that sexual harassment is coercive and deeply offensive to the victim, as well as constituting an invasion of her civil liberties.

7. Protect the Victim

Sexual harassment by its very nature does not lend itself to normal rules of investigative procedure. The victim, if left unprotected, is open to reprisals from her harasser. He is in a position to make her working environment intolerable. As a result she may become both physically and psychologically ill.

Offer the woman the use of the corporation's counseling facilities, assure her that her job is secure, and determine if it is possible to move her harasser. If not, try to transfer her.

8. Set Out a Disciplinary Agenda

There is a range of disciplinary measures that management has at its disposal. Consideration should be given to whether or not this is the first complaint, to the seriousness of the offense, to the length of service, and to the job performance of the harasser. The following seven steps are progressively harsh, leading ultimately to the harasser's dismissal.

1. Issue a warning.
2. Insist on counseling for the harasser.
3. Transfer the harasser.
4. Withhold a promotion or work assignment.
5. Lower performance rating.
6. Put on probation.
7. Fire.

9. Utilize Outside Consultants

Try to avoid the pitfalls of conducting a sexist investigation where the victim is put on trial. Consider the use of outside consultants. Since sexual harassment is a hierarchical, power-based problem, the victim will feel more comfortable with an outside consultant who is not a part of the organizational structure. She will also be more confident that she will receive a fair hearing.

10. Deal with the Harasser in a Productive Fashion

When you issue your first warning to the perpetrator of sexual harassment, explain the implications of his behavior to him. By the time you approach him, be prepared to move either him or his victim. Try to isolate the man, if possible. Failing this, do not attempt to solve the problem by replacing the victim with a plain or older woman. Our research indicates that the perpetrators of sexual harassment are exercising their power, not expressing desire. Warn the new woman of her boss's proclivities and encourage her to report any further incidents of sexual harassment.

If your warning fails and all subsequent deterrents fail, fire him. Not doing so leaves the corporation open to lawsuits, public inquiries, and bad press.

B. UNIONS AND SEXUAL HARASSMENT

A First-Rate Organizing Tool

Historically unions have fought courageously to improve the lot of working men and women. Striving to obtain a fair share of the profits generated by the labor of the workers, they stood in the forefront of progressive social change. Unions have clearly defined their role to protect workers from exploitation and have taken aggressive action to fulfill their mandate.

Sexual harassment is an exploitative practice that creates intolerable working conditions for women. The issue of sexual harassment is no less important than the traditional issues unions have fought for—wages, benefits, occupational health, and safety. Sexual harassment is a pervasive problem that dramatically affects vast numbers of rank and file workers. If unions are to accomplish their goal of ending exploitation and injustice in the workplace, they must address this matter.

In the past there have been some incidents within the trade union movement of discrimination against women members. Many union officials today sincerely wish to redress these wrongs. In both Canada and the United States legislation stipulates that unions have a duty to represent all of their members fairly. A number of unions are now openly encouraging their women members to play a more active role in union affairs. Dealing with the problems of sexual harassment in the workforce may prove an effective way of catching and holding the interest of female union members.

Trade unions are not completely free of sexual harassers themselves. Many sexual harassers are not managers, but male union members. By taking swift and direct action to oppose sexual harassment from supervisors and managers, unions will set an instructive example for their own membership. Where they develop educational programs and strict policies condemning sexual harassment, this will help to purge sexual harassment from within their own ranks.

Finally, sexual harassment provides a unique tool that can be of aid in union organizing campaigns. Nearly nine out of ten working women report that they have experienced sexual harassment; almost half state that they or a woman they know have quit a job or been fired because of sexual harassment on the job. The tragedy is that until recently, although so many women were adversely affected by sexual harassment, there was little discussion between victims. Now that sexual harassment is becoming a topic of common conversation, women on the job will be able to communicate more frankly about their problems. As they meet to discuss their mutual frustrations with sexual harassment, they will naturally begin to share their concerns about wages, job benefits, and so forth. Unionization is an obvious vehicle they can use to improve their situation.

Unions have had difficulties organizing women employees. Large sectors of the female workforce remain unorganized. Sexual harassment could be the key issue to foster communication among women workers and collective action to redress the manifold injustices inflicted on women at work.

TEN-POINT PLAN FOR UNIONS

1. Discuss Sexual Harassment in Union Organizing Campaigns

Train union organizers to recognize sexual harassment and what it means. Design campaign literature to deal with sexual harassment and indicate how a union can help victims. Use discussions of sexual harassment to begin the communication process about the need for unions. Union representatives should develop expertise in this area and endeavor to sit on public panels and in all public forums where sexual harassment is discussed. The benefits a union can provide working women should be pointed out, and the unionization process should be outlined to all such audiences.

2. Education of Union Personnel

It is critical to provide comprehensive education about sexual harassment to union officials and members. The topic can be addressed at union meetings and conferences and in union publications and brochures.

Sexual harassment should be defined, strategies for prevention should be examined, and a full discussion should be held of remedies for sexual harassment victims and the union's role in obtaining such remedies. Special educational sessions can be held for new female union members outlining the protections that the union can provide in this area. The union can demand that management be required to undergo similar education campaigns.

3. Contract Negotiations

When it comes time to bargain for a new contract, the existing union contract should be examined carefully to determine whether it prohibits sexual harassment and provides adequate remedies. Clauses that outlaw discrimination on the basis of sex and provide that there can be no discharge or discipline without just cause go some way toward providing protection, but a comprehensive clause specifically dealing with sexual harassment is more satisfactory.

Consider whether the normal grievance procedure is adequate for sexual harassment complaints or whether special requirements should be set out. For example, it might be better to have a reverse onus of proof in sexual harassment cases. Due to the problems of proving sexual harassment, it could be stated in the contract that once a woman employee complained of sexual harassment, the onus shifted to the alleged harasser to disprove the complaint.

During the contract negoations, bargain for provisions that specifically prohibit sexual harassment and provide protection to victims of such behavior. Since many women are forced to quit their jobs, the contract should extend protection to these women in addition to women who are fired, that is, a carefully worded constructive dismissal clause should be included in the contract. These clauses provide that women do not have to wait to be fired before they can seek redress. If working conditions are made intolerable, women are entitled to interpret them in the same manner as a firing, and to leave the job. The arbitrator who interprets the contract clause will evaluate the woman's story. If she can prove that working conditions were made intolerable, the arbitrator will "construct" a dismissal and provide a remedy for sexual harassment.

4. Utilize the Grievance Procedure

Once the contract covers sexual harassment, encourage victims to come forward with grievances. Actively solicit these complaints in union publications and at union meetings. Once a grievance is lodged, treat it seriously and make it a priority to argue the case, acting as the woman's advocate throughout the various stages of the grievance process, to arbitration if necessary. Encourage sexual harassment victims to make grievance as groups. A number of sexual harassment victims grieving against one manager will have a much greater chance for success than will an individual griever. Since many sexual harassers are repeaters, when an isolated complaint is made, investigate to determine whether there have been any previous victims. If so, urge them to support the initial grievance. In acting with management to select arbitrators to hear sexual harassment grievances, use caution in order to choose arbitrators who are unlikely to be guilty of sexual harassment themselves.

5. Assist Women in Fighting Sexual Harassment in Other Forums

If the contract does not deal adequately with sexual harassment, women victims may be better advised to take their complaints to government agencies (such as human rights commissions, the EEOC, and so on) or the courts, rather than to utilize the grievance procedure. Unions can take an active role in assisting women who are willing to pursue these outside remedies. They can act as an advocate, helping women to put together a compelling case with as much evidence as can be marshaled. Unions have traditionally provided these kinds of services to members seeking unemployment insurance, workmen's compensation, and so forth. This assistance should be extended to victims of sexual harassment seeking compensation from government tribunals and courts. Unions can provide legal counsel or perform the service of referring women victims to sympathetic, knowledgeable lawyers.

6. Other Tactics

There are a variety of more informal techniques that can be employed where women employees are reluctant to pursue a grievance or outside legal remedies. These women can be encouraged to make confidential, informal complaints to union officials. The union representatives can then warn other union members about such harassers and solicit the assistance of the membership in reporting further incidents. In some cases it may be beneficial to put the harasser on notice that his actions have not gone ignored and that further harassment will result in formal grievances.

Where the formal grievance procedure and these other informal tactics fail to provide relief, the union can consider making the problem public. Publicity in the media about sexual harassment at a specific organization would raise corporate eyebrows far and wide and could result in the organization's being forced to take immediate corrective action.

7. Lobbying

Legislative change is needed to address the problems of sexual harassment. Political pressure will be required to push such reforms through the legislatures. Unions can pass local resolutions advocating legal reforms and direct these to the attention of public officials and politicians. Letter-writing campaigns, media gimmicks, and other lobbying techniques can be employed to apply pressure to elected officials for amendments to the appropriate legislation.

8. The Trades: A Special Work Environment

Women are increasingly moving into nontraditional work areas—construction, mechanics, electronics, and other trades. There they are facing extreme and virulent forms of sexual harassment. Most trade occupations are unionized, and the unions in this field hold a great degree of control over the operations of contractors. The union leadership could take a special role in protecting women from sexual harassment on nontraditional worksites. Incoming women employees could be given strategic training for handling sexual harassment, and union officials could furnish them with active support and assistance in coping with the problems caused by this adverse defensive reaction by male supervisors and co-workers. Contract language should be tightened up to deal with sexual harassment, educational programs should be directed at female and male employees and managers, and union hiring-hall procedures should be utilized to enforce sanctions against notorious harassers.

9. Encourage Women to Participate in Union Affairs

Experience indicates that unions that have an active female membership, with women in positions of authority inside the union structure, have a better record on sexual harassment cases. Such unions tend to understand the problem more clearly and to act more effectively on complaints. In an effort to root out this coercive behavior, unions should actively seek from women members greater participation in internal union affairs.

10. Conduct Research

For years sexual harassment has remained a hidden, secret oppression. Out of fear and a realization that complaints would not be treated fairly, women have been reluctant to speak up. Unions are in a unique position to bring forward detailed information concerning the nature and extent of this problem. Extensive surveys and in-depth research could be conducted among union members to uncover the reality of sexual harassment facing working women. Case studies could be explored to determine which strategies proved successful in dealing with sexual harassment. Those findings could be incorporated into educational documentaries and written material for distribution to union members and the public at large.

11

Societal solutions

I. LONG-RANGE GOALS

Sexual harassment is rooted in two systematically exploitative features of
North American society and culture: sex discrimination and a hierarchical, undemocratic workplace. In order to combat sexual harassment,
either or both of these syndromes must be addressed. Viewing women
primarily as sex objects cannot continue. Any equitable analysis requires
that women be recognized as individuals with full rights to explore
employment and other life goals.

An authoritarian, power-ridden work structure provides an excellent environment for coercion and exploitation. The movement toward a
more democratic industrial setting will help to eliminate some of the
notorious abuses of authority. These social changes constitute long-range
goals. They will not be accomplished without lengthy, draining, and
possibly acrimonious struggles.

A. Sexual Equality

Throughout recorded history the principle of sexual equality has never
received serious societal consideration, except from small numbers of
courageous individuals, who have fought bitter private and public battles. Although women have achieved some real gains in the twentieth
century, we are still a very long way from attaining true sexual equality.
Some of the most powerful individuals in our society continue to treat the
proponents of sexual equality with amusement and condescension, if not
open hostility.

Without sexual equality there is little hope of eliminating the multitude of sexist practices and discriminatory attitudes that saturate the
total context of our lives. If we are to redress the balance, we must

examine the inherent sexual biases in our educational system that allow a perpetuation of the notion that women are not capable of sharing fully in the organization and management of society. This translates into a grossly unequal distribution of money and power. As a long-range goal we are faced with the challenge of generating public discussion and education about the innate injustice of not recognizing sexual equality as a critical societal objective.

Public discussion and education alone will not accomplish the societal transformation needed for sexual equality to become a reality. Until a critical mass of women is participating equally in industry, government, and the judicial system, there is no way to ensure sexual equality. The few women in our society holding prominent positions are not particularly effective in eradicating sexist practices and attitudes. They are victimized themselves and often attempt to cope with sexism by becoming "one of the boys" or adopting the attitude that they are superior to other women, a "queen bee" surrounded by a mass of drones.

Despite the fact that women are generally better educated than men, they are still clustered at the bottom of all hierarchical structures. In order to tilt the balance in favor of equalization, we must seriously enforce quotas and affirmative action. Only then will women be able to apply peer group pressure in business, government, and the judicial system in order to outlaw sexual harassment, along with all other forms of sex discrimination.

B. Industrial Democracy

The majority of North American organizations conduct their operations in a traditional, hierarchical manner. The organization is designed like a pyramid, with the workers on the lower levels reporting to managers above them. Decisions are made at the top of the organization, and orders flow down to be carried out by the employees below. In such an environment, a supervisor wields enormous power over subordinates. He can make unilateral determinations about pay increases, promotions, work assignments, discipline, and discharge. The employee in most cases has little or no ability to challenge such decisions. Sexual harassment flourishes under these conditions.

In recent times there has been a growing realization in Europe (and to some degree, similar discussions are taking place in North America) that an autocratic hierarchical work structure may adversely affect the quality of working life. Workers are becoming increasingly restless and intolerant of boring, mindless, repetitive jobs. Industrialists have begun to recognize that these employees' skills have gone untapped. It is becoming clear that the sharing of decision making between management and labor improves workers' self-perceptions and creates a more productive workforce, with a greater potential for job fulfillment.

Joint decision making—industrial democracy—can be introduced in a number of ways. The most obvious is through unionization. The employees of one organization organize collectively to acquire certification and bargaining rights from the appropriate labor relations board. By law the employer must recognize the union as the exclusive bargaining agent for its employees, and both the employer and the union must bargain in good faith over the creation of a series of contracts.

Once the organization is unionized, it is no longer management's prerogative to issue edicts covering wage levels, fringe benefits, discipline, and dismissal. Instead a code of behavior is set out in the contract that is binding on both parties. Management stipulates to pay employees at a certain level and to discipline and discharge only for "just cause." Sexually harassed employees immediately gain a forum in which to dispute a coercive dismissal or other job penalty.

In some contracts management also agrees not to discriminate against employees unfairly and to allow the union a voice in decisions concerning such issues as technological change. A specific grievance procedure is set forth in the contract to allow both management and the union to take action over a breach in the terms of the contract by the other party. When a complaint is lodged, it is generally heard through several levels of appeal inside the organization and is ultimately adjudicated by an impartial, outside arbitrator, who is chosen by both management and the union.

The unionization process is not always simple. Management, in many cases, will fight desperately to keep a union out. Despite labor law provisions, which make it illegal to discipline or dismiss an employee for union activity or to intimidate employees from exercising their rights to join a union, management antiunion tactics are often effective.

Once a union is certified, the battles continue. In the struggle to negotiate the best contract they can get, union members are often forced to strike and to take other collective action.

Despite the conflict such adversary methods create, the rewards are substantial. The workers gain input into the decision-making process. They not only obtain a hand in setting out the rules, but they also gain a powerful advocate in the union to help them seek redress against management when these rules are broken. Women union members can urge the union to bargain for specific contract provisions to outlaw sexual harassment; sexual harassment victims should be actively assisted by the union when seeking compensation.

Apart from unionization, there are a number of other variations on the industrial-democracy theme. Labor-management councils can be formed that can meet frequently to make decisions on a number of fronts—production quotas, work methods, pay scales, and so on. Such councils can also serve as an appeal forum to review disciplinary measures meted out by management. A sexually harassed employee may be able to seek a fair hearing from such a body, which would not be available from management acting alone.

Finally, organizations may be cooperatively owned and operated by the workers themselves. Instead of a rigid separation between the owners and the workers, the employees in such organizations collectively own the business and share the profits (or shoulder the losses). They can determine the policies of the organization as a group and establish appeal structures to review any individual disciplinary action.

All of these steps toward industrial democracy improve the balance of power. Power that has historically been wielded by management, acting according to its own dictates and interests, is being shifted to the employees. Where there is a more evenhanded sharing of decision making, there is a much better chance that coercive, exploitative managerial practices will not be tolerated. In the end result, sexual harassment victims, along with other victimized workers, stand to benefit substantially from collective action to secure a greater measure of equality in the workforce.

II. SHORT-TERM SOLUTIONS

A. Collective Action

We have come to the inevitable conclusion that individual victims of sexual harassment acting on their own behalf run the risk of further victimization. It takes tremendous courage and energy to complain publicly. The victim is almost certain to encounter skepticism and is often forced to prove that her personal life is above reproach. This proof of innocence may extend to the individual's mode of dress, conversation, and social life. An individual's courageous act may help those women who complain later, but she herself is personally open to the possibility of becoming a "sacrificial lamb."

A real and viable alternative lies in collective action. If two or more women register a joint complaint, the organization cannot treat sexual harassment as an isolated incident, placing the burden of proof on the victim. Our research indicates that sexual harassers rarely concentrate on one woman. The woman is usually one in a long list of victims. A woman new to the organization should question long-standing employees about her harasser's behavior with former employees. She should try to track down the other victims both inside and outside the organization. She may find that there are enough women who have suffered at the hands of the harasser that a petition is possible, demanding that management take immediate remedial action.

Collective action is a powerful short-term solution. No one woman will be singled out as the complainant, so personal habits become irrelevant. Collectively, women will be able to withstand the pressure to capitulate. Furthermore, the possibility of reprisals is significantly reduced. The organization will act quickly to attempt to negotiate a settlement. They will appreciate that collectively women have an excellent case to take to a human rights commission or to the courts. The publicity that this would generate could only serve to reflect negatively on the organization and the harasser.

B. Vigilante Tactics

Diana E. H. Russell in her book, *The Politics of Rape*, recommended that since most rape victims cannot expect justice within our judicial system, they should adopt a variety of vigilante tactics by organizing themselves into action groups. The tactics she describes can easily be adapted to sexual harassers.[1]

It would be very damaging to a harasser's career for a group of his victims to picket his place of work, carrying placards describing and condemning his behavior. It is also effective to hand out pamphlets at the same time that provide more specific information and a list of demands. The picketing and pamphleting need not be limited to the harasser's place of work. His home, his church, his clubs, and so on are all excellent places to extend these activities. Picketing and pamphleting could be supplemented with phone calls to his home or workplace, informing anyone who answers that he is a sexual harasser. Another self-help tactic that has been used with some success is to post notices identifying sexual harassers in the women's washrooms at the workplace.

Still another tactic that Ms. Russell suggests is posting pictures of the harasser around the community, warning women of his coercive activities on the job. Unquestionably this is the type of publicity the harasser would prefer to avoid. If the harasser is a well-known person, it is possible that the media may become involved.

Since sexual harassment is generally so difficult to prove in the absence of witnesses or other victims, the use of decoys is an imaginative and effective tactic. As an example, policewomen are often used as decoys in amassing evidence against men who solicit prostitutes, or in some instances where a man is suspected of rape. In sexual harassment cases, the decoy would try to have herself hired into the position vacated by the victim. Presumably the harasser would subject her to the same kind of treatment. She could not only substantiate the victim's allegations but could utilize a hidden tape recorder to record the exact words of the sexual harasser. So long as one party consents to a recording device (in this instance, the decoy), the evidence is admissible in a court of law.

It is unlikely that the victim of sexual harassment can employ the services of a policewoman, but she can hire a woman detective or enlist the help of friends. Failing this, there are enough concerned and outraged women who would be prepared to act on a victim's behalf. Those women, who have worked in the area of violence against women, are sufficiently versed in self-help tactics that they would be ideal collaborators.

Admittedly, these street tactics will provoke criticism and possible reprisals, such as libel suits or criminal charges for harassing telephone calls, but the results could be substantial. The tables will have turned, placing the harasser's career and reputation in jeopardy. Our adjudicative forums both within and outside our places of employment do not dispense evenhanded justice when dealing with cases of sexual harassment. Collective vigilante tactics will force these various forums to respond, recognizing that the victims are both serious and angry enough to take direct action.

C. Sexual Harassment Crisis Centers

Only two sexual harassment crisis centers have emerged in North America, one in New York City and one in the Boston area. With limited funds and staff, they have begun the monumental task of educating victims and the public about the nature and extent of sexual harassment. In addition, they provide a forum of research, counseling, and action. As long as the legal and political systems will not respond adequately to complaints of sexual harassment, these crisis centers serve as a lobby, as an advocate, and as a haven for victims.

On the most fundamental level, crisis centers assure the victims of sexual harassment that their plight is a deep-seated societal problem and not a personal failing. It is essential that women support and promote the extension of such centers across North America. Unlike action groups, sexual harassment crisis centers can engage in the long-term objective of overhauling antiquated, destructive attitudes and practices that allow sexual harassment to flourish.

III. NEW LEGISLATION

Legislative remedies are only as effective as the people who enforce them. As long as human rights agency personnel, court administrators, attorneys, and judges share the sexist attitudes held by the bulk of society, legal solutions will offer little relief.

The legislative and judicial systems, however, do respond to pressure from exploited groups. There is hope that new laws and a less discriminatory enforcement of such laws will improve the situation.

A. Employment-Standards Legislation

Any legislation that enacts a code of civil liberties in the workplace will increase the protection that can be made available to sexual harassment victims. To date, the focus of labor legislation has been on trade unions and collective bargaining. Employees who have not or cannot unionize are left to rely upon employment standards legislation, which sets minimum wages, hours of work, vacation pay, and so on. An overhaul of this legislation would do much to improve the working environment.

One example of positive legislative change involves recent amendments to federal Canadian employment standards legislation. These amendments extend protection to nonunion employees who are dismissed unfairly. Employees who have worked for their employer for twelve consecutive months will have the right to file a complaint if they feel they are discharged without cause. A federal government inspector will try to conciliate the case, and failing that, the issue will be referred to an adjudicator. The adjudicator will hold a hearing, and if it appears that the employee was discharged unfairly, the employee can be reinstated and/or awarded compensation.

This review system is much like the grievance procedure available to unionized employees. Sexually harassed women who find that they are discharged by the harasser will benefit from this type of law. Consideration should be given to enacting similar provisions in other jurisdictions. The obvious shortcoming is that the legislation protects only women who have been dismissed. Women who are forced to quit or who are harassed by the imposition of unfair working conditions will not be covered.

B. Sexual Harassment Legislation

The obvious problem with most of the existing laws is that they do not specifically address the issue of sexual harassment. For a variety of reasons, separate legislation should be enacted to outlaw sexual harassment. Initially the political process of passing new legislation will provide an excellent educational forum and may go some way toward deterring potential harassers. In addition, while sexual harassment is a form of sex discrimination, it is a distinct feature with special characteristics requiring carefully chosen legislative remedies. New laws must be tailored to fit this unique problem specifically.

1. Criminal or Civil Labor Legislation?

The initial question is whether legislation prohibiting sexual harassment should be criminal legislation or civil labor legislation. To put sexual harassment into criminal statutes would be attractive, because criminal law is the most serious form of legislation. There would be great educational value in enacting a law to make sexual harassment a crime. The obvious problem is that a criminal charge must be proved beyond a reasonable doubt, whereas in civil cases, the burden of proof is only the balance of probabilities. The higher standard required in criminal cases could result in far fewer convictions, and for this reason putting sexual harassment laws into civil labor legislation may be preferable.

2. Outright Prohibition or Protection from Coercion?

Sexual harassment laws could be framed in two ways. They could either outlaw sexual harassment itself, or they could be drafted to prevent job-related reprisals from being enforced against women who reject sexual advances on the job. Both approaches have positive and negative aspects.

It is appealing to envision laws that baldly prohibit sexual harassment, but there would be problems in trying to define "sexual harassment." This behavior can manifest itself in a variety of ways. To try to outline all of the possibilities would be too onerous a task. To define sexual harassment in a very general way runs the risk of being too unspecific.

It is likely more feasible to draft sexual harassment laws in such a manner that the sexual advance itself is not prohibited. Instead, it could be made unlawful for anyone to "discharge, discipline, refuse to hire, or discriminate in any other way with respect to terms and conditions of employment against any person for that person's rejection of sexual advances on the job." The drawback with this, of course, is that men can continue to harass so long as the woman does not feel able to object and so long as there are no employment consequences.

3. From Whom Should Women Be Protected?

Since employers, supervisors, co-workers, clients, and customers have all sexually harassed working women, the new law should extend to cover this range. The legislation could be drafted to prohibit employers from penalizing employees for having resisted the sexual advances of another person, whether or not that person is in the employ of the employer.

This protects the sexually harassed woman from any coercive actions from her employer based on her rejection of sexual harassment from management, co-workers, clients, and customers. However, this form of drafting allows a complaint to be lodged only against the employer. To allow complaints to be made against clients and customers would take it out of the realm of labor legislation and put it into a more general criminal law framework.

4. Constructive Dismissal

Since many women are forced to quit their jobs through sexual harassment, the new law should contain a constructive dismissal provision. It should clearly point out that employers are liable not only for firing, refusing to hire, disciplining, and so on, but also for cases where women feel compelled to leave their jobs due to sexual harassment.

5. Forum for Adjudication

The new sexual harassment laws could be enforced by an administrative tribunal or by the courts. Administrative tribunals are supposed to be less expensive, less time-consuming, and less legalistic and formal. However, in many cases the enforcement agency has taken over the control of the process, and it retains the authority to determine which cases go forward to adjudication and when. Courts are time-consuming, expensive, and formalistic, but the litigants retain control over the process. The preferable option would likely be to have an administrative tribunal to hear these cases but allow complainants the right to sue on the basis of this legislation on their own in court if they so wished.

6. Conciliation and Settlement

Most administrative tribunals endeavor to conciliate the vast proportion of the cases that come before them, thus removing the need for a hearing and adjudication. Conciliation can prove to be a useful tool in some instances. A conciliation officer can approach an employer after a complaint has been made and point out that there seems to be a serious problem with sexual harassment in the organization. The officer can make it clear that a full-blown hearing on the question will be of benefit to no one. It can be recommended that instead of adjudication, the organization can agree to compensate the victim of sexual harassment and to implement educational programs or internal dispute-solving mechanisms for the future. The resolution of such a case may be as satisfactory as if a hearing were held, and the sexual harassment victim will be spared the anguish and publicity associated with a hearing.

On the other hand, conciliation can be overused to a debilitating extent. To place all the emphasis on discussion, conciliation, and negotiation is too mild a technique. The coercive authority of the agency must back up any attempts at conciliation. The offending organization must realize that sexual harassment laws are enforced effectively and publicly and that conciliation techniques are only the first stage in the process. Furthermore, conciliation must not be allowed to drag on for lengthy periods of time. It might be useful to make the conciliation procedure optional, at the choice of the complainant. In addition, once a complaint is lodged, the agency could set a hearing date for a month later and then try to conciliate within the parameters of that deadline.

7. The Hearing

Some consideration must be given to whether the hearing should be open to the public and the media or closed to all but the participants in the case. In some cases neither party wants a public hearing. In others one party may want publicity, and the other may not. There is a public-educational value in having such adjudications reported by the media. The public interest will have to be weighed against the private embarrassment and individual damage that may be created by disclosure.

8. The Onus of Proof

Sexual harassment cases are very difficult to prove. There are few witnesses, and the woman is put in the position of trying to allege that her negative employment consequences are attributable to sexual harassment. With such clear-cut problems of proof, one solution would be to create a reverse onus in the new sexual harassment law. The sexual harassment victim would have to prove that she had been employed by the organization and that she had suffered employment reprisals. She would allege that these were due to sexual harassment, and the onus would shift to the organization to disprove that sexual harassment was the cause of the discipline or dismissal.

This type of reverse onus already exists in various labor statutes in a number of jurisdictions. One example involves employees who are discharged for union organizing. The employee makes the allegation that the union activity was the cause of the discharge, and the employer must then disprove this argument. The reasoning behind such a reverse onus is that the employer is the one who took the steps that caused harm to the employee. He knows why he took these steps and is thus in the best position to lay out the evidence. This analysis applies equally to sexual harassment cases. A reverse onus should be part of any new sexual harassment law.

9. Existing or New Forum

If an administrative agency is chosen to enforce the new law, it should not be the EEOC or existing human rights commissions. These agencies administer legislation dealing with race and other minority discrimination. Women are not a minority group. Sexism is different from racism and other discrimination facing minority individuals. Those who are the most concerned about racism are often the least concerned about sexism. Sexual harassment laws must be administered by a separate agency until we reach the point that sexual harassment is no longer so rampant in society that it exists inside human rights agencies.

Women's issues now fall second to the issues that concern other oppressed groups. The genuine liberal position is that race is more important. This attitude keeps sex discrimination perpetually second in a contest where there is never enough time and money to get beyond first place. As a result, a separate women's bureau should be formed to administer the sexual harassment law as well as other legislation dealing with sex discrimination.

10. Penalties: Punishment and Compensation

The new sexual harassment law should provide a comprehensive code of remedies that can be imposed once sexual harassment has been proven. The victim must be given the option of reinstatment and awarded financial compensation for wages lost and other expenses incurred. Fines should also be a possible penalty. The compensation and fines should be assessed against both the organization and the harasser personally.

If the sexual harassment case is not an isolated event but part of a larger problem in the organization, the agency or the courts should be able to force the organization to implement a program that will address this issue. Educational seminars, the establishment of a grievance procedure to adjudicate future complaints, and affirmative-action programs could be considered. Positive efforts to prevent future occurrences and to deal fairly with complaints will provide a welcome response to evidence of sexual harassment.

IV. A SEXUAL TABOO IN THE WORKPLACE

As long as so many men use sex in so many ways as a weapon to keep down the women with whom they work, how can we develop mature, give-and-take working relationships?[2]

The late Margaret Mead asked this question as a prelude to proposing a new sex taboo in the workplace. As Dr. Mead accurately pointed out, with almost half of all adult women in the workforce, there are serious discrepancies. Boys are brought up at home and at school to respond to women in outmoded ways. They become men who cannot be trusted alone with a woman. They are angry and frustrated by having to treat a woman as an equal—either as a female with power who must be cajoled or as a female without power who can be coerced. At the same time we are teaching our daughters to expect a very different working world, one in which both women and men are full and equal participants.[3]

Dr. Mead disagreed that legislation alone will ensure this equitable partnership. It was her contention that basic taboos, "the deeply and intensely felt prohibitions against 'unthinkable' behavior," are what keep the system in balance. Taboos affirm what we hold most precious in our human relationships.

We are, she maintained, in a period of transition that requires new taboos to assist in the development of "decent sex mores" in the workplace. An incest taboo, she believed, will protect women from victimization. Neither men nor women should expect that sex can be used to victimize women who need to keep their jobs, or to keep women from advancement, or to help men advance their own careers. The incest taboo

Dr. Mead proposed flatly asserts, "You don't make passes at or sleep with the people you work with."

This incest taboo, similar to the one that exists between brothers and sisters, would assist men and women in the development of lifelong relationships based on mutual respect.

Dr. Mead looked toward a working relationship that is effortless and that encourages men and women to respect each other as persons.[4] With this incest taboo, Dr. Mead insisted, a woman will be judged solely on her skill, ability, and experience and perceived as a whole person rather than a sex object open to sexual exploitation.[5]

Notes

CHAPTER 2

1. *The New York Times,* August 23, 1977.
2. Sam Janus, Barbara Bess, and Carol Saltus, *A Sexual Profile of Men in Power* (New York: Warner Books, 1977), p. 62.
3. *The Globe and Mail* (Toronto), August 23, 1977, p. 12.
4. *Washington, D.C. Area Feminist Alliance* (Washington, D.C.: Task Force on Violence Against Women of the D.C. Area Feminist Alliance, 1978), p. 1.

CHAPTER 3

1. *The Evening Telegram* (Toronto), February 9–27, 1915.
2. Ivy Pinchbeck, *Women Workers and the Industrial Revolution, 1750–1850* (London: Frank Cass & Co. Ltd., 1930), pp. 310–11.
3. Wanda Fraiken Neff, *Victorian Working Women, An Historical and Literary Study of Women in British Industries and Professions, 1832–1850* (New York: AMS Press Inc., 1966), p. 85.
4. *Report of the Royal Commission on the Relations of Labour and Capital in Canada,* 1889; Susan Mann Trofimenkoff, "One Hundred and Two Muffled Voices: Canada's Industrial Women in the 1880s," *Grow Paper* no. 10 (Toronto: Group for Research on Women, Ontario Institute for Studies in Education).
5. *Report,* vol. 5, p. 368, fn. 4.
6. Ibid., vol. 4, pp. 319–20.
7. Ibid., vol. 4, p. 438.
8. Neff, *Victorian Working Women,* p. 55, fn. 3; Friederich Engels, *The Condition of the Working Class in England in 1844* (Stanford, California: Stanford University Press, 1958).

9. Edward Shorter, "Female Emancipation, Birth Control and Fertility in European History," *American Historical Review* 78 (1973); 605–40.

10. Louise A. Tilly, Joan W. Scott, Miriam Cohen, "Women's Work and European Fertility Patterns," *Journal of Interdisciplinary History* 6, no. 3 (Winter 1976); 447–76.

11. Pinchbeck, *Women Workers*, fn. 2, pp. 86–90, 100.

12. Ibid, p. 243.

13. Neff, *Victorian Working Women*, p. 73, fn. 3.

14. Pinchbeck, *Women Workers*, p. 262, fn. 2.

15. Elizabeth Hasanovitz, *One of Them* (New York: Houghton Mifflin, 1918).

16. Charlotte Baum, Paula Hyman, Sonya Michel, *The Jewish Woman in American* (New York: New American Library, 1975), p. 136.

17. *Report*, vol. 5, p. 368, fn 4.

18. Wayne Roberts, *Honest Womanhood: Feminism, Femininity and Class Consciousness among Toronto Working Women, 1893–1914* (Toronto: New Hogtown Press, 1976).

19. *Boston Daily Times*, January 16, 1839.

20. Lori Rotenberg, "The Wayward Worker: Toronto's Prostitute at the Turn of the Century," in *Women at Work, 1850–1930* (Toronto: Canadian Women's Educational Press, 1974), p. 40.

21. Ibid., p. 38.

22. Jeanne Westin, *Making Do* (Chicago: Follett Publishing Company, 1976), p. 96.

23. Barbara Mayer Wertheimer, *We Were There: The Story of Working Women in America* (New York: Pantheon Books, Inc., 1977), p. 240.

24. *Hansard*, House of Commons Debates, Canada, Session 1890, pp. 3164–65.

25. Ibid., p. 3169.

26. Ibid., pp. 365–67.

27. Ibid., pp. 366–67.

28. *R. v. Jones* (1934), 63 C.C.C. 341.

29. Debates of the Senate of Canada, Session 1920, p. 701.

30. Mary Bularzik, "Sexual Harassment at the Workplace: Historical Notes," *Radical America*, 1978, Vol. 12, No. 4, pp. 25–28.

31. Ibid., p. 31.

CHAPTER 5

1. *The Globe and Mail* (Toronto), August 17, 1977.

2. 1977 Criminal Code, s. 153 (1) (b).

3. *R.v. Johnston*, 1948 C.C.C. 59.

190 SEXUAL HARASSMENT ON THE JOB

4. *R. v. Jones*, 63 C.C.C. 341; *R. v. Blanchard* (1941), 75 C.C.C. 279; *St.-Hilaire v. R.*, 1966, 3 C.C.C. 31 (Que. C.A.).

5. 390 F. Supp. 161 (1975), U.S. Dist. Ct., D. Arizona.

6. 418 F. Supp. 233 (1976), U.S. Dist. Ct., N.D. California.

7. 422 F. Supp. 553 (1976), U.S. Dist. Ct., New Jersey.

8. *Williams v. Saxbe*, 413 F. Supp. 654 (1976), U.S. Dist. Ct., Dist. of Columbia, is an excellent example of such a case, although space does not permit a full examination of its findings.

9. 561 F. 2d 983 (1977), U.S. Ct. of Appeals, Dist. of Columbia Circuit.

10. 316 A.2d 549 (1974), S. Ct. of New Hampshire.

11. *Samms v. Eccles* (1961), found in Wright & Linden, *Canadian Tort Law*, 6th Edition (Toronto: Butterworths, 1975), pp. 52–54.

CHAPTER 6

1. Working Women United Institute, 593 Park Avenue, New York, New York, 10021.

2. Lin Farley, *Hearings on Sex Discrimination in Employment*, Testimony given before the New York State Assembly Labor Committee, December 8, 1976, p. 5.

3. Alliance Against Sexual Coercion, P.O. Box 1, Cambridge, Massachusetts, 02139.

CHAPTER 7

1. Paula Kane and Christopher Chandler, *Sex Objects in the Sky* (Chicago: Follett Publishing Co., 1974), p. 112.

CHAPTER 8

1. Evelyn Reed, *Problems of Women's Liberation* (New York: Pathfinder Press Inc., 1972), p. 81.

2. Michael Korda, *Male Chauvinism: How It Works* (New York: Random House, Inc., 1973), p. 108. Reproduced by permission of Random House, Inc.

3. From *Games Mother Never Taught You* by Betty Lehan Harragan (New York: Rawson Associates Publishers, Inc., 1977), pp. 289–93. Copyright © 1977 by Betty Lehan Harragan. Reprinted by permission of Rawson Associates Publishers, Inc.

4. *Toronto Star,* June 5, 1978.

5. Harragan, *Games Mother Never Taught You,* p. 299.

6. Ibid., p. 297.

7. Charles Winick and Paul Kinsie, *The Lively Commerce* (New York: Quadrangle/The New York Times Book Co., Inc., 1971).

CHAPTER 9

1. John T. Molloy, *The Woman's Dress for Success Book* (Chicago: Follett Publishing Co., 1977), pp. 34–35.

2. Ibid., p. 38.

3. Margaret Hennig and Anne Jardim, *The Managerial Woman* (New York: Anchor Press/Doubleday & Co., Inc., 1977), p. 173.

CHAPTER 11

1. Diana E. H. Russell, *The Politics of Rape: The Victim's Perspective* (New York: Stein and Day Publishers, 1974), p. 286.

2. Margaret Mead, "A Proposal: We Need Taboos on Sex at Work," *Redbook,* April 1978, p. 31.

3. Ibid.

4. Ibid., p. 33.

5. Ibid., p. 38.

Index

STATUE
OF LIBERTY
ENLIGHTENING
THE WORLD

By Rodman Gilder

THE NEW YORK TRUST COMPANY

100 BROADWAY

TEN ROCKEFELLER PLAZA

MADISON AVENUE AND FORTIETH STREET

718
$385

19644

PRINTED IN LETTERPRESS AND PHOTOGRAVURE
BY WILLIAM E. RUDGE'S SONS IN JUNE 1943

nov. 1943

The New York Trust Company wishes to make special acknowledgement to Harry T. Peters for his valued counsel and for access to his superb collection of prints; to George H. Eckhardt for his guidance; and to the author, Rodman Gilder, Director, American Scenic and Historic Preservation Society; Trustee, New York Society Library; Trustee, City History Club; Past Member of Art Commission, City of New York; and author of "The Battery."

⚜ FOREWORD ⚜

For many years, The New York Trust Company has used a representation of the Statue of Liberty as its symbol. Such use was prompted by an enduring regard for the statue and belief in the ideals for which it stands.

Our interest in the statue dates from the formation in 1889 of the New York Security and Trust Company, whose incorporators were represented through William L. Strong on the American Committee for the Statue of Liberty and its Finance Committee. The Statue of Liberty itself had then been dedicated on Bedloe's Island only three years before, but was already strongly identified with the harbor and city of New York — a name featured in our corporate title adopted in 1905. The Liberty National Bank, formed in 1891, naturally used the symbol during its thirty years of separate existence. Through this bank, which·was merged with The New York Trust Company in 1921, we acquired the model of the great monument cast by Bartholdi. This small statue now stands in the lobby of our Main Office, located in lower Manhattan, a short distance from the Battery from which the famous statue may be viewed.

This model and a counterpart whose present whereabouts is unknown, if indeed it still exists, were the first bronze castings made by the sculptor from the clay "sketch." As was the custom, refinements were made in the mould and finishing, especially affecting the crown and torch. Our model is signed by Bartholdi and dated "1875 — Registered in Washington, August 31, 1876." The second date refers to the deposit of the two models in the United States Patent Office under the law of the day. Upon the disposal of patent models by the Patent Office, the two small statues passed into private ownership — one of them eventually coming into our care as an irreplaceable and treasured possession.

Today, when the forces of liberty are struggling once more against the forces of oppression, it seems fitting to consider some of the motives underlying the creation of the greatest of all symbols of human freedom — the Statue of Liberty. To that purpose, this book is dedicated.

John E. Bierwirth
PRESIDENT

ORIGINAL BRONZE MODEL
OF THE STATUE OF LIBERTY

One of two casts by the sculptor registered in the United States Patent Office.
Now in the lobby of the Main Office of The New York Trust Company.

STATUE
OF LIBERTY
ENLIGHTENING
THE WORLD

More than half a century ago, the torch of the Statue of Liberty was raised in New York Harbor, a beacon to guide the free men of the world. The statue has come to be regarded as the token of the solemn pledge of one free people to the downtrodden of other lands that in the United States of America there will always exist equality under the law, and that in one land the rights of man will always be respected and guarded.

Although the statue itself is little more than one-third as old as the Nation, the ideals forged into the metal and built into the stone of the base are as eternal as liberty itself. They go directly back to the American Revolution, when a small band of brave men built strong foundations upon which arose the structure of a great nation.

Millions have seen the monument on Bedloe's Island from the Battery and from ships and many thousands visit it every year; yet not every American has actually laid eyes on the statue in its full grandeur. Nevertheless, its deep significance is understood throughout this entire "nation conceived in liberty." The towering statue has a profound symbolic meaning for every American soldier and sailor going forth from the port of New York to defend his own and his country's liberty. When they return in triumph, our vic-

ÉDOUARD RENÉ
DE LABOULAYE

1811–1883

As proof of the friendship and the community of emotions of the people of the two countries, Laboulaye pointed out that the people of the United States honored the remembrance of common glories, and loved Lafayette and his volunteers as they revered American heroes. He declared that this common heritage was of far greater importance in America than the political acts of the French government.

Adapted from *Harper's Weekly*, December 15, 1866.

torious fighting men will greet this mighty symbol — as they have in the past — with shouts and often with tears.

More than 18,000,000 immigrants, it is estimated, have entered this country through the port of New York since the monument was unveiled. For them the first sight of Liberty was an experience never to be forgotten.

₹ *Origin of the Idea* ₹

In 1865, a little group of French men-of-letters, artists and politicians met at the home of Édouard René de Laboulaye near Versailles, France. Of all Frenchmen, only Lafayette had exceeded Laboulaye in his love for the United States, and it was said that the mantle of that hero descended upon his shoulders. Better than any of his countrymen, Laboulaye recognized the bond of a common love for liberty that existed between the people of France and the United States.

Although a subject of Napoleon III, this outspoken republican had in 1850 printed a discourse on the American Constitution and "the utility of studying it," had written a learned "Political History of the United States," a paper on the youth of Benjamin Franklin, and a novel, "Paris in America," in which a character says: "The folly of love and the madness of ambition are sometimes curable, but no one was ever cured of a mania for liberty." In the same book, liberty is described as the "daughter of the Gospel — sister of justice and pity — mother of equality, abundance, and peace."

It was decided that the French should give to the Americans some great token that would be a symbol of eternal friendship. This was to be a gift from a people to a people, not from a government to a government.

🗽 *The Sculptor Bartholdi* 🗽

One of Laboulaye's guests was a bearded young Alsatian sculptor, Auguste Bartholdi. The Franco-Prussian War a few years later found Bartholdi taking part, as an organizer of the Garde Na-

AUGUSTE BARTHOLDI

1834–1904

An early portrait of Bartholdi, showing him as a young man with fire and inspiration

Adapted from *Scribner's Monthly,* June 1877.

tionale, in the hopeless defense of his native Alsace against this latest invasion from the east. He also served on the staff of Garibaldi in the Army of the Vosges. After the total defeat of the French Emperor and armies, and while civil war was raging in Paris, Bartholdi decided to make his long-deferred visit to the United States.

As he reached these shores, the definite plan for the monument which he was to build to Franco-American friendship became clear in his mind. "The picture that is presented to the view when one arrives at New York," he declared, "is marvelous: when — after some days of voyaging — in the pearly radiance of a beautiful morning is revealed the magnificent spectacle of those immense cities, of those rivers extending as far as the eye can reach, festooned with masts and flags; when one awakes, so to speak, in the midst of that interior sea covered with vessels — some giants in size, some dwarfs — which swarm about puffing, whistling, swinging the great arms of their uncovered walking beams, moving to and fro like a crowd upon a public square, it is thrilling. It is indeed, the New World, which appears in its majestic expanse with the ardor of its glowing life. Was it not wholly natural that the artist was inspired by this spectacle? Yes, in this very place shall be raised the statue of Liberty, as grand as the idea which it embodies, casting radiance upon the two worlds. If, then, the form of the accomplished work is

BARTHOLDI'S STATUE OF LAFAYETTE

Union Square, New York.
Presented to the City by French residents of New York.

Adapted from *Scribner's Monthly*, June, 1877.

Adapted from *Scribner's Monthly*, June, 1877.

BARTHOLDI'S OWN PRELIMINARY SKETCH
OF THE STATUE OF LIBERTY ENLIGHTENING THE WORLD

"The Statue was born for this place which inspired its conception," wrote Bartholdi. "May God be pleased to bless my efforts and my work and to crown it with the success, the duration, and moral influence which it ought to have."

Note in the background Brooklyn Bridge, then under construction; it was opened in 1883.

---

mine, to the Americans I owe the thought and the inspiration which gave it birth."

"To the sculptor form is everything and is nothing; it is nothing without the spirit — with the idea it is everything," said Victor Hugo in a personal message written later to Bartholdi, whose project the aged author encouraged from the beginning. Bartholdi's sculpture at its best was inspired by the spirit, the idea of his subject. His most famous work in France is the colossal stone "Lion of Belfort" on a mountain side — a lion at bay, unyielding and defiant. The idea was the superb defense of Belfort against seventy-three days of shattering Prussian bombardment. The idea of France bringing timely aid to our newborn nation is expressed in Bartholdi's statue — in Union Square, New York — of the youthful, ardent Lafayette stepping ashore from a small boat, pressing his sword against his heart as he offers heart and sword to General Washington.

Although the monument to the friendship of the two nations was conceived by the artist as a colossus on a pedestal, Bartholdi was resolved that it should not seem colossal, except to those who came near its base. It was to be larger than any known statue ancient or modern, but in the immense picture surrounding it, in a harbor all of twenty square miles in area, it was to "appear simply in harmony with the whole, and have the normal aspect of a statue in a public square."

The site chosen by Bartholdi was the small island about a mile and a half southwest of the tip of Manhattan. Before 1664, when the city was called New Amsterdam, the island belonged to one Isaack Bedloo, who came here from Calais, France. Its later names included Love Island (after Governor Lovelace), Oyster, Kennedy's, and Liberty Island. When Bartholdi arrived, he saw on Bedloe's Island the star-shaped ramparts of Fort Wood (named

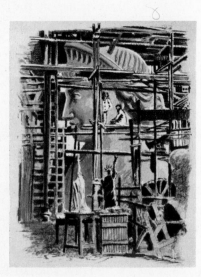

THE HEAD OF
BARTHOLDI'S STATUE

In the workshop of Gaget, Gauthier & Cie., 25 Rue de Chazelles, Paris. Here Bartholdi's chief assistants were the sculptor Simon; supervisor of copper work, Bergeret; and the modeller, Baron.

Note the two small "Models of the Committee" on benches in the foreground.

Adapted from *St. Nicholas*, July, 1884.

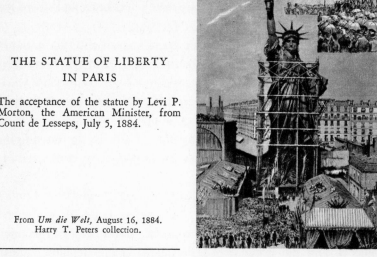

THE STATUE OF LIBERTY
IN PARIS

The acceptance of the statue by Levi P. Morton, the American Minister, from Count de Lesseps, July 5, 1884.

From *Um die Welt,* August 16, 1884. Harry T. Peters collection.

after Col. Eleazar D. Wood, a hero of the War of 1812). This fort had been built in 1811, upon much earlier fortifications, to command the main channel of the harbor. In his imagination, the sculptor saw the pedestal and statue of his monument rising from the centre of the fort.

Bartholdi, following the advice of Laboulaye, set about acquainting himself with our country and travelled as far west as San Francisco. He met, among many others, President Grant; Lieutenant-General Philip H. Sheridan, who had studied first hand the conduct of the Franco-Prussian War; Peter Cooper, manufacturer and philanthropist; John W. Forney, newspaper editor, politician, and European Commissioner for the projected exposition in Philadelphia; and Charles Sumner. In New England, he was cordially received by the scientist Agassiz and the poet Longfellow. Sumner and Longfellow, ideal subjects for a sculptor, made the deepest impression upon him. They listened to his story and examined his sketch in water colors which foretold how the colossal statue would look in the midst of the vast "upper bay" of New York.

After Bartholdi's return to Paris, Laboulaye, then a member of the Chamber of Deputies, organized a "Union Franco-Américaine" whose first public appeal for Statue of Liberty funds, in October, 1875, was signed by twenty-one men, including descendants of fighting French noblemen who helped this country win its independence—Noailles, Rochambeau, and Lafayette. Two American signatures appeared, those of John W. Forney and Elihu B. Washburne, our Minister to France, the only foreign envoy who stuck to his post during the dreadful siege of Paris. Washburne had been, for a time, Grant's Secretary of State.

🗽 *Money for the Statue* 🗽

Contributions came in from ordinary citizens, deputies, cabinet officers, and the popular old President of the Republic, Marie Edmé Patrice Maurice MacMahon, a hero of the Crimean War, Marshal of France, who in 1870 had been wounded, overwhelmed and captured at Sedan. The City of Paris gave $2000. No contribution was asked or received from the French Government.

The fund was not large enough to finish the whole work in time for the Philadelphia Exposition in 1876; but the right forearm, hand and torch were there for the more than nine million visitors to see. After the fair, this exhibit was displayed, on the Fifth Avenue side of Madison Square, New York City, until in 1884 it was sent back to Paris.

THE ORIGINAL MODEL OF THE STATUE OF LIBERTY

This clay model was completed by Bartholdi in 1875 and approved by the Franco-American Union. It is in the Bartholdi Museum in Colmar, France.

Inset:

BARTHOLDI'S MOTHER

Charlotte Beysser Bartholdi was the model for the Statue of Liberty.
This painting is also in the Bartholdi Museum in Colmar, France.

National Park Service.

Adapted from *St. Nicholas*, July, 1884.

THE HEAD OF THE STATUE

Exhibited in Paris before being sent to America.

At the Paris Exposition of 1878, the colossal head of Liberty was exhibited and was found to be spacious enough to accommodate forty visitors at a time.

"La Liberté Éclairant le Monde," a hymn by the playwright, Émile Guiard, was set to music by Charles Gounod, composer of "Faust," and was sung at the Paris Opera. The refrain, translated, was: "The rays of my torch, piercing the darkness, bring lost ships to safe anchorage and carry my light to the oppressed."

With the sanction of the French Government, a lottery was organized for the benefit of the fund. Three hundred thousand tickets were sold at one franc, then worth about twenty cents. Two hundred small terra cotta replicas of the statue were also sold — each signed by Bartholdi and registered—at 1000 francs in France and, to cover duty and shipping costs, at $300 in this country. These were almost exact copies of the original "study model" whose height was 1.25 meters (about 4 feet). Two bronze copies of the "study model" were sent here and registered in the United States Patent Office in 1876.

The Union Franco-Américaine announced in 1880 that the fund was complete. Contributions had been received from 5000 subscribers, including 181 cities and ten municipal chambers of commerce.

The unique task that Bartholdi and his associates had set themselves attracted wide attention: they had no less than 300,000 visitors to their workshop from far and near. Ex-President Grant showed his interest by visiting the shop on his journey around the world in 1877.

🎋 *Building of the Monument* 🎋

In Egypt, at twenty, Bartholdi had gazed with deep emotion upon the colossal, centuries-old "granite beings, in their imperturbable majesty . . . whose kindly and impassible glance seems to disregard the present and to be fixed upon the unlimited future." He said that he learned then that the treatment of a colossal statue must be entirely different from that of heroic, life-size, or smaller sculpture. "The details of the lines ought not to arrest the eye . . . the surfaces should be broad and simple, defined by a bold and clear design, accentuated in the important places . . . it should have a summarized character such as one would give to a rapid sketch."

Starting with the 1.25-meter model, a complete statue 2.85 meters high was built, followed by another four times as high, this latter being about one-fourth the size of the completed masterpiece. At each stage, the sculptor made changes in order to conform to the principle of the utmost simplicity in the final work. Bartholdi's final modifications in design had to be made in the one-fourth-size model of plaster supported by its wooden frame. No further changes were possible.

The statue was divided into about 300 sections, and each section enlarged to four times its size by the painstaking, mathematical

process of "pointing up," in this case involving many thousands of measurements and as many verifications. Against the plaster surface of each of these enlarged sections was built and fitted precisely a stout mould of laminated wood. Into each wooden mould, a sheet (one square meter or larger) of virgin copper, 2.5 millimeters or about one-tenth of an inch in thickness, was pressed by means of rammers, levers, and mallets large and small. In the case of complicated shapes, the copper had to be heated. Wrought iron bands and rods gave rigidity to each of the copper sections, which were feather-edged and held together with one-fifth-inch flush-headed copper rivets.

The "noble rust," as Italians call it, which gives copper and bronze so beautiful a surface color, has—aided by the salt-laden air of New York Harbor — covered the Statue of Liberty with a

Harper's Weekly, October 30, 1886.

malachite green that does not disintegrate the metal as rust devours iron.

The iron skeleton of the statue, now anchored deep in the base of the masonry pedestal, was designed by the noted bridge-builder, Alexandre Gustave Eiffel, who later designed and built the Eiffel Tower. Between the skeleton and the exterior of the statue is a secondary iron structure.

In designing the interior structure, Eiffel took into account the possible violence of gales on the Atlantic seaboard and provided a generous margin of strength. (The well anchored statue was virtually uninjured on July 30, 1916, by the tremendous Black Tom eruptions in Jersey City which destroyed some $22,000,000 of munitions and other property.) Galvanic action was avoided by insulation between all iron and copper parts. (This now consists of asbestos, soaked in shellac.) Folds of the statue's drapery gave ample opportunity for expansion or contraction of the copper resulting from changes in temperature. Lightning is conducted by copper rods into the earth.

🔥 *Liberty Rises in Paris* 🔥

To honor the centenary of the surrender—which the French fleet and army made possible—at Yorktown on October 19, 1781, the first rivet was ceremoniously placed in the statue by the then American Minister to France, Levi P. Morton, Vice President of the United States in President Benjamin Harrison's administration, 1889–1893, and Governor of New York State from 1895 to 1897.

From *Leslie's Weekly,* June 20, 1885. Harry T. Peters collection.

THE TORCH OF THE STATUE OF LIBERTY AS IT WAS ENVISIONED BEFORE PLACEMENT

The statue, 151 feet 1 inch in height, set up without a pedestal in the Rue de Chazelles, on high ground three-fifths of a mile northeast of the Arc de l'Étoile, towered above the skyline established by Baron Haussmann and, to the amazement of all Paris, topped even the Vendôme Column. Its completion was celebrated at a dinner given to Bartholdi, May 21, 1884, by Henry F. Gillig, at which the sculptor received the compliments of the French and American guests, including Senator Jules François Jeannotte-Bozérian, former United States Minister Edward F. Noyes, and Count Ferdinand de Lesseps, engineer of the Suez Canal.

Senator Bozérian, declaring that Bartholdi's masterpiece was a work of filial piety as well as of patriotism and art, said:

"On the day that I, with many others, first harnessed myself to the success of our work, which is now reaching its happy conclusion, M. Bartholdi said to me, 'Come with me to the opera. You will understand later the special reason for my invitation.' I accepted. We entered a stage box, in a corner of which sat a lady of imposing appearance. Finding myself near Bartholdi, I said to him, 'That is the statue of Liberty Enlightening the World.' He pressed my hand, saying: 'Yes, it is.' Do you know who that lady was? It was Bartholdi's mother." She had, indeed, posed for the

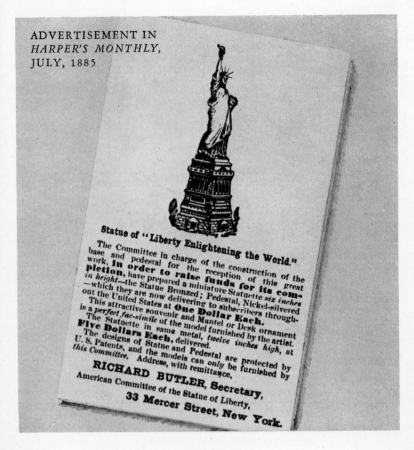

ADVERTISEMENT IN
HARPER'S MONTHLY,
JULY, 1885

Statue of "Liberty Enlightening the World."

The Committee in charge of the construction of the base and pedestal for the reception of this great work, **in order to raise funds for its completion,** have prepared a miniature Statuette *six inches in height*—the Statue Bronzed; Pedestal, Nickel-silvered —which they are now delivering to subscribers throughout the United States at **One Dollar Each.** This attractive souvenir and Mantel or Desk ornament is a *perfect fac-simile* of the model furnished by the artist. **Five Dollars Each,** in same metal, *twelve inches high,* at The Statuette delivered. The designs of Statue and Pedestal are protected by U. S. Patents, and the models can *only* be furnished by this Committee. Address, with remittance,

RICHARD BUTLER, Secretary,
American Committee of the Statue of Liberty,
33 Mercer Street, New York.

Statue. Charlotte Beysser Bartholdi was the inspiration of her son. It was she who kept afire in him his desire to make this statue and it was fitting that she should thus be immortalized.

Three weeks later, the sculptor was honored with a banquet by United States Minister Morton. On this occasion, Admiral Peyron announced that the French Government would furnish a vessel to convey the colossus to New York.

On the Fourth of July, 1884, in the presence of members of the French Cabinet, and others, Count de Lesseps, representing the Union Franco-Américaine, formally presented the statue to the United States in the person of Mr. Morton, who had been authorized to receive it.

The statue, weighing about 220 tons, of which the copper weighed about 88 tons, was dismantled. The sections were numbered and packed in 210 wooden cases and at Rouen put aboard the government steamship *Idsère,* which sailed May 21, 1885, for New York.

National Park Service.

THE TORCH OF THE STATUE OF LIBERTY
In Madison Square, New York, after the Philadelphia Exposition, in 1876, to 1884.

Before the departure of the vessel, American residents of Paris presented to the city a reduced copy of the statue. First set up in the Place des États Unis, it was moved in 1889 to the downstream end of the long Isle des Cygnes and there re-dedicated by Marie François Sadi Carnot, President of the Republic, who received it from the American minister plenipotentiary, Whitelaw Reid, editor and publisher of the *New-York Tribune.*

At this ceremony, Eugene Spuller, Minister of Foreign Affairs, declared that the two great republics "united in the past by services rendered are united at present by a common principle, and will be united in the future by the benefits that Liberty will produce for humanity."

🐦 *This Side of the Atlantic* 🐦

Great monuments are often long a-building. The Washington Monument on the banks of the Potomac took thirty-six years—the Bunker Hill Monument twenty-eight. The Statue of Liberty was inaugurated eleven years after the French began to raise funds for the sculpture; and the American campaign for money to build the pedestal lasted about nine years.

By the time the *Idsère*—loaded with the hammered copper and wrought iron of the largest and in some respects the most significant statue known to history—was sighted off Sandy Hook on June 16, 1885, New York and the nation were ready to receive appropriately the extraordinary gift from the people of France. But this state of mind had been reached with no undue haste.

Although it was known here that $10,000 had already been contributed in France to the fund for building the statue and that Bartholdi was continuing his work, no money whatever was collected by the end of 1876 to build the pedestal and provide for the reception of the gift.

William M. Evarts, William H. Appleton, Samuel D. Babcock, John Jay, and William H. Wickham called a meeting at the Century Club to organize an American Committee for the Statue of Liberty. On January 2, 1877, Richard Butler, Joseph H. Choate, Frederic Coudert, James F. Dwight, George Jones (one of the cofounders of *The New York Times*), Edward Moran, James W. Pinchot, Theodore Roosevelt (father of the future President Theodore Roosevelt), H. F. Spaulding, Anson Phelps Stokes and other substantial citizens attended. Evarts was elected chairman, Spaulding treasurer, and Butler secretary. The original committee of 114 was later enlarged to more than 400. The Executive Committee consisted of Joseph W. Drexel, Parke Godwin, V. Mumford Moore, James W. Pinchot, and Frederick A. Potts. Louis de Bébian, Henry Hentz, Edward Kemp, Charles Lanier, Henry G. Marquand, William L. Strong, and S. V. White formed the Finance Committee, whose duty was to raise $125,000, the amount then deemed necessary.

The prompt action of a sub-committee on legislation—Evarts, Godwin, Pinchot, Clark Bell and Ex-Governor of New York, Edwin D. Morgan—resulted in the passage on Washington's Birthday, 1877, of a joint resolution of Congress which stated that "Liberty Enlightening the World" was to be given and erected by French citizens and that the pedestal was to be built by private subscription. The resolution authorized and directed the President to accept the statue when presented "and to designate and set apart for the erection thereof a suitable site upon either Governor's or Bedloe's Island, in the harbor of New York; and upon the completion thereof shall cause the same to be inaugurated with such ceremonies as will serve to testify the gratitude of our people for this expressive and felicitous memorial of the sympathy of our sister republic; and he is hereby authorized to cause suitable regulations to be made for its future maintenance as a beacon, and for the permanent care and preservation thereof as a monument of art, and of the continual good will of the great nation which aided in our struggle for freedom."

The Finance Committee met with many serious difficulties. Some

From *Leslie's Weekly*, November 6, 1886.

"THE GRAND DEMONSTRATION ON LIBERTY DAY,
OCTOBER 28 — THE MILITARY AND CIVIC PROCES-
SION PASSING DOWN LOWER BROADWAY WITH THE
NAVAL PAGEANT IN THE DISTANCE."

Veteran firemen, dragging their apparatus, were the principal feature of
the parade, here viewed from approximately 100 Broadway.

---

rich patrons of the arts were slow to accept the merits of the statue.
Less solvent citizens held back because they felt that the many rich
men of the nation's commercial metropolis could easily contribute
the required money. The New York public was apathetic. And
to raise money for this purpose outside of New York City was
difficult.

THE ILLUMINATION OF NEW YORK HARBOR

Illumination of New York Harbor on the first clear night
after the unveiling of the statue.

Ground was broken on Bedloe's Island in April, 1883, but exca-
vating was delayed until October. By January 4, 1884, the fund
had reached $125,000. This amount was clearly inadequate. The
foundation without the pedestal cost $93,830.61. It was explained
that the miscalculation was the result of hidden masses of con-
crete and masonry under Fort Wood, within whose ramparts the
monument was to be erected.

In December, 1884, President Arthur recommended to Congress an appropriation to complete the pedestal. (The massive
base, fifty-three feet deep, was already built.) A joint resolution
to this effect died in committee. A later attempt to draw on the
Federal Treasury failed. Governor Grover Cleveland vetoed, on
constitutional grounds, a bill passed by the State Legislature to

enable the City of New York to contribute $50,000 to the pedestal fund.

Only fifteen feet had been built of the eighty-nine-foot pedestal. This had been designed by the distinguished American architect, Richard M. Hunt, who had received a nine-year professional training in France. Sealed into the cornerstone was a history of the statue, and other items.

The treasurer of the American Committee announced early in March, 1885, that only $3000 was left of the $182,491.40 laboriously collected during the previous eight years, and that there was no prospect of further contributions.

🗽 *The* World's *Campaign* 🗽

These were the circumstances when a newspaper stepped into the breach to bring success as the press has done in so many other instances of worthy projects threatened with failure. The New York *World*, recently bought by Joseph Pulitzer, started on March 15 a remarkable campaign to raise the $100,000 still needed for the pedestal. Pulitzer had emigrated from Hungary to the United States in time to serve in the Union Army in 1864; twenty years later, as the new editor of the *World*, he had played an important part in the election of Cleveland to the Presidency.

The *World*, with the largest newspaper circulation (less than 150,000) in the United States, contended that, as the statue was a gift of the French people, the money for the pedestal should come from the people of our whole nation. It rejoiced when a subscription of $500 was received from a resident of Chicago. The newspaper itself contributed $1000, and called upon the poor and rich to save New York and the nation from the disgrace of failure to complete the project. Almost daily it hammered away. A cartoon, appearing repeatedly at the head of Statue of Liberty news, showed Uncle Sam, hat in hand, soliciting subscriptions for the pedestal. The *World* encouraged all sorts of theatrical, musical and sports

From *Leslie's Weekly*, July 2, 1887. Harry T. Peters collection.

"WELCOME TO THE LAND OF FREEDOM — OCEAN STEAMER
PASSING THE STATUE OF LIBERTY—SEEN FROM THE STEERAGE
DECK"

---

benefits for the fund. It publicized a plan of the American Committee to sell statuettes of "Liberty" at one to five dollars each. Illustrated sheet music composed in honor of the statue was lithographed and sold for the fund.

The press with few exceptions praised and aided the *World*. The Philadelphia *News* collected subscriptions. *The New York Times* made a cash contribution.

The *World* printed the name of every contributor. The list on July 12, 1885, for example, included "Little Wallie, May, Van Velsor, and Little Georgie, 10 cents each . . . Mix's fifth contribution, 1 cent . . . Total to date $92,090.83."

On August 11, less than seven months after the campaign started, the *World* announced the completion of its fund, which had come from about 121,000 contributors. Although business concerns and individuals had given amounts up to $2,500, eighty per cent of the money had been contributed in amounts of less than one dollar. The check sent by the *World* to the Committee was for $101,091. By common consent, $1000 of this was spent on a very elaborate testimonial for Bartholdi, designed by James R. Whittemore of Tiffany & Co. This featured a life-sized head in silver of the French sculptor, a large revolving globe of silver with France and the principal rivers of the world inlaid in gold, and a miniature of the statue. The design included a tribute to the power of the press in the form of the latest type of mammoth newspaper press shown in silver repoussé.

🦎 *Liberty Comes to New York* 🦎

The reception of the French vessel *Idsère*, 1000 tons, which brought the statue to New York, took place on June 19, 1885. Major General Charles P. Stone — a veteran of the Mexican and Civil Wars — chief engineer of the pedestal, received, on a tug in the harbor, the title deeds conveying the statue from France to the United States.

Then began the enormous task of assembling the statue and anchoring it to the pedestal. Bartholdi came in November, 1885, to give aid and counsel to General Stone, David H. King, Jr., builder, and their engineers, mechanics and workmen. The great skeleton was set up, the surrounding auxiliary structure installed, and the hundreds of hammered copper sections of the statue were fitted together, held by more than 300,000 copper rivets.

🦎 *Dedication of the Statue* 🦎

In a heavy mist with occasional showers of cold rain, on October 28, 1886, the Statue of Liberty was dedicated. New York City declared a general holiday and the City of Brooklyn closed its schools for the day.

A grand military and civic parade was reviewed during the fore-

STATUE OF LIBERTY NATIONAL MONUMENT

Proposed development by United States Department of Interior, National Park Service.

---

noon at Madison Square by President Grover Cleveland, Secretary of State Thomas F. Bayard of Delaware, Secretary of War William C. Endicott of Massachusetts, Secretary of the Navy William C. Whitney of New York, Secretary of the Interior Lucius Quintus Cincinnatus Lamar of Georgia, Governor David B. Hill and staff, and other French and American notables of the day.

The parade crossed City Hall Park, proceeded down Park Row and Broadway and disbanded at the Battery. The President and the Governor boarded U.S.S. *Despatch* at West Twenty-third Street, accompanied by the Americans and Frenchmen who were to take part in the afternoon exercises at Bedloe's Island. The little vessel led the other craft down the North River and into the Upper Bay. Behind her, steamed in double column the entire motley flotilla of nearly 300 tugs, yachts and excursion steamers carrying military and other organizations — each vessel in her designated position. The limited area and wharfage of Bedloe's

Island prevented the landing of all but participants in the un-veiling. The vessels bearing the great floating audience took their assigned positions around the broader eastern end of the pear-shaped island close to the anchored squadron of eight white-hulled, steam-propelled, full-rigged warships of the U.S. Navy under the command of Rear Admiral Stephen B. Luce, war veteran and founder of the Naval War College. At anchor also lay several French warships.

As the Commander-in-Chief approached, "the men-of-war's men were seen springing aloft in the rigging. Spryly they ran out along the yards and stood elbow to elbow," the *New-York Herald* re-ported. "The rainbow of fluttering bunting that arched each frigate and corvette contrasted prettily with the blue suits of the jolly tars." The Presidential Salute of twenty-one guns blazed away from the warships and the harbor fortifications, filling the air with white smoke.

On a large platform at the foot of the pedestal, within the star-shaped ramparts and facing a seated audience of about 2500, were already assembled governors of states, members of Congress, the American Committee, officers of the Army and Navy, and the orators of the day. The President — followed by the members of his cabinet and others — was escorted to his seat. Amid the tre-mendous din, the rendering by Gilmore's band of "Hail to the Chief!" counted for little. During a lull, the Rev. Dr. Richard S. Storrs began a solemn prayer, parts of which were drowned out by the enthusiastic blasts of steam whistles. The mist obscured many of the vessels, but when the whistles blew, the great size of the flotilla was appreciated. It was said that a million people, afloat and ashore, saw through the mist at least a part of the inauguration.

Bareheaded in the cold drizzle, the aged Count de Lesseps, his white upturned mustache unwilted, was the first orator; he spoke in French.

Senator Evarts, former Secretary of State, began reading his address. At the end of an eloquent passage he received a round of hearty applause. Bartholdi, with three others, had gone up into the statue and had laid hold of the rope with which he was to pull away the rain-darkened French flag, which enshrouded Liberty's head, and thus unveil his masterpiece. This was the culmination of the labors of the best part of his life. The applause, he thought, marked the end of Evarts' oration, when the unveiling was to take place. He pulled the rope.

The masters of the hundreds of steam craft, discovering the giant countenance of Liberty, unanimously saluted her with their whistles. Senator Evarts stopped reading. In a momentary lull, the Senator was about to continue when U.S.S. *Tennessee,* flagship of the squadron, fired a broadside. The band struck up "My Country, 'tis of Thee." When this was over, the Senator went on to the end of his address, while the din slowly subsided.

During the whole time Evarts was on his feet President Cleveland — who possessed a keen sense of humor — apparently gave the inaudible speech his most grave and concentrated attention.

The President, having taken the trouble to compress his oration, accepted the statue in one paragraph packed with meaning:

"The people of the United States accept with gratitude from their brethren of the French Republic the grand and complete work of art we here inaugurate. This token of the affection and consideration of the people of France demonstrates the kinship of republics, and conveys to us the assurance that in our efforts to commend to mankind the excellence of a government resting upon popular will, we still have beyond the American continent a steadfast ally. We are not here today to bow before the representation of a fierce warlike god, filled with wrath and vengeance, but we joyously contemplate instead our own deity keeping watch and ward before the open gates of America and greater than all that have been celebrated in ancient song. Instead of grasping in her hand thunderbolts of terror and of death, she holds aloft the light which illumines the way to man's enfranchisement. We will

Adapted from T. Johnson engraving, *Century Magazine*, October, 1888.

EMMA LAZARUS 1849-1887

With strong faith in America as the refuge of the oppressed, she wrote *"The New Colossus,"* which is inscribed on a tablet inside the pedestal of the Statue of Liberty and appears on the half-title page of this book.

---

not forget that Liberty has here made her home, nor shall her chosen altar be neglected. Willing votaries will constantly keep alive its fires and these shall gleam upon the shores of our sister Republic thence, and joined with answering rays a stream of light shall pierce the darkness of ignorance and man's oppression, until Liberty enlightens the world."

The French delegation consisted of fifteen men — including Vice-Admiral Jaurès, General Pélissier, Deputies Spuller and Desmons, and Napoleon Ney — but the only French official orator was the Minister to the United States, W. A. LeFaivre.

In his address, Chauncey M. Depew, later United States Senator from New York, and at this time counsel for the New York Central and other railroads, touched upon the fraternal relations between this country and France and said, "This Statue of Liberty rises toward the heavens to illustrate an idea which nerved the three hundred at Thermopylæ, and armed the ten thousand at Marathon; which drove Tarquin from Rome and aimed the arrow of Tell; which fired the farmer's gun at Lexington, and razed the Bastille at Paris; which inspired the charter in the cabin of the *Mayflower* and the Declaration of Independence from the Continental Congress."

Assistant Bishop Henry C. Potter — who was soon to get under way the building of the Cathedral of St. John the Divine, Morningside Heights, New York, removed his rain-soaked mortar-board and pronounced the benediction.

When the *Despatch* headed upstream, with the President standing in the cold rain on the forward uncovered deck, the guns of the warships and forts again roared out a salute.

❦ *The Statue as Inspiration* ❦

While the pedestal on Bedloe's Island was building, and at the time of the inauguration of the monument, many artists and poets were inspired by the colossal statue and the idea it symbolized. Noah Davis, James Boyle O'Reilly, Ella Wheeler Wilcox, Esther Singleton, and others joined the chorus of praise.

John Greenleaf Whittier, then nearly eighty years of age, wrote a poem of six stanzas including these two:

> Unlike the shapes on Egypt's sands
> Uplifted by the toil-worn slave,
> On Freedom's soil with freemen's hands
> We rear the symbol free hands gave . . .

> Rise, stately symbol! holding forth
> Thy light and hope to all who sit
> In chains and darkness! Belt the earth
> With watch-fires from thy torch uplift!

John Hay called Edmund Clarence Stedman's poem "the most powerful, vibrant poem of occasion anyone has written in our time." The following is one of the stanzas, in which Liberty speaks:

> "O ye, whose broken spars
> Tell of the storms ye met,
> Enter! fear not the bars
> Across your pathway set;
> Enter at Freedom's porch,
> For you I lift my torch,
> For you my coronet
> Is rayed with stars. . . . "

"The New Colossus," best known of the Statue of Liberty poems, was written in 1883 to aid the pedestal fund by New York-born Emma Lazarus, an early advocate of what is now called the Zionist movement. Twenty years after she had published her sonnet (see half-title page of this book) it was cast in bronze and placed, by the philanthropist Georgina Schuyler, on the interior wall of the pedestal.

The New York Trust Company collection.

HAIL AMERICA

Like other great artists, Joseph Pennell, the famous illustrator, was inspired by the Statue of Liberty and used it a number of times in his etchings and lithographs. This mezzotint, of which he made forty impressions in 1909, is possibly his finest view of the Statue of Liberty. The Statue was also the central figure in Pennell's famous Liberty Loan poster, considered by many to be the most effective of American war posters of the period 1917-1918. (In reverse as in the original.)

SOME OF THE POSTAGE STAMPS SHOWING THE STATUE

Julian Hawthorne's tribute was in prose:

"Though the bronze goddess stands motionless and firm, she seems but a moment ago to have assumed the attitude which she will retain through centuries to come. She has stepped forward, and halted, and raised her torch into the sky. There is energy without effort and movement combined with repose. Her aspect is grave almost to sternness; yet her faultless features wear the serenity of power and confidence. Her message is the sublimest ever brought to man, but she is adequate to its delivery. In her left hand she holds a tablet inscribed with the most glorious of our memories, the birthday of the Republic. No words are needed to interpret her meaning, for her gesture and her countenance speak the universal language, and their utterance reaches to the purest depth of the human soul."

Since the Statue of Liberty has stood at the principal gateway of the nation, this cherished national monument — as great in significance as it is in size — has become increasingly an inspiration not only to poets and artists but to all our people. Pictures and small replicas of it are in numberless American homes. The annual total of visitors from all parts of the country is expected to increase when the National Park Service of the Department of the Interior carries out its plans to enlarge the wharfage and improve the facilities at Bedloe's Island.

When the 77th Division, composed of men from metropolitan New York was organized during the First World War, it appropriately adopted the Statue of Liberty as its insignia. This is the division of which the famous so-called "Lost Battalion" was a unit. The warriors of the 77th, whose homes were in the shadow of the statue, received their baptism of fire on the battlefields of the country whose people had given the statue to their native land. Reconstituted during the present war, the 77th Division, wearing the same insignia, again is fighting for the cause of liberty.

Although the statue has not been used on our coins, it has carried far and wide its message of liberty on millions of our postage stamps and on those of at least five other countries.

🗽 *Special Events* 🗽

From time to time, special attention is drawn to the Statue of Liberty — as when President Theodore Roosevelt in 1904, on the occasion of Bartholdi's death at the age of seventy, cabled a message of condolence to Madame Bartholdi "in the name of the American people."

In 1916, when France had been fighting for her life for more than two years against the ancient enemy, President Wilson came to New York and after sunset on December 2, from the deck of the Presidential yacht, U.S.S. *Mayflower,* off Bedloe's Island, dedicated the first flood-lighting system of the statue. At a banquet in New York that night, the President said: "There is a great responsibility in having adopted Liberty as an ideal because we must illustrate it in what we do ... Throughout the last two years there has come more and more into my heart the conviction that peace is going to come to the world only with Liberty." Other speakers were the French Ambassador, Jules J. Jusserand, Chauncey M. Depew, who had also spoken at the inauguration of the statue, and Ralph Pulitzer, the son of Joseph. Said the French envoy:

"Not to a man, not to a nation the statue was raised, not to a man, famous and useful as he may have been, not to a nation great as she may be. It was raised to an idea — an idea greater than any man or any nation, greater than France or the United States — the idea of Liberty!"

From Bedloe's Island on October 28, 1936, exactly fifty years after the unveiling of the statue, at a period when Laboulaye's grandson, André, was French Ambassador to the United States, President Franklin D. Roosevelt broadcast an address, to which President Albert Lebrun and our Ambassador William C. Bullitt responded by radio. President Roosevelt said, "Citizens of all democracies unite in their desire for peace. Grover Cleveland fifty years ago recognized that unity of purpose on this very spot . . . Liberty and peace are living things. In each generation — if they are to be maintained — they must be guarded and vitalized anew."

In war and in peace, the serene and majestic figure, typifying the hopes and aspirations of mankind, will remain, in the words of Laboulaye, "a symbol that braves the storms of time. It will stand unshaken in the midst of the winds that roar about its head and the waves that shatter at its feet."

Photograph by I. M. Levitt, Assistant Director of the Fels Planetarium of the Franklin Institute, Philadelphia, Pennsylvania.